RESEARCHING TEACHER EDUCATION: NEW PERSPECTIVES ON PRACTICE, PERFORMANCE AND POLICY

Multi-Site Teacher Education Research Project (MUSTER)

Synthesis Report

Keith M Lewin and Janet S Stuart
March 2003

Educational Papers

Department for International Development: Educational Papers

This is one of a series of Education Papers issued by the Policy Division of the Department For International Development. Each paper represents a study or piece of commissioned research on some aspects of education and training in developing countries. Most of the studies were undertaken in order to provide informed judgements from which policy decisions could be drawn, but in each case it has become apparent that the material produced would be of interest to a wider audience, particularly those whose work focuses on developing countries.

Each paper is numbered serially, and further copies can be obtained through DFID Education Publication Despatch, PO Box 190, Sevenoaks, TN14 5EL, UK – subject to availability. A full list appears overleaf.

Although these papers are issued by DFID, the views expressed in them are entirely those of the authors and do not necessarily represent DFID's own policies or views. Any discussion of their content should therefore be addressed to the authors and not to DFID.

Address for Correspondence

Centre for International Education
University of Sussex Institute of Education,
Falmer,
Brighton,
Sussex
BN1 9RG _ UK

T   +44 +1273 678464
E   cie@sussex.ac.uk
F   +44 +1273 678568
W   www.sussex.ac.uk/usie/cie

© Keith M Lewin and Janet S Stuart
March 2003

DFID

Educational Papers

No.1 SCHOOL EFFECTIVENESS IN
DEVELOPING COUNTRIES:
A SUMMARY OF THE
RESEARCH EVIDENCE.
D Pennycuick (1993)
ISBN: 0 90250 061 9

No. 2 EDUCATIONAL COST-BENEFIT
ANALYSIS.
J Hough (1993)
ISBN: 0 90250 062 7

No.3 REDUCING THE COST OF
TECHNICAL AND
VOCATIONAL EDUCATION.
L Gray, M Fletcher, P Foster, M King,
A M Warrender (1993)
ISBN: 0 90250 063 5

No. 4 REPORT ON READING
ENGLISH IN PRIMARY
SCHOOLS IN MALAWI.
F Williams (1993) Out of Print
Available on CD-Rom and
DFID website

No. 5 REPORT ON READING
ENGLISH IN PRIMARY
SCHOOLS IN ZAMBIA.
E Williams (1993) Out of Print –
Available on CD-Rom and
DFID website

See also No. 24, which updates and
synthesises No.'s 4 and 5.

No. 6 EDUCATION AND
DEVELOPMENT: THE ISSUES
AND THE EVIDENCE.
K Lewin (1993)
ISBN: 0 90250 066 X

No. 7 PLANNING AND FINANCING
SUSTAINABLE EDUCATION
SYSTEMS IN SUB-SAHARAN
AFRICA.
P Penrose (1993)
ISBN: 0 90250 067 8

No. 8 Not allocated

No. 9 FACTORS AFFECTING
FEMALE PARTICIPATION
IN EDUCATION IN SEVEN
DEVELOPING COUNTRIES.
C Brock, N Cammish (1991)
(revised 1997).
ISBN: 1 86192 065 2

No.10 USING LITERACY: A NEW
APPROACH TO POST-
LITERACY METHODS.
A Rogers (1994) Out of Print –
Available on CD-ROM and
DFID website. Updated and
reissued on No 29.

No.11 EDUCATION AND TRAINING
FOR THE INFORMAL
SECTOR.
K King, S McGrath, F Leach,
R Carr-Hill (1994)
ISBN: 1 86192 090 3

No.12 MULTI-GRADE TEACHING:
A REVIEW OF RESEARCH
AND PRACTICE.
A Little (1995)
ISBN: 0 90250 058 9

Educational Papers

No.13 **DISTANCE EDUCATION IN ENGINEERING FOR DEVELOPING COUNTRIES.**
T Bilham, R Gilmour (1995)
Out of Print – Available on CD-ROM and DFID website.

No.14 **HEALTH & HIV/AIDS EDUCATION IN PRIMARY & SECONDARY SCHOOLS IN AFRICA & ASIA.**
E Barnett, K de Koning,
V Francis (1995)
ISBN: 0 90250 069 4

No.15 **LABOUR MARKET SIGNALS & INDICATORS.**
L Gray, AM Warrender, P Davies,
G Hurley, C Manton (1995) Out of Print – Available on CD-ROM and DFID website.

No.16 **IN-SERVICE SUPPORT FOR A TECHNOLOGICAL APPROACH TO SCIENCE EDUCATION.**
F Lubben, R Campbell,
B Dlamini (1995)
ISBN: 0 90250 071 6

No.17 **ACTION RESEARCH REPORT ON "REFLECT" METHOD OF TEACHING LITERACY.**
D Archer, S Cottingham (1996)
ISBN: 0 90250 072 4

No.18 **THE EDUCATION AND TRAINING OF ARTISANS FOR THE INFORMAL SECTOR IN TANZANIA.**
D Kent, P Mushi (1996)
ISBN: 0 90250 074 0

No.19 **GENDER, EDUCATION AND DEVELOPMENT - A PARTIALLY ANNOTATED AND SELECTIVE BIBLIOGRAPHY.**
C Brock, N Cammish (1997)
Out of Print – Available on CD-ROM and DFID website.

No.20 **CONTEXTUALISING TEACHING AND LEARNING IN RURAL PRIMARY SCHOOLS USING AGRICULTURAL EXPERIENCE.**
P Taylor, A Mulhall (Vols 1 & 2)
(1997) Vol 1 ISBN: 1 861920 45 8
Vol 2 ISBN: 1 86192 050 4

No.21 **GENDER AND SCHOOL ACHIEVEMENT IN THE CARIBBEAN.**
P Kutnick, V Jules, A Layne (1997)
ISBN: 1 86192 080 6

No.22 **SCHOOL-BASED UNDERSTANDING OF HUMAN RIGHTS IN FOUR COUNTRIES: A COMMONWEALTH STUDY.**
R Bourne, J Gundara, A Dev,
N Ratsoma, M Rukanda, A Smith,
U Birthistle (1997)
ISBN: 1 86192 095 4

No.23 **GIRLS AND BASIC EDUCATION: A CULTURAL ENQUIRY.**
D Stephens (1998)
ISBN: 1 86192 036 9

No.24 **INVESTIGATING BILINGUAL LITERACY: EVIDENCE FROM MALAWI AND ZAMBIA.**
E Williams (1998)
ISBN: 1 86192 041 5No.25

Educational Papers

No.25 **PROMOTING GIRLS' EDUCATION IN AFRICA.**
N Swainson, S Bendera, R Gordon, E Kadzamira (1998)
ISBN: 1 86192 046 6

No.26 **GETTING BOOKS TO SCHOOL PUPILS IN AFRICA.**
D Rosenberg, W Amaral, C Odini, T Radebe, A Sidibé (1998)
ISBN: 1 86192 051 2

No.27 **COST SHARING IN EDUCATION.**
P Penrose (1998)
ISBN: 1 86192 056 3

No.28 **VOCATIONAL EDUCATION AND TRAINING IN TANZANIA AND ZIMBABWE IN THE CONTEXT OF ECONOMIC REFORM.**
P Bennell (1999)
ISBN: 1 86192 061 X

No.29 **RE-DEFINING POST-LITERACY IN A CHANGING WORLD.**
A Rogers, B Maddox, J Millican, K Newell Jones, U Papen, A Robinson-Pant (1999)
ISBN: 1 86192 069 5

No.30 **IN SERVICE FOR TEACHER DEVELOPMENT IN SUB-SAHARAN AFRICA.**
M Monk (1999)
ISBN: 1 86192 074 1

No.31 **PRODUCTION OF LOCALLY GENERATED TRAINING MATERIALS.**
I Carter (1999)
ISBN: 1 86192 079 2

No.32 **SECTOR WIDE APPROACHES TO EDUCATION.**
M Ratcliffe, M Macrae (1999)
ISBN: 1 86192 131 4

No.33 **DISTANCE EDUCATION PRACTICE: TRAINING & REWARDING AUTHORS.**
H Perraton, C Creed (1999)
ISBN: 1 86192 136 5

No.34 **THE EFFECTIVENESS OF TEACHER RESOURCE CENTRE STRATEGY.**
Ed. G Knamiller, G Fairhurst (1999)
ISBN: 1 86192 141 1

No.35 **EVALUATING IMPACTS (OF EDUCATION PROJECTS & PROGRAMMES).**
Ed. V McKay, C Treffgarne (1999)
ISBN: 1 86192 191 8

No.36 **AFRICAN JOURNALS – A SURVEY OF THEIR USAGE IN AFRICAN UNIVERSITY LIBRARIES.**
A Alemna, V Chifwepa, D Rosenberg (1999)
ISBN: 1 86192 157 8

No.37 **MONITORING THE PERFORMANCE OF EDUCATIONAL PROGRAMMES IN DEVELOPING COUNTRIES.**
R Carr-Hill, M Hopkins, A Riddell, J Lintott (1999)
ISBN: 1 86192 224 8No.38

Educational Papers

No.38 **TOWARDS RESPONSIVE SCHOOLS – SUPPORTING BETTER SCHOOLING FOR DISADVANTAGED CHILDREN** (case studies from Save the Children). M Molteno, K Ogadhoh, E Cain, B Crumpton (2000) ISBN: to be confirmed

No.39 **PRELIMINARY INVESTIGATION OF THE ABUSE OF GIRLS IN ZIMBABWEAN JUNIOR SECONDARY SCHOOLS.** F Leach, P Machankanja with J Mandoga (2000) ISBN: 1 86192 279 5

No.40 **THE IMPACT OF TRAINING ON WOMEN'S MICRO-ENTERPRISE DEVELOPMENT** F Leach, S Abdulla, H Appleton, J el-Bushra, N Cardenas, K Kebede, V Lewis, S Sitaram (2000) ISBN: 1 86192 284 1

No.41 **THE QUALITY OF LEARNING AND TEACHING IN DEVELOPING COUNTRIES: ASSESSING LITERACY AND NUMERACY IN MALAWI AND SRI LANKA.** D Johnson, J Hayter, P Broadfoot (2000) ISBN: 1 86192 313 9

No.42 **LEARNING TO COMPETE: EDUCATION, TRAINING & ENTERPRISE IN GHANA, KENYA & SOUTH AFRICA.** D Afenyadu, K King, S McGrath, H Oketch, C Rogerson, K Visser (1999) ISBN: 1 86192 314 7

No.43 **COMPUTERS IN SECONDARY SCHOOLS IN DEVELOPING COUNTRIES: COSTS AND OTHER ISSUES.** A Cawthera (2001) ISBN 1 86192 418 6

No.44 **THE IMPACT OF HIV/AIDS ON THE UNIVERSITY OF BOTSWANA: DEVELOPING A COMPREHENSIVE STRATEGIC RESPONSE.** B Chilisa, P Bennell, K Hyde (2001) ISBN: 1 86192 467 4

No.45 **THE IMPACT OF HIV/AIDS ON PRIMARY AND SECONDARY EDUCATION IN BOTSWANA: DEVELOPING A COMPREHENSIVE STRATEGIC RESPONSE.** P Bennell, B Chilisa, K Hyde, A Makgothi, E Molobe, L Mpotokwane (2001) ISBN: 1 86192 468 2

No.46 **EDUCATION FOR ALL: POLICY AND PLANNING - LESSONS FROM SRI LANKA.** A Little (2003) ISBN: 1 86192 552 0

No.47 **REACHING THE POOR - THE COSTS OF SENDING CHILDREN TO SCHOOL** S Boyle, A Brock, J Mace, M Sibbons (2003) ISBN: 1 86192 361 9

Educational Papers

No.48 **CHILD LABOUR AND ITS IMPACT ON CHILDREN'S ACCESS TO AND PARTICIPATION IN PRIMARY EDUCATION - A CASE STUDY FROM TANZANIA**
by H.A Dachi and R.M Garrett
(2003)

ISBN: 1 86192 536 0

NOW AVAILABLE – CD-ROM
containing full texts of Papers 1-42

Other DFID Educational Studies Also Available:

REDRESSING GENDER INEQUALITIES IN EDUCATION. N Swainson (1995)

FACTORS AFFECTING GIRLS' ACCESS TO SCHOOLING IN NIGER. S Wynd (1995)

EDUCATION FOR RECONSTRUCTION.
D Phillips, N Arnhold, J Bekker, N Kersh,
E McLeish (1996)

AFRICAN JOURNAL DISTRIBUTION PROGRAMME: EVALUATION OF 1994 PILOT PROJECT. D Rosenberg (1996)

TEACHER JOB SATISFACTION IN DEVELOPING COUNTRIES. R Garrett (1999)

A MODEL OF BEST PRACTICE AT LORETO DAY SCHOOL, SEALDAH, CALCUTTA.
T Jessop (1998)

LEARNING OPPORTUNITIES FOR ALL.
DFID Policy Paper (1999)

THE CHALLENGE OF UNIVERSAL PRIMARY EDUCATION.
DFID Target Strategy Paper (2001)

CHILDREN OUT OF SCHOOL.
DFID Issues Paper (2001)

All publications are available free of charge from DFID Education Publications Despatch, PO Box 190, Sevenoaks, TN14 5EL, or by email from dfidpubs@eclogistics.co.uk

Foreword: The Multi-Site Teacher Education Research Project

This Research Report synthesises the findings from a four-year programme of research on Teacher Education supported by DFID. It is focused on insights from Ghana, Lesotho, Malawi, and Trinidad and Tobago. The research in South Africa is presented in a separate book.

The research was co-ordinated from the Centre for International Education at the University of Sussex. Participative workshops were used at different times in the project to develop the framework for the research, design data collection and analysis methods, and consolidate research findings into a range of publications. Principal Researchers were identified in each country who convened country research teams to undertake the research. This created ownership, grounded research activity in national contexts, and contributed to building future research capacity.

The dissemination of research insights from MUSTER is taking many forms. Thirty Discussion Papers have now been produced and are available from the MUSTER Website (http://www.sussex.ac.uk/usie/muster). These include country baseline studies, along with many analytic sub-studies by research team members. A special double issue of the International Journal of Educational and Development containing 13 articles has been published (May 2002). Contributions have also been made to a special edition of the International Journal of Educational Research on Teacher Education. Other outputs include a book on Changing Patterns of Teacher Education in South Africa: Policy, Practice and Prospects; a collection of Teacher Educators' Resource Materials developed from MUSTER research; various locally published research reports, and individually published articles in different academic journals. Five national workshops have been organised for policy makers and practitioners to disseminate findings directly to communities of stakeholders in each country. MUSTER research has also been presented at various international conferences including the Oxford Conference and the U.S. Comparative and International Education Society. Four country reports (Ghana, Lesotho, Malawi and Trinidad and Tobago) are being published as DFID Research Reports. A CD-ROM will be made available of the major MUSTER publications.

Keith Lewin and Janet Stuart

Acknowledgements

MUSTER has depended on the collaborative endeavours of a large number of researchers and the co-operation of many teacher educators, teacher education students, Ministries of Education, and training institutions. To all these actors we express our gratitude. Most particularly the research has relied centrally on the efforts, insights, skills, and persistence of the research teams and the Principal Researchers, often working under difficult circumstances with many competing pressures on their time. The range of research products and their quality is testimony to the immense amount of work and goodwill that all those involved have committed to MUSTER.

Beryl Clough was an unstinting, conscientious, committed and caring Project Secretary for the MUSTER project who cheerfully coped with all its crises, deadlines and financial aberrations. Sadly she passed away before the completion of the Project and is sorely missed by all involved. This report, and the other outputs from MUSTER, have benefited greatly from her dedication, sense of duty, and willingness to go the extra mile. We hope it does justice to her memory.

The Researchers

MUSTER research was co-ordinated from the Centre for International Education, Institute of Education at the University of Sussex in partnership with five link institutions each of which convened research teams to collect and analyse data. The institutions and the Principal Researchers were:

- The Institute of Education, University of Cape Coast, Ghana (Dr. K.Akyeampong)
- The Institute of Education, National University of Lesotho (J.P.Lefoka)
- The Centre for Educational Research and Training, University of Malawi (D.Kunje)
- The Faculty of Education, University of Durban-Westville, South Africa (Dr.M.Samuel)
- The School of Education, University of the West Indies, Trinidad and Tobago (Dr. J.George).

Four Sussex faculty co-ordinated the MUSTER research providing advice, direct research support in–country, and assistance with data analysis and report publication. These are Professor Keith Lewin, Dr Janet Stuart, Dr David Stephens (1997-1999), and Dr Yusuf Sayed (1999-2001). Dr Julie Coultas (Research Officer 1998/1999) assisted with statistical analysis and advice to parts of the research. Three doctoral students have been attached to the project and have worked with the relevant country teams – Alison Croft (Malawi), Dominic Furlong (Ghana) and John Hedges (Ghana). John Hedges also acted as a Research Officer (2000/2001) to support the dissemination programme. Each country has organised its research teams differently. A full list of research teams in each country is included in Appendix 1.

Contents

Contents - Continued

Contents - Continued

Figures

Abbreviations

BAGET	Bachelor of General Education and Training	MANEB	Malawi National Examinations Board
BTC	Blantyre Teachers' College	MDG	Millennium Development Goals
CIE	Centre for International Education	MIITEP	Malawi Integrated In-service Teacher Education Project
COSC	Cambridge Overseas School Certificate	MOE	Ministry of Education
		MSCE	Malawi School Certificate of Education
CPD	Continuing Professional Development	MSSSP	Malawi Schools Support Systems Project
CXC	Caribbean Examinations Council	MUSTER	Multi-site Teacher Education Research
DEO	District Education Officer		
DEP	Diploma in Education (Primary)	NQT	Newly Qualified Teacher
		NTTC	National Teacher Training College
DFID	Department for International Development	NUL	National University of Lesotho
DO	District Officer	OJT	On the Job Training
DPTE	Diploma in Primary Teacher Education	PEA	Primary Education Advisor
		PRESET	Pre-service Education for Teachers
DRT	District Resource Teacher		
EFA	Education For All	PTC	Primary Teachers Certificate
ESL	English as a Second Language	PTR	Pupil-teacher Ratio
FCUBE	Free Compulsory Universal Basic Education	SPSS	Statistics Package for Social Sciences
FPE	Free Primary Education	SSCE	Senior Secondary Certificate of Education
GCE	General Certificate of Education	SSR	Staff Student Ratio
GER	Gross Enrolment Ratio	SSS	Senior Secondary School
GES	Ghana Education Service	TDC	Teachers Development Centre
GNP	Gross National Product	TP	Teaching Practice
GTZ	Gesellschaft fur Technische Zusammenarbeit	TPP	Teaching Practice Preparation
		TTC	Teacher Training College
ICT	Information and Communication Technologies	UCC	University of Cape Coast
IJED	International Journal of Educational Development	UDE	University Department of Education
		UNDP	United Nations Development Programme
INSET	In-service Education for Teachers		
		UDW	University of Durban-Westville
JC, JCE	Junior Certificate of Education	UPE	Universal Primary Education
JSS	Junior Secondary School	UT	Untrained Teacher
JUSSTEP	Junior Secondary School Teacher Education Project	UWI	University of the West Indies

Executive Review: Researching Teacher Education: New Perspectives on Practice, Performance and Policy

1.   Introduction

The MUSTER research project has undertaken extensive empirical studies of different aspects of primary teacher education as it is practised in Ghana, Lesotho, Malawi, South Africa[1] and Trinidad and Tobago. The variety, richness and nuances of the data and its interpretation cannot be captured in a single global summary. This would do violence to the differences in context and culture, the variations in inputs, processes and outcomes, and the profile of needs that each teacher education system seeks to meet.

However, it is possible to offer some synthetic observations which have germinated from the many sub-studies and which highlight some emerging priorities for teacher education and development that resonate across the case study countries, and perhaps for those confronting similar challenges. This executive review therefore focuses on cross-cutting issues, and invites the reader to pursue individual themes in the main text of this report, and in the various MUSTER publications. In particular the four country reports published by MUSTER offer comprehensive analyses of each system and reach specific conclusions and recommendations at national level (Akyeampong 2001, Lefoka and Sebatane 2002, Kunje, Lewin and Stuart 2002, George and Quamina-Aiyejina 2002). Each has been the subject of a national dissemination workshop. MUSTER research in the fifth country, South Africa, has been consolidated and published as a separate book (Lewin, Samuel and Sayed 2003), In addition a special double edition of the International Journal for Education and Development (Vol 22, Nos 3 and 4) carries fourteen contributions by MUSTER authors (Stuart and Lewin 2002).

This review is organised in six sections. The first section identifies a range of key policy challenges for teacher education, and details emerging priorities. The next three sections sequentially reflect on insights and issues concerned with the selection and admission of trainees, the initial teacher education curriculum, and the characteristics of teacher education Colleges. This leads to a discussion of structures for initial training and some alternative models. The fifth section develops an analysis of the roles external assistance can play in improving quality and effectiveness. Section six briefly outlines some developmental scenarios that arise from the cross-case analysis undertaken within MUSTER.

2.   On Policy Challenges and Priorities

In Ghana, Lesotho, and Malawi the challenge posed for teacher education by national targets for enrolment and pupil-teacher ratios for primary schooling is immense. None of these systems can produce enough new teachers to meet projected demand. Each needs to increase the output of trained teachers several-fold (Lewin 2002). In Ghana output would have to increase three or four times if all children were to be enrolled at primary level and

---

[1] The bulk of the South Africa work is published in Lewin, Samuel, Sayed (2003) and this report focuses largely on Ghana, Lesotho, Malawi, and Trinidad and Tobago.

Executive Review

taught by trained teachers. In Lesotho, more than five times current output is needed. Projections of demand in South Africa suggest substantially rising demand for teachers (Crouch with Lewin 2001) which is very sensitive to the demographic impact of HIV/AIDS. Demand is rising as the numbers entering primary teacher training have fallen to minimal levels. Malawi has already adopted a mixed-mode approach to training that is relatively low cost and high volume which could meet demand with imaginable levels of expansion. However, quality is widely questioned, the programme cannot be delivered as originally intended, and places are unlikely to be filled without recruiting from those completing just two years of secondary schooling (Kunje and Chirembo 2000, Stuart and Kunje 2000). Trinidad and Tobago is the only case where demand is well within the capacity of training institutions. Here there is a window of opportunity to invest in quality improvement and extending the role of colleges into professional support pre- and post-training, something that is largely absent in the MUSTER countries.

Though the detail is complex, the MUSTER conclusions are clear. The Millennium Development Goals (MDG) relating to education cannot be met unless the supply of teachers is adequate to keep pupil-teacher ratios within reasonable limits, and the quality of their training is sufficient to result in minimum acceptable levels of pupil achievement. The costs of existing methods of training are such that simple expansion of existing capacity is often not financially viable. Improvements in efficiency and effectiveness are needed that can lower costs and expand output within sustainable budgets. It may also be necessary to consider alternatives to two or three years full-time, pre-career training. Traditional teacher education programmes are heavily 'front-loaded' with most investment at the beginning of a teaching career. Their unit costs can exceed those of university education and may be 50 or more times the annual cost of a primary school place. If the average length of teachers' careers is declining, as it is in some cases as a result of HIV/AIDS, and if the numbers which have to be trained are much larger than current capacity, teacher education programmes with lower costs are needed. The alternative is to revise MDG targets for universalising access and achieving gender equity in primary schooling.

MUSTER has explored the process and practice of teacher education across a range of countries in great detail. Several common threads emerge related to policy issues, which are outlined below.

First, the simple observation is that across the MUSTER countries policy on primary teacher education is fragmented, incomplete, and more often than not simply non-existent. Despite the obvious importance of policy on teacher education to the achievement of nationally and internationally agreed goals to universalise primary schooling, improve quality, and enhance equity in access and retention, the development of coherent, medium term, financially sustainable teacher education policy, tailored to meet the demand for new teachers, has been widely neglected.

Executive Review

In Ghana, College reform has not been a priority since FCUBE (Free Compulsory Universal Basic Education) was announced. The recent introduction of the 'In-In-Out' programme to replace three-year fully residential training has not evolved from a considered strategy to supply the number of teachers needed to meet the objectives of FCUBE. A Teacher Education Task Force has now been established, as a sequel to the MUSTER national workshop, and time will tell if it will succeed in the development of an integrated policy. Lesotho continues to train far fewer teachers than it needs to implement Free Primary Education (FPE). It has also established a Task Force on Teacher Education to build on the MUSTER research and has ambitions to develop a strategic plan. Malawi has grappled with the implications of its FPE programme and has attempted to meet the need for trained teachers through the innovative Malawi Integrated Inservice Teacher Education Programme (MIITEP) programme of mixed college- and school-based training. The suspension of this programme, with the consequence that no new teachers were enrolled in training for more nearly three years, reflects the absence of national teacher education policy and of any real sense of urgency to address the problems of initial training. The recent creation of a Teacher Education Division within the Ministry, the inclusion of teacher education more prominently in the Policy and Investment Framework, and the agreement on the funding of three extra MIITEP cohorts are positive signs Trinidad and Tobago policy on teacher education has no clear locus of control or chain of accountability. Unlike other Eastern Caribbean States, where partnerships exist between Ministries, Colleges and the University of the West Indies, responsibilities are ill-defined, as is policy The MUSTER national conference has developed some momentum to resolve this unsatisfactory situation (George and Quamina-Aiyejina 2002) and created an opportunity to revitalise the college system and capitalise on its strengths.

It is self-evident that national planning must directly address questions of teacher supply and demand, quality, curriculum and deployment. To be plausible such policy needs to have clarity about its goals (what are the skills and competencies newly trained teachers should possess?), methods (how are these to be acquired?), costs (what resources are needed?) and timescale (how long will it take to achieve the desired outcomes?). If such policy is developed alongside the evolution of sector-wide agreements with external development partners, as is the case in several of the MUSTER countries, then it should be an integral part of the process which produces agreed spending plans and identifies performance goals. This has yet to become a reality.

The first priority is therefore for policy makers to actually develop policy which has national standing and is integrated into the medium term planning process. There are a number of other priorities which can be identified.

The second issue is to recognise that what is possible and sustainable is constrained in different ways in the different countries. Most simply put, any medium term policy has to

Executive Review

recognise the realities imposed by demography (which determines the numbers of pupils and hence teachers needed each year), teacher attrition (retirement, alternative career choices, the impact of HIV/AIDS), and enrolment rate targets (achieving and sustaining universal enrolment up to a specified grade level). It also has to start from existing training capacity and recognise the constraints of infrastructure on the rate at which output might grow in quality and quantity. Our analyses indicates how different the situations are in the different countries, and also draw attention to some of the constraints and opportunities imposed by history, politics and finance. In three of the countries the choice is between mass methods that could produce trained teachers in sufficient quantity to meet demand, and those which might improve quality but would limit the number of pupils with access to teachers with any training at all. The MUSTER analyses of supply and demand, and of efficiency and costs, need refinement, periodic up-dating, and integration into frameworks for policy at national level.

A third area of policy concern relates to the mechanisms through which teacher education is resourced, and its performance monitored. Typically budgetary systems use historic budgeting loosely related to actual or projected student numbers. The arrangements vary, but none of those we have explored seem sufficient to provide a stable financial environment conducive to the efficient management of colleges. Where budgetary allocations are unpredictable, release of funds irregular, and auditing and accountability weak, it is difficult to see how consistent development can take place. Under these circumstances it is also unlikely that training institutions can develop their own medium term strategic planning and gain the commitment of their staff to a common set of goals. Training systems are not large and complex in comparison with school systems. It should be possible to include teacher education budget lines in Medium Term Expenditure Frameworks and ensure that what is allocated is disbursed regularly. Given the relatively small number of institutions involved there is no obvious reason why they should not stand in a direct relationship with a Ministry department and budget. Where we have observed the effects of decentralising the budget to intermediary levels, this seems to introduce an unnecessary layer of bureaucracy and delay.

MUSTER research has not identified existing funding mechanisms which reward efficiency and penalise waste. Neither, as noted above, is funding generally linked to any formula related to the number of students, or their successful graduation. It is also true that salary costs per student (predominantly lecturers' salaries) vary across training institutions within the same country, largely as a result of variations in student-teacher ratios. This suggests that norms on staffing are seldom applied, resulting in under-staffing of some institutions and over-staffing of others. It is also significant for costs that the average size of training institutions is often small, and falls below 500 trainees in many cases. This is often smaller than the size of typical secondary schools and many primary schools. Economies of scale are available if it is possible to increase average size and distribute fixed costs across more trainees. Expenditure on learning resources in training institutions is often minimal and no

Executive Review

mechanisms seem to exist to ensure that learning resources are replenished at some minimum level. No ring-fencing or other procedures are used to protect spending on books, learning aids etc., with predictable results. There are many mechanisms that could be used to regularise the flow of funds and create at least some incentives to increase efficiency. These could improve the chances that training institutions will develop cumulatively within a stable financial environment that could offer better value for money.

Fourth, boarding-related costs are high and often the largest element of training institution costs. These costs may be necessary and can be efficiently managed. The policy questions revolve around the length of time boarding is essential, and whether any element of cost recovery should be introduced. The latter is especially relevant where trainee teachers are paid stipends as untrained teachers from which they would otherwise have to fund their own living costs.

Fifth, policy on initial teacher education should be linked to that on subsequent In-service Training (INSET) and Continuing Professional Development (CPD). This is generally not the case. However effective initial training is, it leads into the stage of 'newly qualified teacher' (NQT), a critical period when new teachers require support and guidance and often receive little systematic induction. Training institutions should play a full role in INSET and CPD, since these activities should cross-fertilise and feed back into more effective initial training. In principle, an 'initial' qualification is precisely that, and not a terminal stage in a career ladder. The balance between the time and money spent on initial training and subsequent INSET and CPD is a critical policy question. If most investment is front-loaded (i.e. at the beginning of a teacher's career), if teacher attrition is high and rising, if career lifetimes as primary teaches are shortening, and if substantial effort is to be directed to changing school practice through direct support for whole school development, then it may make sense to shorten periods of initial training in favour of more training inputs for NQT's as their careers develop. Amongst other things, this has the benefit of directing more investment of training resources towards those on the job and likely to remain so.

Sixth, none of the countries within MUSTER (with the exception of South Africa), has begun to address the question as to whether non-government resources have a role to play in expanded and more effective teacher education. Historically much was provided through not-for-profit non-government institutions. It may or may not be the case that these questions should be reopened. Where resources are a major constraint on teacher education, and internal efficiency of public institutions is low, some forms of public-private partnership need to remain among the options. The detailed case that might be made for partnerships is necessarily located within each system and may or may not be attractive.

Finally, it seems to us, the constructive and effective development of teacher education requires direct association with Ministerial authority, clear lines of administrative control and

Executive Review

accountability, and strategic delegation of some measure of autonomy to training institutions, at least in professional arenas. The latter would seem essential if teacher education institutions are to move away from patterns of organisation and operation which closely resemble secondary schools, to become professional development institutions working to facilitate the learning of adults and their induction into new roles as self-confident, competent and creative young professionals.

The policy problems we have identified in MUSTER suggest that at their core are several causes. First, primary teacher education policy has often been seen as an afterthought to policy on Education for All and the MDGs, neither of which foreground teacher education issues . It is almost as if it is a residual concern that has had to be addressed in the wake of policy on universalising schooling, which has had a much higher public profile and much catalysis for development agencies. Second, the locus of control over teacher education has been ambiguous, and is often a subsidiary function within a department of a line Ministry. Third, and partly as a result, resources have not flowed in ways consistent with demand for newly trained teachers. Fourth, key stakeholders (parents, teachers unions, educational administrators, college lecturers) have been slow to assert the importance of re-conceptualising teacher education in the wake of primary curriculum reform and universal access, as also have been some other development partners.

3.   On Selection and Admission

Policy on trainee selection is generally poorly articulated and lacking any evidence base. Predominantly trainees are selected as a result of meeting minimum academic requirements. Other selection methods – interviews, aptitude tests, language tests – are rarely used and are not consistently applied. Yet we can find no studies of the predictive validity of such selection methods. The attempts MUSTER made to test this do not show that school-leaving achievement scores are good predictors of college performance. It is widely argued that academic selection criteria should be raised to increase the quality of trainees. This is unwise unless there is confidence that these are good predictors of subsequent performance. It is unrealistic where there simply are not enough minimally qualified applicants in the pool currently available, which is the case in some countries. Two policy implications flow from this. First, there is a case for considering whether selection should include things other than academic results from secondary school examinations and, if so, what procedures are viable and cost-effective. Second, where academic achievement levels are thought to be too low, the question is whether content upgrading in subjects should be a priority at training institution level, or whether some sort of access programmes at school level might be more effective (school costs are generally much less than college costs). We note that in two of our case-study countries (Malawi and Trinidad and Tobago), trainees are appointed as untrained teachers before initial training. In principle this provides an extended opportunity to assess suitability and to base selection on performance as an untrained teacher. However, since

Executive Review

trainees are already appointed to the teaching profession, and links between the experience-based programme and the training institutions are weak or non-existent in the two cases, this opportunity is largely lost. It does not have to be.

The second set of issues relates to the characteristics of those selected. The detailed data indicate many factors that shape the starting points from which the trainees progress. Some of these may be thought fairly obvious (e.g. low levels of academic qualification), others are not so obvious (e.g. the range and extent of previous experience as teachers, the relatively high ages of some entrants). MUSTER has also provided insights into attitudes and dispositions to teachers and teaching which can be used to inform the management of professional learning. Trainees do not enter training with no preconceptions, but many. How they learn, what they internalise, and how motivated they are to remain teaching in primary schools, are all bound up with these cognitive and affective qualities. It is these that, at least from one point of view, frame the 'zones of proximal development' which trainers can use in delivering the curriculum. Yet neither curriculum developers nor tutors seem to take cognisance of what students bring with them, or to seek to understand it more fully. In the worst cases training proceeds on assumptions about the characteristics of those trained which are demonstrably false. The first step in ameliorating these problems is to acquire information and insight about the trainees, however they have been selected. It is their characteristics that matter in defining their learning needs and shaping the curriculum process.

4.   On the Curriculum for initial training

The MUSTER analyses of teacher education curriculum issues lead to many insights into the quality and relevance of material for existing programmes. The picture these paint is one that suggests that investment in curriculum development is long overdue and that much which is currently available falls short of what is needed and what is possible. Large parts of the teacher education curriculum seem to have been adapted from the academic curricula of school or university, rather than designed for adult learners or for the acquisition of professional knowledge and skills. They seldom recognise the role of relevant experiences, nor the different motivation and learning styles of adults. The curriculum needs to be reconceptualised, but in ways that keep in touch with local context and realities. The following are points for consideration.

Firstly, the curriculum must be matched to the needs of the learners, recognising areas of both strength and weakness. Primary trainees are usually a 'mixed ability' group; they will have done different subjects at high school, and a number may well have been 'slow learners'. Many may find maths and science particularly difficult. The subject courses must take this into account, by such means as setting, providing remedial support, self-study materials, or whatever is needed. This could include subject upgrading to school-leaving level through recognised and effective distance learning methods.

Executive Review

Second, a fresh look has to be taken at all the traditional components. Curriculum developers have to be realistic about what can be achieved within the given time, taking account of the age, experience and academic level of the entrants. Many programmes seem to assume that everything has to be taught during initial training, and consequently most of the curricula we analysed are grossly overloaded. The resulting stress on both tutors and students tends to lower morale and lead to less efficient teaching and learning.

The curriculum should be slimmed down to concentrate on helping the student acquire relevant core skills and competences, and the basic subject knowledge needed at that stage. This might mean less focus on the subject as a traditional discipline, and more on understanding the main concepts from a learner's viewpoint, as expressed in the terms **science education, language arts education**, etc. In so doing, students are likely to come to a clearer and more useful, if narrower, understanding of the subject itself, as well as the primary school syllabus. The languages of instruction should have a special place in the training of primary teachers, especially where lower primary is taught in the vernacular and upper primary in English. Trainees need to be fully fluent and competent in both, and to understand the strengths as well as the difficulties of bilingualism.

Such a slimmed-down curriculum should, however, include key frameworks drawn from psychology and sociology about how children learn, how individuals differ, and about the role of schools in the society. This is a problem area. Firstly, 'foundations' courses often try to teach far too much of the theory. Secondly, the texts and the research on which they are based are often drawn exclusively from rich country contexts. There is an urgent need here for both research and curriculum development to bring theories developed elsewhere into dialogue with local cultural practices and the students' own experiences of growing up. The aim should be to compare what is considered universal with what is culturally specific and contextual, so that students come to understand themselves and their pupils more clearly. Then, taking a problem-solving approach to their work, the young teachers are better equipped to deal with the realities of their classrooms .

Third, the role of the personal in professional education has to be recognised. Trainees do not come empty-handed, they bring much baggage in the form of images, ideas and experiences about teaching. One task for the tutors is to help them unpack and articulate these, so some can be thrown away, others refashioned or replaced. This does not require special techniques or resources, but it does imply an open approach from the tutors, and the use of methods such as autobiographical essays, role-play and discussion, to elicit memories and allow attitudes to be re-examined.

This links to the need for the whole curriculum to pay more attention to the 'affective side'. It is paradoxical that while most trainee teachers and their tutors rate personal attitudes and interpersonal skills as key characteristics of good primary teachers, the training curriculum

Executive Review

allows little space or opportunity for fostering personal growth and attitudes conducive to professional responsibility.

Fourth, the processes by which the curriculum are delivered need to be rethought. Theories of professional learning stress how public propositional knowledge, situational understanding, and personal experience have to be brought together. Such theories emphasise the importance of practice, and of reflection on practice, in developing skills. New information, ideas and skills have to be used before they are fully understood and internalised. Therefore, preparing and developing teachers means providing them with appropriate inputs of relevant knowledge, information and concepts stage by stage. Learning to apply and use the ideas and skills needs support, coaching and constructive feedback, thus 'scaffolding' the learning. Therefore learning to teach requires extensive opportunities for guided practice in a conducive environment.

This highlights the role of the school. For practical reasons, most training programmes have Teaching Practice in one or two large blocks, or during an internship year, often at the end of the course. Yet shorter, alternating, periods of time on and off campus are more effective, as they allow new information, ideas and skills to be internalised gradually through application and practice; equally, the experiential knowledge gained from attempting to teach can be thought about and refined before the next trial. This is difficult logistically when colleges are residential and/or in rural areas.

Fifth, attention must be paid to modes of assessment. Written terminal exams have a role to play but should be complemented by assignments linked to practice in schools which might use the classroom as a resource. Ghanaian experience suggests this is difficult, both because of conservative attitudes, and because alternative methods are thought to be too time-consuming to be used with large numbers of students. However difficult, new attempts must be made to find more appropriate methods of assessing professional learning and professional competence. In particular, the assessment of TP is often just a ritual, sometimes a farce. Aims in some systems (e.g. South Africa) to provide more holistic assessment of performance in an authentic environment, based on demonstrated competences integrating knowledge, skills and attitudes are laudable, but difficult to achieve.

Sixth, we suggest that curricula need to be more precisely designed for specific contexts – preparing teachers for bilingual teaching, large classes, few resources etc – for specific school phases e.g. lower or upper primary, and for specific groups of trainees, such as experienced but unqualified teachers, or school leavers. One practical approach might be a more modular curriculum, where trainees took those subjects and contents they needed, but care would be needed to ensure integration and coherence.

Executive Review

Finally, we suggest that in any teacher education curriculum the overall aims and desired outcomes need to be clarified, so that everyone is aware of the kind of teacher they are trying to produce – whether this be framed in terms of an effective instructor engaged to deliver a given curriculum efficiently, or in terms of a more autonomous professional expected to exercise their own judgement reflectively. The curriculum strategy then needs to be consistent with these aims and outcomes, and stakeholders should be supported in understanding and carrying out their roles in achieving it.

There are some general dimensions to curriculum problems raised by the MUSTER research. Amongst the most important are:

The lack of mechanisms for curriculum development, evaluation and renewal.
None of the MUSTER countries have systems for teacher education curriculum development; as a result it is ad hoc and sporadic.

Teacher Education and Structural Change.
Educational reform focused on schools often proceeds in advance of reforms in teacher education curricula. In principle teacher education should lead rather than lag behind wider reforms, so that new entrants can be prepared to adopt new curricula and teaching methods. It is, however, unrealistic to expect new teachers to be focal points for change as new members of the profession in junior positions. There are risks, exemplified in some of the MUSTER countries, that reforms that simultaneously seek to transform pedagogy, curriculum content, and the organisation of learning and teaching, may over-stretch infrastructure and capacity for change.

Cross-Cultural Borrowing and Innovation.
International borrowing is inevitable and often useful for the development of teacher education. However, models and theories developed in one context should not be imported uncritically to others. Some aspects will resonate more easily across cultures than others. Teacher education curricula are needed that, while sometimes using cross-national insights as points of departure, also build on local teacher knowledge, experience, and examples of good practice, in order to develop culturally relevant and effective teaching strategies. If innovations are to work, they need to be grounded and contextualised, and to make sense to those expected to carry them out. Moreover, strategies for innovation should recognise the importance of establishing a favourable climate of opinion to adopt new practices. Innovations that are pushed from the centre, rather than pulled by effective demand from communities of practice, will always be more difficult to sustain.

Executive Review

5.   On Colleges

The college systems that MUSTER has explored have their specific histories which draw attention to the contributions they have made to educational development in the past. The strong impression from MUSTER data is that whatever the historic impact of teacher education institutions had been, those which we researched were no longer playing key roles in the development of their national education systems. There was little evidence that most staff were engaged directly in curriculum development, either at school level or in Colleges. Professional links with school system were often fragile or non-existent and practising primary teachers were conspicuous by their general absence from activities organised in the colleges. Many colleges can be characterised by physical and intellectual isolation and many appeared held down by the weight of tradition, by lack of vision, and poor management. Any reconceptualisation of teacher education has to consider whether colleges have a role, and if so, what that role should be.

In principle training institutions could be 'powerhouses of change' responsible for a number of different facets of teacher education: initial training, INSET, training of trainers for school- and district-based support, curriculum development, research, development of teaching materials, etc. As developmental institutions distributed geographically across school systems, they should be ideally situated to be centres of support, inspiration and innovation not only for new teachers but for NQTs and experienced teachers as well. If this were to become a reality then a number of issues need consideration, which necessarily differ in detail in different cases. These include:

College governance.
Most colleges exist uneasily in an ill defined area between Ministries, higher education, and schools. Forms of governance need to be identified that support an academic and professional atmosphere, and which might encourage the development of cultures of research on practice linking staff and programmes into problems of school development and students' achievement. This may imply some form of University affiliation to provide access to expertise, enhance the status of training institutions, and expand the intellectual horizons of staff.

Staffing.
It is essential to develop a cadre of professional teacher educators, who are capable of working both within and outside the institution in creative and innovative ways. This implies a pay and career structure that recognises the kinds of work they do and the responsibilities they carry. It should be policy to recruit primary trainers from experienced and committed primary teachers and provide the necessary academic upgrading, or if taking secondary-trained teachers, to provide appropriate orientation including a period observing/teaching in primary schools. Gender issues must be borne in mind to ensure women candidates are

Executive Review

not disadvantaged by selection criteria or mode of training. The development of a cadre implies induction programmes for new recruits, and regular opportunities for continuing professional development, including where appropriate post-graduate degrees. Teacher educators should be expected to work with and in schools and carry out research, to keep up to date with international developments and to help adapt these to local conditions.

Links with Schools.

Colleges need to establish closer relationships with schools. We found few examples of good practice. Possible partnership arrangements include: selected 'professional development' schools, near or on the campus; the linking of initial training of students to the professional development of the co-operating teachers; the use of trained mentors to undertake part of the supervision and assessment, etc. Tutors could spend in schools time teaching, training, or doing research; equally, experienced teachers could be seconded to colleges for specific tasks.

College Strategic Planning.

A strategy of 'whole college development' is attractive. Such an approach would require a senior management team with a clear vision of change and administrative support and resources to carry it out. This presupposes medium term policy on teacher education and confirmation of the role colleges can play. It also assumes the existence or appointment of groups of tutors prepared to commit themselves to their own professional development and that of the training system.

6.   On Structures

Teacher education systems develop within national contexts which condition their form. New ideas for methods and structures have to recognise the realities of differing needs, circumstances and resources. Suggested improvements have to be formulated within the assumptions, processes and expectations of the wider national education system. There is thus no 'one-size-fits-all' solution to the problems of teacher education MUSTER has explored. However there are some structural questions that recur across systems. The basic structural issues for teacher education systems revolve around where training should take place, how long it should take, and what, if anything, should happen before and after periods of initial training leading to certification.

There are three common options as to institutional location. These are colleges of education, university education departments, or in schools. In reality the choices between these locations are not free. College-based systems for primary training are common in many low income countries and reflect how training systems have developed. Colleges are often the only post-secondary institutions in their geographic area and may be associated with post-secondary opportunities for particular groups who have a political stake in the continuity of the institutions. College systems seem likely to persist unless or until essentially political decisions are taken to adopt another arrangement. South Africa has taken the step of making all initial training university-based or affiliated with universities. However, the circumstances under which this has come about are unique (see Lewin, Sayed & Samuel 2003).

College-based systems may have advantages in terms of local location linked to communities or clusters of schools, a focus on a single profession and a responsiveness to educational needs, a role in pre-service and in-service education, and lower costs than tertiary level institutions. Our research suggests that these potential advantages are not necessarily converted into realities. They also have to be balanced against the risks of parochialism associated with the local (especially when colleges are rural and physically and intellectually isolated), the limits of expertise and insight associated with training institutions divorced from research, and the high costs that may be associated with small size.

University-based training offers the prospect of inputs from staff with high levels of disciplinary expertise, connection to insights from research relevant to learning and teaching, multi-disciplinary perspectives, and superior teaching resources associated with large-scale institutions. On the other hand critics suggest that university-based training may be a long way removed from the issues of practice in primary schools, high levels of academic knowledge in disciplines are largely irrelevant, and tutors' career advancement is likely to depend more on research recognition than training competence.

School-based training has become increasingly common in rich country systems. There are many good pedagogic and professional development reasons why training located in the work environment is potentially attractive because of its direct links with practical problems, advice from successful teachers, and socialisation into professional norms and standards. However, the basic assumptions of school-based training – namely that there are sufficient schools to offer appropriate training environments and enough qualified teachers to act as professional mentors to trainees – are often difficult to meet in low income countries. Most schools may not be appropriately resourced as training sites, lacking both qualified teachers and enough teaching and learning materials. Nor do staff necessarily see their role as including training new teachers and they are unlikely themselves to have any training as trainers. Under these circumstances, school-based training may simply become a form of 'sitting by Thabo', with new teachers simply copying what is done around them whether or not this is good practice. The MIITEP experience does suggest that with enough support, some elements of school-based training are possible even in very resource-poor circumstances. But expectations of what can be achieved have to be realistic: serious investment has to be made in print-based handbooks and manuals for trainees and for trainers, while field-based peripatetic resource persons and selected members of school staff have to be trained in supervision and support.

Executive Review

School-based training is generally associated with various forms of distance education, as it is in MIITEP. Distance education methods are attractive because they allow teachers to be trained while on the job, which saves the costs of replacement. It should also reduce the direct costs if a proportion of the training is self-instructional and based on print or other low cost media. However, the problems of distance learning are well known. For primary teachers in rural Africa there are particular problems. The materials have to be at the right language level for ESL learners and cover a wide range of topics, as the trainees may have access to few other printed resources. In so-called predominantly 'oral' cultures students may find book-based learning particularly difficult; aural media such as radio programmes or audio-cassettes may be more effective, if the technology is available and motivation can be maintained. Video is much more expensive, and unlikely to be as cost-effective as alternatives. Though new information technologies based on computers and the internet appear to offer many potential benefits, these are yet to be demonstrated in practice in mass systems of teacher education in Africa. They have high initial costs and carry risks of rapid obsolescence of hardware and software. Regular face to face contact with peers and a tutor are likely to remain essential components of training, albeit supplemented by other methods.

The questions of how long training should take and what should happen before and after the period of initial training are important, but as with the question of where training should be located there is no single answer. A wide range of possibilities can be imagined some of which are shown below.

Modes of Training

Mode 1	Conventional full-time college-based training preceded by no experience
Mode 2	Conventional full-time college-based training preceded by pre-course experience and followed by mentored induction into schools
Mode 3	Untrained teaching experience followed by conventional full-time college-based training
Mode 4	Mentored pre-training experience followed by conventional full-time college-based training and mentored induction into schools
Mode 5	Mentored pre-training experience followed by a short period of conventional college-based training followed by school placement with INSET support
Mode 6	Mentored pre-training experience followed by alternating short periods of conventional full-time college-based training followed by mentored induction into schools
Mode 7	Mentored pre-training experience followed by wholly school-based training on the job leading to mentored distance support

There are many other possible mixes which carry different resource and cost implications. We can note four key observations. First, extended full-time institutional training is only one of many options. Second, what comes before and what comes after core periods of training may be just as important as what occurs in the core, though rarely is it systematically considered as part of the training process. Thirdly, there is no necessity for core periods of training to be continuous or front-loaded in terms of costs or training inputs. Fourth, mixed mode methods, which make use of distance education and learning while working, are clearly options which have potential cost advantages. The resource implications of different approaches can only be identified when their component parts are specified in particular country contexts.

The analytic questions related to future policy and practice focus on which of these (and other possible modes) are feasible, relevant to short to medium term needs, and are likely to be cost-effective. Is a new and different balance of inputs attractive to meet new needs and disquiet over both costs and effectiveness of existing patterns of delivery? There are opportunities to reconsider how investment in teacher education and training is best organised and delivered, given the shortfalls in teacher supply generated by enrolment expansion, the new emphasis in many countries on changing curricula to improve pupils' achievement, the consequences of financial constraints, and the importance of improving quality and effectiveness.

7. On External Assistance

Several issues stand out from the MUSTER research for those who provide external assistance. First, a number of points have already been made relating to the formation of policy on teacher education. Where teacher education, and more broadly the education system as a whole, is partly externally financed, it is incumbent on agency representatives to promote a strategic approach to teacher education and ensure it is appropriately considered in medium term planning. Where such policy does not exist it should be encouraged and the evidence base for its development supported. International development targets related to primary education and the EFA agenda cannot be realised without an adequate supply of qualified and competent teachers. Teacher supply is the main constraint on the achievement of these goals in a good number of the poorest countries.

The second point is that evidently it is not sufficient to make external finance available either through projects or as part of more general budgetary support. Availability is not the same thing as disbursement; disbursement is not the same thing as resources reaching end users in ways that result in valued outcomes. Where teacher education institutions are starved of funds (resulting in erratic and often very low salary payment, near zero allocation to learning materials, and lack of maintenance to the point where facilities are closed for long periods), regeneration of effective training systems is impossible.

The third point is that judgements do have to be made in the round about the profile of external assistance whether within a sector plan or without. More specifically, assistance directed to school level designed to improve access, retention and quality has to include support for teacher development, since it is teachers who determine, more than anything

Executive Review

else, the quality of learning that takes place. How this is articulated with the initial training system, and its institutions, is a core question. Initial training of itself is always unlikely to result in the transformation of teaching and learning in schools in the short term: new teachers are likely to be less skilled than experienced teachers, their organisational status is such that they have less influence on curriculum and school policy and practice, their numbers are small compared to those established in the profession etc.. Nevertheless, new teachers, and the institutions that train them, are in principle one of the few vectors for introducing new practices to improve pupil learning. Others may exist or be developed (e.g. teachers' centres and peripatetic advisory teachers). So a key question for those who provide external assistance is whether to include initial training institutions in development plans or to by-pass them in favour of direct support into the school system. A strategy of benign neglect of colleges, which does seem by implication to have been followed in some cases, seems an opportunity missed. Unless of course the judgement is made that such institutions really have reached the point where they are largely ineffective and not amenable to significant reform.

Fourth, external support has a comparative advantage in some spheres but not in others. Most obviously, subsidy of development budgets for capital assets (predominantly buildings) may be the only way in which physical capacity can be expanded. Like other forms of assistance this can, of course, result in plant which is suited to purpose with appropriate durability and recurrent costs; it may also be poorly designed, expensive and difficult to maintain with local resources. Technical assistance is the other common form of support. This also needs to be tailored to purpose. Few believe that agency support of staff directly delivering services is cost-effective. More attractive is expert assistance with curriculum development, especially in those areas of the curriculum that are most internationalised (e.g. mathematics, science, international languages). This can also give access electronically or otherwise to networks which allow developers to share their experience across institutions and countries. Such international experts need to work very closely with national experts with a view to creating sustainable capacity in the future. This is sometimes easier said than achieved. External support for learning materials production as well as development can also be useful. Views may differ on the value of supporting low volume, low quality domestic production of print material (which often has a high import content), rather than buying in from the lowest cost international provider. The fact is the latter may be considerably cheaper and more cost-effective, but it requires foreign exchange. External assistance is often the only source of staff development for college staff, especially where this involves periods spent outside the country acquiring new skills and evaluating different approaches to training. Training institutions generally account for a small proportion of the education budget and relatively small amounts of external assistance can have a substantial impact on their quality. Their staff ought to be aware of the most recent developments in their fields of study elsewhere and be able to adapt and develop these sensitively and realistically for local use.

Executive Review

Fifth, teacher education is a certification process that carries with it a license to practise as well as salary benefits. Inevitably this means that curricula in action are heavily influenced by the form and content of the assessment system. MUSTER research identifies this as an area of general weakness. Different arrangements exist in different countries for the setting, taking and marking of assessment tasks and various rubrics are followed that can include continuous assessment, project work, and assignments alongside the fairly universal fixed-time closed-book written examinations and the assessment of teaching practice by tutors. There is evidence that much assessment is narrowly limited and excludes many things identified in curricular materials as valued learning outcomes. Professional knowledge and skill are rarely reliably assessed and much teaching practice evaluation is ritualised to the point where it is unlikely to be valid and reliable. Assessment and certification techniques require expertise and systematic application. External assistance can and should make a direct contribution to the development of reliable and valid examination systems with the objective of ensuring curriculum relevance, technically robust selection, and cost-effective assessment.

Sixth, the management of many teacher education systems and their institutions is weak. Few systems provide training or support for senior management who are likely to have been promoted from teaching positions. None of the colleges we undertook research in had a strategic medium term plan, and as far as we can establish none had been asked to produce one. If they had it is likely they would have needed assistance. Management information systems were also lacking, with basic information often incomplete or simply not collected or retained. The extent to which management expertise, procedures and systems can be transferred across systems depends on differences in organisational culture, infrastructure and resources, and levels of institutional autonomy. However, much is known about more and less efficient and effective management, and external assistance can help such knowledge to be shared in ways which are sensitive to what will and will not make a difference within a particular system.

Finally, the list of possibilities for constructive assistance would not be complete without a further observation. Innovation almost invariably requires resources. Poorly financed systems under pressure rarely have these available. Crisis management informs action more often than tested solutions to problems of learning and teaching. External assistance can be crucial to develop work that would otherwise not occur. It can and does also support experiments with innovative curricula and alternative delivery systems, some of which may promise cost-effective methods of meeting expanded demand. This has to be seen as what it should be. It is development support for limited periods beyond which such innovations need to become self-sustaining. If this is not so, then such assistance begins to resemble recurrent budgetary support, which needs a different kind of justification. It should be support for innovations grounded in the systems to which they are applied, not simple transplants of blueprints developed elsewhere for different purposes.

Executive Review

8. **Some Scenarios for the Future**

Teacher education appears to be one of the most conservative parts of many education systems. It seldom is the source of curriculum innovation, theorised pedagogy, or radical reconceptualisations of professional learning. It often lags behind schools in the adoption of new practice and patterns of learning and teaching. This is a signifier that political will and bureaucratic courage may be needed for the implementation of real changes designed to improve efficiency and effectiveness. The case of South Africa, where changes in teacher education were part of more general system-wide transformation, is instructive but unique (see Lewin, Samuel & Sayed 2003). There the will and the vision has existed to challenge old orthodoxies, wasteful resource allocation, and ineffective training methods.

The MUSTER research leads to much food for thought about future patterns of teacher education. One way of encapsulating some of the possibilities is to formulate some possible scenarios. Three portraits are developed in the main text. These are summarised below.

8.1 **Scenario 1: More of the Same – Roosting Egrets[2]**

More of the Same (MOS) is what will happen in the absence of coherent development policy and medium term strategic planning. The strengths and weaknesses will remain, inertia will define curricula and learning experiences, working practices will continue to deliver the curriculum at current levels of efficiency, and increased output will be difficult to achieve where it is needed at sustainable levels of cost.

This scenario is only attractive if there is a reasonable balance between supply and demand for new teachers and the quality of training is regarded as appropriate. The former only applies in Trinidad and Tobago, and the latter in none of the MUSTER countries.

For all the reasons MUSTER has highlighted – e.g. the changing characteristics of new entrants, the gulf between curricular content and process and the realities of schools coping with post-EFA surges in enrolments, the lack of innovation in colleges designed to promote closer professional interactions with schools, the lack of systematic support for induction of NQTs – MOS is not really an option. It is however the default condition and the most likely outcome unless energy, commitment and resources are directed towards the challenges MUSTER has identified.

---

[2] Egrets are birds of habit that return to the same spot each evening to roost day in day out.

8.2   **Scenario 2: Managed Evolution - Weaver Birds at Work[3]**

Managed evolution is a real possibility where medium term policy (identifying goals, resources, implementation modalities, and time-scale) can be realised and integrated into sectoral plans for education. This is a prior condition since without such policy, updated periodically to reflect changing needs, development cannot be purposefully managed. It implies prioritisation of teacher education as a critical arena for support, manifested through secure forward planning of resource allocation over a long enough period to allow development plans to come to fruition. It also assumes that teacher education has a defined and effective locus of control within Ministry of Education structures (e.g. Departmental status with Director level representation). Though there may be potential in decentralising some aspects of teacher education, this may be premature if existing institutions have weak self-management capacity, small size, and common needs.

The incrementalism implied in this scenario invites strategic thinking which identifies those aspects of teacher education that impinge on quality, efficiency and effectiveness and which can be changed without radical reforms and which have gains which outweigh their costs. These may or may not be sufficient to develop systems in ways which respond to the volume of demand for new trained teachers. They may lead to revised time-scales for the achievement of EFA and MDG targets.

MUSTER identifies a raft of incremental changes that have more or less applicability to different systems. These include:

Improved selection and preparation for initial training

Pre-training teaching experience as an untrained teacher is common. Only in Trinidad and Tobago is this institutionalised as an On-the-Job Training Scheme. The development of OJT-like schemes has several attractions – trainees can be selected partly on the basis of their performance over time, rather than initial academic qualification; trainees contribute to reducing teacher shortages through the work they do; managed OJT schemes could greatly enrich the skills and competencies of those entering training. At the same time, pay and conditions of service need to be improved to the point where they can attract and retain people with appropriate qualities.

Curriculum Development

Teacher education curricula suffer in varying degrees from fragmentation. In most systems curricula are not developed dynamically or incrementally, neither are they suffused with contributions from teacher educators at college level. Written materials for trainers and for trainees are in short supply and often derived from a variety of sources which lack coherence

---

[3] Weaver birds in their many varieties both follow set patterns to build nests and display astonishing ingenuity in adapting to different sites with different local conditions to construct efficiently durable nests which all differ in detail but serve the same purpose.

Executive Review

or consistency in approach. Revitalised teacher education systems could transform this situation through systematic and cumulative approaches to developing and enriching the curriculum and its learning materials base at college level, and through coherent national level programmes to generate more relevant core materials within an agreed framework.

Changed Working Practices
Working practices in teacher education differ widely. However, MUSTER data indicates that there is considerable scope to improve quality through more effective management focused on trainees' learning experience. Training institutions need to be much more demand-led, in terms of being responsive to the needs of trainees, rather than to the preferences, priorities and familiar practices of those who work in them. In many cases lecturing to large groups of up to 100 is favoured, though it is not necessary where student-staff ratios are below 20:1. Few colleges make much use of experienced teachers drawn in to inform discussions about pedagogy, class management, and curriculum realities. Even fewer college staff spend periods in schools in a professional development role which could help inform their college-based teaching.

Teaching Practice
All the MUSTER training systems include periods of teaching practice in schools. This can have high costs associated with supervision by college tutors. Trainees' experience of teaching practice suggests that it can be very valuable, but that for many learning is not coherently managed, and supportive supervision is not consistently available. There is little clear thinking on what learning outcomes can and cannot be achieved through existing patterns of teaching practice, most of which have not undergone any fundamental reappraisal since they were first introduced. There is considerable scope for improvements, such as integrating teaching practice much more closely and extensively with college work, re-evaluating the merits of college-based micro-teaching and other methods of acquiring professional skill which can be more resource-efficient than largely unsupported teaching practice, and arranging teaching practice placement and support more effectively.

Infrastructure and Learning Materials
Most colleges in MUSTER countries have poor physical facilities and infrastructure, few learning materials, and underutilised space as a result of periods of neglect. They are nevertheless frequently the only post-secondary institution in an area with a concentration of educational professionals, and thus the only source of advice and support to practising teachers. Impoverished facilities compromise the effectiveness with which training can be conducted and have a depressing effect on morale. Relatively small investments could transform at least some of these institutions into much more vibrant, accessible and attractive professional development nodes with outreach capabilities.

Teacher Educator Staff Development

The college lecturers are a neglected resource. Their main needs are: better personnel management, deployment and induction, and a clearer career structure linked to staff development and promotion opportunities, which would attract, motivate and retain suitable tutors. These things are achievable without excessive costs, but require different approaches to staff development which could improve morale, create incentives and rewards for improved performance, and attract new talent into the profession.

Changes in approaches to learners

Teacher educators may need to develop or rediscover culturally appropriate 'visions' of what an effective teacher is. They should provide opportunities for growth and development of personal attributes that can help trainees become confident and competent in their diverse professional roles. Student teachers need to be treated as adult learners and helped to study in more independent and proactive ways, so they experience themselves new ways of learning and teaching; they need to learn to reflect in ways that enable them to improve the quality and effectiveness of their teaching.

8.3   Scenario 3: Radical Reform – Soaring Eagles[4]

Radical reform requires vision, courage and persistence to reshape teacher education in fundamental ways. It will usually require substantial investment up-front before benefits are apparent, and the conversion to new approaches of those embedded in the comfort zones of the old. It is the most exciting but the most risky option as entrenched interests rarely embrace new practices without strong incentives; such changes are usually linked to wider political reforms.

Some possibilities here are:

Reprofiling the structure and length of training

Conventional teacher education systems are heavily front-loaded in terms of the investment of resources i.e. most if not all the resources are committed to pre-career full-time residential training. Where demand is high long periods of pre-career training will be expensive and slow to produce large numbers of new teachers.

Alternatives which provide shorter periods of introductory training, followed by periods of work as assistant teachers, and interspersed with subsequent training inputs building on the base acquired from school experience, could be both more efficient (those who are trained are on the job, therefore costs are lower), and more effective (theory and practice are placed in dialogue, college-based work has to respond to real problems and skill needs). It is therefore possible to conceive of training which is 'drip fed' over time rather than provided

---

[4] Eagles cover large distances with remarkable skill and adapt to different environments with apparent ease, flexibly applying themselves to the problems of survival in different and changing environments.

Executive Review

in a single long period pre-career. There are many possibilities of detailed configurations which could include short intensive (e.g. 3 months) residential training, vacation workshops, complementary distance learning support, local cluster groups to support trainee teachers on the job etc. If this were linked to incremental progression up the career structure – e.g. trainee teacher, assistant teacher, junior teacher, fully qualified teacher – it could provide incentives to stay with the programme and accumulate skills and competence.

A variant of this approach could seek to move the locus of training activity to schools, as is the case in many high income countries. Conceptually it is easy for this to appear attractive. However, MUSTER empirical evidence draws attention to some important stumbling blocks. These include: the scarcity of school locations representing good practice relative to the numbers of trainees, the shortage of those likely to possess mentoring skills at school level and their willingness to invest substantial time in the activity, and the difficulties of moderating the school-based experience and ensuring appropriate and valid assessment and certification. Circumstances will differ and it may be that some of these problems can be overcome. In the short to medium term it is possible to imagine movement towards more school-based training through alternating periods of On-the-Job training and college-based work.

Mixed-mode training programmes, which combine college-based work with different types of distance learning, already exist. MIITEP in Malawi is an example. The research on MIITEP indicates the many difficulties that exist in realising the technically coherent model in practice where infrastructure is weak. MUSTER countries do not currently use modern information and communication technology (ICT) in teacher education. The reasons for this in the African countries are self-evident. The costs are high, connectivity is low, and relevant content is yet to be created. This situation may change over the next decade. Until it does it will remain the case that print material offers far more durable opportunities for support for training at a distance, though of course it lacks the interactivity that ICTs could potentially provide[5].

A different conceptual model of learning to teach

Many of the curricula we analysed seemed premised on the idea that if students are given enough knowledge and skills at college these can be applied unproblematically, like 'recipes', to any classrooms. A more useful model is one that sees teaching as interactive problem-solving, requiring a thoughtful and reflective approach to practice. Thus learning to teach means acquiring not only knowledge and skills, but also a situated understanding of pupils and how they learn, along with repertoires of skills and strategies for dealing with unique and ever-changing circumstances. The aim of the training should be the development of

---

[5] Interactivity is only of value where it suits the purpose (i.e. it provides a pathway to desired learning outcomes), and is available at affordable price levels. Interactivity that requires responses from people can quickly become very expensive in staff time, or simply inoperable when the volume of messages requiring considered response overloads the capacity to respond.

Executive Review

professional reasoning ability, rather than the acquisition of pre-defined behaviours (Akyeampong 2001). Such a model requires an epistemological shift towards a view of knowledge that recognises the value of teachers' personal, experiential and craft knowledge as well as the public propositional knowledge offered in college. For such a different model to take root will require time, debate, and professional development among lecturers, curriculum developers, MOE personnel, and the wider educational community. This is consonant with the new more learner-centred and constructivist-based approaches to teaching and learning in many reform programmes for school curricula, and could be a more suitable preparation for them.

Transforming College Practices

Two radical suggestions emerge from MUSTER data. First, none of the colleges in the research have strong and free-flowing professional links with schools. They play little role in curriculum development and implementation at school or any other level, and seldom provide central resources for teachers' INSET and CPD. With a different mandate, managerial commitment, and appropriate resources they could become developmental institutions with substantial outreach to schools. Their staff could acquire responsibilities to improve learning and teaching at school level directly as well as through the training of teachers.

Secondly, and even more radically, college lecturers could be appointed on different types of contracts than those which prevail. Most college staff are drawn from the ranks of practising teachers in mid-career. For many this becomes their occupation through until retirement. Employment practices usually privilege those with higher levels of academic qualifications and this can have the effect of excluding those with extensive primary experience in favour of those who have taught at secondary level and who are more likely to have degree level qualifications. The staffing of a developmental college might not look like this. It could be staffed by experienced and effective teachers, given appropriate professional development, and seconded from primary schools for, say, five year periods. Permanent college staff could be required to work in schools periodically to give them relevant and recent experience and ensure that their training activities were closely grounded in the realities of schools and learning problems. With imagination groups of staff could be periodically tasked with development activities related to curriculum implementation, improving training effectiveness and supporting the induction of NQTs.

Changing the Relationships between Content and Professional Skills and Competences.

All the college systems MUSTER has researched have difficulties in striking an appropriate balance between up-grading content skills in subjects (and in the medium of instruction), and developing pedagogic and professional skills. Most attempt both simultaneously with more or less successful integration. Where the entry level characteristics of trainees suggest that subject-based knowledge and skill, or language fluency, are inadequate, the radical choice may be to develop pre-course bridging programmes focused specifically on these. This could be in the training institution. But it could also be undertaken in nominated secondary schools given this task. The latter is likely to be more cost-effective. If initial training programmes really could assume students' mastery of basic content and language skills, then they would be free to focus sharply on professional and pedagogic competencies.

A Flood of Materials

Learning material for trainee teachers and NQTs located within national contexts in MUSTER countries is scarce. Yet print material is relatively cheap, durable and can be immensely helpful to those starting teaching in school environments where good practice may not be common and informed advice is difficult to come by. Colleges, which could and should be a major source of such material, often do not produce text material in volume and are unable to ensure trainees leave with a portfolio of supporting manuals, enrichment materials etc. This problem is more readily resolvable than textbook supply to all children since the numbers are much smaller. The radical proposition may not sound radical – flood the trainee teachers with quality support materials. It is radical in the sense that it has yet to be prioritised or realised in the systems we have researched.

9.   Concluding Remark

The last scenario has explored some of the more radical options available that would challenge current practice and can provide an agenda for reform. In conclusion several possibilities stand out that could make real differences. These include:

- More strategic use could be made of untrained teachers supported by orientation programmes and school-based apprenticeship-like relationships (on-the-job training). If this process was managed effectively it could become a step on a pathway to initial qualification. The experience of working as a teaching assistant would discourage some, reinforce the aspirations of others, and allow the unsuitable to be selected out.

- Initial training could be organised in a more modularised way to allow training to be acquired as and when needed. Investment in skill and competency would be cumulative and could take place through a variety of routes (full-time, part-time, day release, residential, distance etc) and in a variety of locations (in school, at teacher centres, in colleges and universities). It would have to be linked to a progressive career structure that regulated promotion to different grades to experience, qualification level and competence. The important difference is that it would not be a single-shot qualification process but a continuous pathway leading to higher levels of competence.

Executive Review

- A staircase of training linked to posts of responsibility and rewards offers the opportunity to embed the training process more firmly in the school and the learning needs of its pupils. So also might the modularisation of the training curriculum. It would make it possible for more training to take place in closer proximity to professional practice both in space and time. It might allow possibilities for schools (and colleges) to acquire some of the attributes of learning institutions. It could obviate the need for special induction and support of NQTs if a seamless web of Continuing Professional Development began to develop which could include the induction of NQTs.

- Teacher educators at all levels, whether school or college-based, need to have induction and continuing professional development. This should ensure that they are aware of recent developments, can judge whether these should be incorporated into training, have perspectives that run beyond their direct experience, and have a rich range of material to draw on to support and stimulate trainee teachers.

- Colleges could then move away from being monotechnic institutions focused purely on residential long course qualifications, towards becoming dynamically integrated nodes of innovation, professional development activity, and advisory support. They could be challenged locally and nationally to make a real difference to learning in schools and the development of the human potential of the populations they serve.

Whether these kinds of proposals are feasible or desirable is necessarily a question for different systems to address. It may be that incremental changes based on the kind of evidence that MUSTER has accumulated are both more attractive and more likely to gain political support. The teacher education systems MUSTER has undertaken research on are 'not broken but they do need fixing'. If teacher educators are to retain public support for their activities, if EFA and MDG targets are to be realised, and if new approaches to learning and teaching which have developmental significance are to be adopted, then all the options should be aired and considered judgements made about which will make a real difference to the next generations of learners and teachers.

Chapter One   **1 The MUSTER Project**

1.1   Introduction

The Multi-site Teacher Education Research (MUSTER) project grew from several roots. During the early 1990s the Centre for International Education (CIE) at the University of Sussex Institute of Education built up links with Universities in a number of low and middle income countries. Teacher education emerged as a common focus of interest. The consensus was that teacher education in many countries was under-theorised, practice was often not demonstrably effective, and existing systems were unable to deliver the numbers of qualified teachers needed at sustainable levels of cost to meet the demands imposed by commitments to Education for All. Consequently, in 1997 the CIE approached the UK Department for International Development[6] (DFID) with a proposal for a collaborative multi-country programme of research into teacher education.

The original proposal for the research identified two separate sets of reasons for such research into teacher education. One set was policy-related, the other was concerned with insights into the nature of teacher education.

On policy MUSTER noted that:

- All countries have systematic arrangements in place for teacher education and allocate substantial resources to initial training, in the belief that it enhances the quality of teaching and student achievement.
- Despite this there is widespread evidence that achievement of students is unsatisfactory, and that teaching methods in schools are slow to change in ways that reflect approaches deemed to be effective. Though many factors are involved in low school achievement, one strategy is to improve the quality of training given to teachers before they begin teaching and enhance the support available for the development of professional skills in the first years of employment.
- Little research has been carried out into the effectiveness of teacher education in most low income countries. Training programmes persist which are based on models developed by the former colonial powers. More recently contemporary models from the UK, USA, Australia and New Zealand have been influential, though their impact and feasibility is largely untested in low income countries. Ministries and development agencies trying to devise more efficient and effective programmes have few locally-based research findings to guide them; nor do they have the capacity to assess formatively which strategies are working in the manner intended.
- In high income countries, where teachers have to be qualified before their first employment, there are clear conceptual and practice differences between pre-service (PRESET) and in-service (INSET). In many low income countries teachers begin working in classrooms with no training, and gain initial professional qualifications much

---

[6] Formerly the Overseas Development Administration (ODA).

1 The MUSTER Project

later, if at all. In several Commonwealth Caribbean countries this pattern is effectively a policy. By default it is also the case in many African systems. The curriculum in many Teacher Training Colleges (TTCs) and University Departments of Education (UDEs) in these countries often does not recognise and build on the prior teaching experience trainees possess.

- It is extremely rare for the responsibilities for training to be shared with schools in which new teachers work in many parts of Africa. Little support is generally available for the professional development of unqualified and newly qualified staff. Mentorship relationships are rarely formalised and the value of initial training may be compromised by subsequent lack of access to advice and role models of good practice.

- Teacher education budgets in most low income countries are heavily constrained. There are indications that costs can be very high relative to other forms of education and training. It is therefore important to generate indications of the costs of different patterns of initial teacher education and identify any areas where more can be achieved within sustainable budgets.

On the nature of teacher education MUSTER pointed out that:

- The actual ways in which teachers acquire and use professional knowledge are not well understood. Over the last 15 years these have been conceptualised and discussed within a rapidly growing literature grounded in the experience of high income countries. Empirical studies and theoretical conceptualisation associated with these developments (e.g. teacher thinking, teacher reflection, the differences between novices and experts) have revealed the complexity of the training task.

- The great bulk of published studies have been carried out in high income countries (e.g. UK, USA, Canada, Australia). There are some exceptions (e.g. Tatto et al 1991, Lockheed & Verspoor 1991, Dove 1985, Avalos and Haddad 1981, World Bank 1978) but these are limited in scope and now becoming dated. Superficially teacher education programmes in many low income countries have remained substantially unchanged since their development under colonial administrations. This is despite radically changed demands from school systems on teachers, often arising from Universal Primary Education (UPE), the commitments to Education for All, and related reforms of the school curricula. In addition, the work of teaching is intimately bound up both with the teacher's identity and sense of self and with the norms, values and expectations of the communities they serve. When these things change, some fundamental reappraisal grounded in context is needed.

- Though attempts have been made to reform teacher education the limited evidence suggests that much has remained at the level of rhetoric rather than being implemented in teacher education institutions. The general theorising which can provide models and concepts for new practice has frequently not found its way into national teacher

1 The MUSTER Project

education curricula. The reasons for this need to be identified in advance of further efforts to promote more effective practice. These may differ from system to system.

- Once consequence is that there is a need to identify which aspects of teacher education theory and practice developed in high income countries might be transportable, and which carry assumptions about the cultural roles of the teacher, pedagogic preferences, and infrastructure availability that compromise their value and restrict their relevance.

From these premises and concerns, a research proposal was designed to look at teacher education from four different but complementary aspects. These were to:

- Identify who becomes a teacher, what images, experiences and motivations they bring with them, and how these change during training and induction.
- Analyse the curricular processes by which new teachers acquire and learn to apply the understanding, skills and attitudes needed to become effective professional practitioners in their local schools.
- Profile training college staff, their career structures and their working practices
- Explore the varied patterns of initial qualification, and link these to considerations of supply, demand, costs, and benefits.

The overall aims were to reach conclusions that could improve the quality of initial teacher education programmes through a better understanding of the processes, and to point towards more effective and efficient methods of meeting demand within realistic resource constraints. Part of the MUSTER problem diagnosis indicated that published research on teacher education was rarely grounded in the context of low income countries, and that teacher education policy was almost never based on evidence derived from particular systems. An additional goal therefore became to build local research capacity at each of the sites chosen for the research, to catalyse subsequent work which could continue after MUSTER was complete and contribute to the development of evidence-based policy.

In summary MUSTER had ambitions to.

- enhance understanding of how new teachers acquire the knowledge, skills and attitudes needed to teach in different systems, and identify the professional learning experiences, including teaching practice, which are most useful and valuable to new teachers given the qualities that they bring with them to initial teacher education.

- categorise different types of pre-service provision leading to initial qualification in each system and profile their institutional bases, identify patterns of overall costs and costs per qualified teacher, and consider implications for efficiency, effectiveness and the prospects of meeting demand in sustainable ways.

1 The MUSTER Project

- build research capacity in-country focused on issues in teacher education using both quantitative and qualitative techniques, and strengthen the resource base of young researchers with field experience through in-project training.

1.2 The Research Partners

The choice of research sites grew out of already established links7 between the Centre for International Education (CIE) and the other educational research institutions listed above. In Malawi, joint research had already been carried out with untrained teachers (Stuart and Kunje 1997). A CIE link visit to Trinidad coincided with the decision of the UWI School of Education's Research Committee to focus, inter alia, on teacher education. The Institute of Education at the National University of Lesotho was interested in working more closely with the National Teacher Training College, whose Director wished to encourage research among his staff. Researchers at both ends of the link with the Institute of Education at Cape Coast University in Ghana had been involved in the reform of teacher college curricula. The South African link developed from a long-standing relationship with the Faculty of Education at the University of Durban-Westville and its associated policy and research centres, which fed into the development of new approaches to teacher education designed to meet the challenges posed by the transformation to democracy and the deconstruction of apartheid.

Ghana, Lesotho, Malawi, and Trinidad and Tobago all have single national teacher education systems that are centrally controlled and relatively homogenous. In these locations it was possible to undertake studies within a common framework with some comparative elements. In South Africa the 1990s were a period of dramatic transition. Teacher education was diverse, fragmented, and undergoing radical change. For these reasons it became clear that MUSTER research needed to take a different form. The scope of the research was broadened to capture some of the diversity that existed and a network of researchers was convened from other institutions including the Universities of the Western Cape, Witwatersrand, and Pretoria. Though several references are made to the South African research in this report it is not reported in detail. A separate book is available that synthesises the fruits of the research in South Africa (Lewin, Samuel and Sayed 2003).

1.3 The Research Process

The Sussex team made a formal proposal to DFID after preliminary contacts had been made with potential link partners, and Principal Researchers identified. When this was agreed contracts were drawn up between Sussex and the other institutions. The first task for each

---

[7] The Higher Education Links scheme run by the British Council had at various times supported staff exchanges between CIE and all the other institutions.

local research team was to conduct a Baseline Study on the current state of teacher education using secondary sources. These were presented at the first MUSTER workshop at Sussex in March 1998, where an overall research design was developed collaboratively building on the concerns listed above.

During this two-week workshop common research elements emerged across the countries. These included needs to focus on:

- teacher preparation for the basic cycle of formal education (generally primary, but in some cases including junior secondary)
- a sequential consideration of the stages through which trainees pass – enrolment in training, the training process, and induction into the first years of teaching as a trained teacher
- enquiry into the teacher education curriculum as locally conceptualised and implemented, exploring inputs, experiences, and outcomes
- a profiling of institutions which provide initial teacher education, the staff who deliver the curriculum, and their professional needs and career trajectories
- analyses of supply and demand, and their implications for costs and financing of sustainable systems for teacher education
- an awareness of gender in the professional and institutional aspects of training, and how gender issues are addressed in the training and induction process.

These concerns, together with the original themes, were distilled into four Strands – Becoming a Teacher, Curriculum Issues, College Issues, and Costs and Resources. Each was approached through questions in the three sequential Arenas – Inputs, Processes, and Outputs. A grid was developed to locate research questions within each stand and arena (see Chapter 2).

On the basis of the grid of questions each country team began to design sub-studies, and develop research instruments along common lines agreed at the workshop A mixture of quantitative and qualitative methods were used to complement each other, enhance both depth and breadth, and allow corroboration of insights. During the next 9 months country plans were finalised and work was begun on sub-studies within each country. These were supported from Sussex through in-country visits and through the e-mail network.

Progress was reviewed at the second MUSTER workshop in Durban, South Africa, in July 1999. This provided the opportunity for the research teams to consolidate draft reports on sub-studies, identify gaps, discuss data analysis, design instruments for further data collection, and plan the completion of sub-studies and country reports which would synthesise findings.

1 The MUSTER Project

In July 2000 the researchers convened for a further workshop at Sussex. This was focused on refining draft reports of further sub-studies, editing the Discussion Papers which were being produced, and planning the country reports. Time was also allocated to sharing ideas about the main issues and findings that had emerged from the research. A dissemination strategy for MUSTER was developed which included an extensive publication programme, a website, and a series of national level policy-orientated symposia. Preliminary work was undertaken to plan these and attract stakeholders. The symposia were held during 2001 and 2002 and each attracted key decision makers. The MUSTER principal researchers met as a group for a fourth time during the South African and Lesotho symposia, and for a fifth meeting around the Oxford International Education Conference in September 2001, which hosted an additional session based on MUSTER findings.

1.4 Themes and Variations

There were local variations to the overall pattern outlined above. This was deliberate and reflected the specific circumstances of each system and the enthusiasms of the researchers to explore in more depth particular issues. Thus, in addition to the core research programme based on the research matrix questions, a variety of sub-studies were conceptualised (see Chapter 2 for examples). Three D. Phil. studies were developed to address specific questions in very considerable detail. John Hedges explored issues to do with the induction and posting of new teachers in Ghana, focusing on problems and issues confronting new teachers in rural locations. Dominic Furlong developed research on financing teacher education in Ghana using data collected across the College system. Alison Croft studied the training and development of infant teachers in Malawi, focussing particularly on how teachers use the local culture and environment effectively in resource-constrained classrooms.

1.5 Reporting and Dissemination of Findings

The first method of dissemination was to create a MUSTER Discussion Paper series. These are listed at the end of this volume and are available free on the MUSTER website. This series included the Baseline Studies written at the beginning of the research period as well as many other thematic contributions. MUSTER Country Studies (Ghana, Lesotho, Malawi and Trinidad and Tobago) which synthesise findings at a country level, are published as DFID Research Reports. The South African material is published by Heinemann as a book. Other documentary outputs are extensive and are indicated in Appendix 2.

Alongside the publication programme five national workshops have been organised for policy makers and practitioners to disseminate findings directly to stakeholders in each country. The first of the national dissemination workshops took place in April 2001 in Maseru and in Pretoria. It was possible to schedule the MUSTER researchers to meet for a fourth time as a group at these conferences. This provided the opportunity to update progress towards completion of the research and plan the contributions to the Oxford

Conference. The Malawi national workshop took place in November 2001 in Lilongwe, the Trinidad and Tobago workshop in January 2002 at UWI, and the Ghana dissemination in July 2002 in Accra. These workshops were well attended and resulted in a variety of national Task Groups being established to take the ideas from MUSTER forward into policy and practice. (See Appendix 3 for details).

1.6 Overview of Report

This Research Report is organised in three parts. In the first part Chapter 2 elaborates on the key research questions that shaped the empirical work, and details aspects of the research strategy and the design, the development and use of the research methods chosen, and includes some reflections on the research process. Chapter 3 outlines the contexts within which the research was undertaken and provides an overview of their teacher education systems to locate subsequent discussion of research findings.

The second section consists of six thematically-based chapters exploring the findings from different parts of MUSTER. These Chapters are broadly organised around the strands that constituted the MUSTER planning framework. Chapter 4 explores the characteristics of beginning teachers and their perceptions and motivations. Chapter 5 analyses the teacher education curriculum. Chapter 6 takes this analysis further and focuses specifically on teaching practice, since this is widely regarded as one of the most useful and one of the most problematic areas of the training curriculum. Chapter 7 examines what happens when newly qualified teachers enter the school system, and what might be the impact of the training. Chapter 8 synthesises insights into the training institutions, their organisation and their staffing. Chapter 9 addresses questions of supply and demand, costs, and resource utilisation, and highlights the prospects for achieving development goals at sustainable levels of cost using existing training methods.

The last section (Chapter 10), in summarising findings across the MUSTER data, comments on policy options for the future under a number of headings that include selection questions, curriculum issues, college development potentials, support for newly qualified teachers, the role of external assistance, and the implications of resource demands for future training.

Chapter Two   **2 Doing The Research**

2.1   The Research Questions

The original questions in the proposal emerged from discussions during link exchange visits, international debates on Teacher Education, the particular interests of the Sussex Team, and suggestions from the DFID. At the first MUSTER workshop much brainstorming went on. This produced inter alia a list of 'really interesting questions' that invited enquiry because they were ones which team members felt were both important and currently poorly understood in each system. What finally emerged was a selection of key questions based on what could realistically be researched in each country with the resources available. It was agreed that the research would aim to:

- Identify who becomes a teacher, what images, experiences and motivations they bring with them, how these change during training and induction, and how they relate to the role and identity of the teacher.
- Analyse the curricular processes by which new teachers acquire and learn to apply the understanding, skills and attitudes needed to become effective professional practitioners in their local schools.
- Gain a deeper understanding of the training colleges, their development and organisation, and the career patterns and perspectives of their staff.
- Explore the varied patterns of initial qualification, costs, and benefits in the context of supply and demand for teachers

Four Strands - Becoming a Teacher, Curriculum Issues, College Issues, and Costs and Resources - and three Arenas - Inputs, Processes and Outputs – were used to collect together research questions which could be used to guide sub-studies. The grid developed and changed over time and was modified in the light of insights from the baseline studies, and by operational constraints. A simplified version (Fig.1) is presented here and linked to Chapters of this report where research questions included in this version are addressed. The full range of research questions and sub-questions exists within the Discussion Papers which capture data from the various sub-studies in more detail.

2 Doing The Research

Figure 1: **The Muster Matrix: An Overall View of Arenas and Strands[8]**

	Arena 1: Inputs	Arena 2: Process	Arena 3: Outputs
Becoming a teacher	◊ Who becomes a teacher and what characteristics do they have? (4) ◊ What do they bring in terms of images, expectations and experiences and how are these culturally located? (4)	◊ How do Trainees experience training programmes? (5 and 6) ◊ How do trainees value their training? (5 and 6)	◊ How do Trainees' attitudes and career intentions change as a result of training? (7) ◊ How do trainees value their training in retrospect? (7) ◊ What is the experience of NTQs after training? (7)
Curriculum	• How was the teacher education curriculum developed and what influenced it? (5) • What is to be taught, and how, and what are the underlying pedagogic assumptions? (5)	• How is the curriculum delivered? (5) • How are the practical elements of the curriculum realised? (6)	• How far are stated aims and objectives achieved? (7) • What are the competencies, in terms of the knowledge, skills and attitudes of the graduating NQTs? (7)
Colleges	* Who becomes a teacher educator and how? (8) * What induction and professional development programmes are available for teacher educators? (8)	* How do teacher educators perceive their work? (8) * How do they perceive the acquisition of knowledge skills and attitudes by young teachers? (8)	* What needs should be prioritised for the development of college staff? (8)
Costs and Resources	◆ What are the national levels of supply and demand for primary teachers? (9) ◆ How are budgets and other resources for training institutions configured? (9)	◆ What are the indicators of internal efficiency in the allocation of resources? (9) ◆ What are the costs of training and How are they profilrd? (9)	◆ What is the future demand for initial training and are the costs sustainable? (9)

[8] Numbers in brackets refer to Chapters where the questions are discussed.

DFID

2 Doing The Research

2.2   The Research Process

MUSTER was conceived as a collaborative multi-site research project that would maintain a core agenda of common research themes. It was also designed to allow the special circumstances and concerns of national researchers to be reflected in variations to a common design and extension into themes specific to particular countries. Some key features of the research process are worth highlighting.

Baseline studies: these were developed to profile the current status of teacher education systems, identify research literature, official reports, curriculum documents and planning material on teacher education, and analyse the key issues that were of most concern in each system. These baseline studies served the purpose of providing a focus on an initial task that was of itself useful (in most cases no recent reviews of teacher education policy and practice existed), and which could provide the basis for the detailed exploration of the issues raised. The baseline studies provided an evidenced counterpoint to assumptions and assertions about the nature and quality of teacher education circulating amongst communities of stakeholders (e.g. see Kunje and Chimombo 1999, Quamina-Aiyejina et al 1999) Lefoka, Jobo, Khiba et al 2000, Akyeampong and Furlong 2000).

Research Matrix: MUSTER developed a grid of core research questions around which there was a consensus. Fig. 1 shows a simplified version of this matrix. This two-dimensional grid identified four strands and three arenas. It was used to guide the development of country research plans and the sub-studies designed to explore the major research questions. Detailed plans identified the data collection methods that would be used for each sub-study. The framework went through several iterations and proved a useful heuristic tool to focus discussion and develop particular components of the research; in the event data relevant to each cell was collected and analysed in all the countries, albeit in different degrees of depth and breadth.

Sub-studies: the research plans that were developed were deliberately segmented in terms of sub-studies. These were configured as research projects with specific foci that could be undertaken and written up in a fairly self-contained way. There were several reasons for this approach. First, some members of the research teams had little experience of acting as independent researchers. Sub-studies enabled individuals and groups to take responsibility for particular pieces of research of manageable scale which could be guided by more experienced researchers. Second, the intention was to build up from the sub-studies to synthetic research reports that would address the larger research questions. Using sub-studies reduced the risk that a particular aspect of the MUSTER research would not come to fruition (if a sub-study could not be completed, there would at least be several others to address related research questions). Third, the completion of sub-studies provided milestones against which to judge the progress of the research and offer more support if

2 Doing The Research

deadlines were slipping or quality needed enhancing. Many of the sub-study reports were produced in good draft form early on and circulated as part of the MUSTER Discussion Paper series; some were later refined into journal articles.

Local Variations: certain studies were undertaken at some sites and not others, as noted above. This allowed the important differences in the significance of different research questions in different contexts to be captured. It also gave more ownership of parts of the research to the research teams and allowed space for local agendas. The local variations included a study of On-the-Job Training Scheme in Trinidad and Tobago, an analysis of patterns of assessment for teacher education in Malawi, detailed observations of college classes in Lesotho, and a wider survey of trainee teacher attitudes in Ghana. In the case of South Africa the research team decided first to focus on the experience and developmental initiatives of UDW, one of the major providing institutions that was historically disadvantaged. Subsequently the scope of the research was widened to include consideration of the four most important pathways to becoming a teacher – college-based training, university training, distance programmes in public institutions, and franchised arrangements with private sector providers.

Symmetrical and Sequential Design: the research was planned to move from baseline studies which provided an overview of recent developments in teacher education and the issues these raised, through detailed research sub-studies, back to a synthetic country report which could have an evidenced basis for conclusions it reached about practice and policy. This country report, and its findings, could then be used during the dissemination process, along with those aspects of more detailed work relevant to future planning. Finally, the sub-studies and the country reports could be used to create comprehensive and synthetic research reports at country level and above.

Communications: MUSTER Principal Researchers were linked into a network of communication through e-mail which allowed frequent sharing of insights, research instruments and support for data analysis and for report writing. The co-ordinators visited the research sites to support the design, development and analysis of data, and individual researchers visited Sussex for periods of writing and reflection. The MUSTER workshops provided opportunities to consolidate products, share insights, and collaboratively plan future activities.

2.3   **Research Methods**

MUSTER used a wide range of research methods, drawing on both quantitative and qualitative techniques of data collection and analysis. This was designed to gain as full a picture as possible of the complex issues. There were also cultural reasons for using a variety of approaches. As one principal researcher put it:

2 Doing The Research

.... The socio-political values of African societies and the attitudes they promote
present those researching into the lives and experiences of its people with a different
set of methodological challenges. This reality required the picking and choosing of a
combination of research approaches, across what is often seen as the methodological
divide of qualitative and quantitative research [....] to enhance the validity of findings
and their interpretation. (Akyampong et al 2000: 4)

There was a tension between collecting data that would be directly comparable across sites
using common instruments, and wanting to respond to the local situation in different ways.
The process of designing instruments collaboratively was commenced at the first workshop
(March 1998). The Sussex team subsequently drew up research memoranda for the different
strands, containing draft instruments that could be adapted locally. In the case of survey
data, draft instruments were developed which had a high degree of commonality. This was
largely retained after piloting, though in some cases particular wording was modified to
reflect local variations in expression and interpretation to enhance construct validity. There
was more variation in the methods used to acquire qualitative data, though broad themes
were agreed which were then explored through interviews, focus groups etc. These varied
in the detail of their realisation.

The main data collection methods, how they were applied, and any special features that were
employed to meet specific circumstances are indicated below. Where appropriate we link
methods to particular strands and arenas. More detailed accounts of the methods used in
each case are available in the relevant Discussion Papers.

2.3.1 Surveys

Questionnaires were used to collect data on student teachers at the points of entry to and
exit from their training course, and from Newly Qualified Teachers (NQTs). The Entry
Questionnaire contained sections on biodata (age, sex, family background, schooling etc),
on memories of schooling, expectations of college, and career plans, using a mixture of
closed and open-ended questions. A final section contained a number of Likert-type
statements about pedagogy, the role and status of teachers, and other professional issues.
Although the open-ended questions produced rich data, they proved difficult and time-
consuming to code and analyse. The Exit and NQT questionnaires were therefore drawn up
at the Durban workshop to a closed-response format so they could be quickly analysed by
computer, using SPSS. They contained a similar section on biodata, evaluations of the
college experience including Teaching Practice (TP), careers plans, and for NQTs items
about induction and early experiences in school. A revised list of Likert items was developed
and included. Because of the time scale, these surveys were cross-sectional rather than
longitudinal, with different cohorts being surveyed.

2 Doing The Research

In Lesotho (one college) and Trinidad and Tobago (two colleges) it was possible to survey trainees from each training institution. In Malawi, two Colleges were sampled out of six, and in Ghana four out of thirty eight. Overall the entry samples included 400 student teachers in Ghana, 90 in Lesotho, 176 in Malawi, and 299 in Trinidad. These samples have their limitations, particularly as regards gender. Over two-thirds of the student teachers in the samples in Lesotho, Malawi, and Trinidad and Tobago were female. In Ghana only about a third were female. In Ghana and Lesotho these proportions were broadly consistent with the intake in previous years. However, in Trinidad and Tobago, and in Malawi, the samples had an over-representation of females when compared to the overall proportions enrolled in training. In Malawi this was due to the fact that one of the colleges used in the sample was all female. In Trinidad and Tobago the reason appears to be because of differential response rates between males and females. Further information on the samples can be found in MUSTER country reports and discussion papers (e.g. Akyeampong and Lewin 2002, George, Mohammed et al 2001, Kunje et al 2001, and Lefoka, Molise et al 2001).

Similar, though slightly smaller, samples were used for the Exit questionnaire. Administering questionnaires in the colleges to entering and exiting students ensured fairly high response rates. The NQTs were more difficult to contact and responses were lower: data was collected from 134 respondents in Ghana, 64 in Lesotho and 64 in Malawi. The Lesotho team drew up a separate questionnaire to elicit views on teaching practice from 120 recently returned third-year students.

A predominantly closed-item questionnaire was used in Ghana, Malawi and Lesotho for college tutors. It requested information on qualifications and career paths, views of the college, its curriculum and their students, and contained a Likert item section inviting agreement or disagreement with a range of statements, many of which paralleled those given to students.

The main strength of the surveys was to capture broadly comparable data across the different countries. This was particularly useful in analysing the origins, characteristics and attitudes of those entering teaching. The Likert sections enabled us to make some tentative estimates about how far attitudes might be changed by training (Akeayampong and Lewin 2002, Coultas and Lewin 2002).

The researchers were aware that many of the survey respondents indicated quite high levels of satisfaction with aspects of the teacher education curriculum although interviews often revealed more general discontent. These sometimes contradictory results had to be interpreted carefully. There was a general consensus that questionnaires may be seen as 'official' instruments, and respondents did not wish to criticise the colleges because of traditions of respect for elders and for those in authority, and this could have led to patterns of response that exaggerated levels of satisfaction. Judgements were made to mediate the

2 Doing The Research

interpretation of responses accordingly. Another problem was language; all the instruments were designed in English – the medium of instruction. After piloting there were uncertainties that respondents understood all the questions in the same way as the researchers, and further attempts were made to try to improve wording and presentation to reduce this problem. In addition there were problems with the administration of some survey instruments. In some cases student respondents were under pressure from exams or other events and were unwilling to devote time to questionnaires; in other cases it was judged more productive to collect some data using other methods since levels of cooperation were problematic. These difficulties were recognised in the interpretation of data and the decisions made on sampling which were designed to be as representative as circumstances allowed.

2.3.2 Interviews

These were used widely in a variety of forms wherever the research teams felt comfortable with this approach. Key informants in colleges and Ministries were interviewed for background information, and to provide views on policies. Semi structured interviews with samples of college tutors were used in the four sites to elicit both information about their careers, and their perspectives, attitudes and beliefs about their work in preparing teachers (see Stuart et al 2000) In Trinidad and Tobago the experience of teaching practice was explored in depth using interviews with college tutors, students, principals and cooperating teachers in the schools (see George, Worrell et al 2000, parts 1 and 2). Similar methods were used there to explore the views of NQTs (Morris & Joseph, 2000).

2.3.3 Focus Groups

These were used in a limited number of places for specific purposes. In cultural contexts where much respect is given to those in authority, the one to-one interview may not always elicit full and open answers, especially where there is a large perceived power distance. Interviewing students in groups proved useful, encouraging respondents to speak out, and allowing for alternative views and underlying assumptions to emerge. For example, in Ghana groups were used effectively with NQTs to discuss their first year of teaching, and also with trainees about their TP (see Akyeampong et al 2000). Similarly in Malawi and Lesotho small groups of students in college were brought together to give their views on the curriculum.

2.3.4 Observations

These were used both in college lecture halls and school classrooms. Tutors were observed teaching in all four sites, most extensively in Lesotho, where eight tutors were observed 3 or 4 times each, and in Malawi, where 16 tutors, drawn from two colleges, were each observed once. In Ghana and Trinidad and Tobago smaller samples were observed. No

2 Doing The Research

schedules were used, but observers noted down key points of the classroom events and processes with as much detail as they could, in some cases supplemented by tape recordings.

Classroom observations were used in all the studies of NQTs, albeit with small samples (6 in Lesotho, 8 in Trinidad and Tobago, 11 in Ghana.), again using simple notes. Small numbers of untrained teachers were also observed to give some insight into differences. In Malawi NQTs were observed using the standard TP assessment instrument to explore how far their teaching differed from those of their untrained colleagues.

2.3.5 Combining classroom observation with interview

In several of the studies in both colleges and schools observations and interviews were used together to try to elicit teachers' and tutors' views about their work in more depth. The shared experience of the lesson provided a context for the interview; more deliberately, the interviewer could use incidents from the lesson to probe some of the underlying assumptions and reasoning (e.g. Croft 2002a). The importance of taking time to build up rapport and trust was emphasised in interactions between researchers and respondents (See Hedges 2002a). In the Trinidad and Tobago TP study, the researchers observed not only the lessons but also the post-lesson conferences, and then interviewed students and tutors. Such forms of triangulation enabled researchers to gain a more holistic view of the processes by drawing out the participants' meanings (George, Mohammed, et al 2001).

2.3.6 Autobiographical essays and student diaries

These were used to supplement the Entry Questionnaire. A small sample of students (18 in Ghana, 27 in Lesotho, 20 in Malawi, 16 in Trinidad and Tobago) were asked to write about good and bad experiences of schooling, their best and worst teachers, and their current hopes and expectations. The essays were coded and analysed qualitatively by theme, along with the open-ended questions on similar topics in the entry questionnaire. They provided very valuable information on the kinds of images and experiences of schooling and of teachers that trainees bring to their training.

A small group of trainees in Lesotho were given diaries in which to write comments about their classes, what they were learning, and their problems. Language, time and the unfamiliarity of diary keeping made this difficult to sustain, but some rich insights were obtained that cast a new light on students' lives.

2 Doing The Research

2.3.7 Document analysis

Documents were used extensively. The Baseline studies were compiled from secondary sources. Past student files were accessed where appropriate. Curriculum documents were analysed using Eraut's (1976) scheme that identifies aims and objectives, content, pedagogy, and teaching-learning materials to see whether they form a consistent curricular strategy. In some sites exam papers were also analysed to ascertain the coverage of syllabus topics and the cognitive demands made.

2.3.8 Tests

In the four sites tests in Maths and English were drawn up using items from, or similar to, the local school-leaving examinations which are used for college entrance. In Malawi and Ghana pedagogical knowledge tests were also devised. These tests were administered cross-sectionally to entering and exiting cohorts since it was not possible to follow cohorts longitudinally.

2.3.9 Financial analysis and modelling supply and demand

Statistical analysis was undertaken based on school census data, national planning reports and budgetary allocations. This was supplemented with data collected at institutional level to establish patterns of expenditure. Interviews were conducted with those with financial responsibilities at different levels. Supply and demand was modelled using simulations adapted for each country to derive projections of future needs linked to national policy goals. This was used to profile budgetary demand and ascertain whether current methods and costs of training were likely to prove sustainable.

2.4 Reflections on the Research Process

A project as large as MUSTER inevitably experiences dilemmas and difficulties as well as successes. Many things did not go according to plan and many adjustments had to be made (Lewin and Stuart 2002). During the fieldwork Lesotho experienced political unrest and occupation by SADC troops. For much of the research period MIITEP in Malawi was suspended as government and agencies negotiated over funding. At the end of the third year, South Africa finally announced a new national policy to incorporate Colleges of Education into the higher education system, ending a period of uncertainty and confusion about policy on the location of initial training. In Ghana elections created uncertainties about the implementation of the 'In-In-Out' system in 2001. An election was announced to coincide with the Trinidad and Tobago national dissemination workshop, causing it to be rescheduled. At Sussex staff changes occurred which had to be accommodated, and new members of the team had to be inducted into the MUSTER research.

2 Doing The Research

Towards the end of the project we set up various structures to enable all participants to reflect on the project and identify aspects of the experience that might inform future collaborative research of a similar kind.[9] The comments below are drawn from some of these reflections.

2.4.1 Collaboration and participation

The original proposal for the research was made from Sussex on the basis of general discussions that emerged from various academic link programmes maintained by CIE with the five partner countries. This followed from the nature of the DFID research commissioning process at the time. Thus, the first research framework that emerged was not a product of formal collaboration for this purpose, but a distillation of issues and questions that had arisen as teacher education issues were debated with colleagues within the link programmes. Ideally, perhaps, a developmental proposal should have been made at the outset to allow a detailed research framework to be developed through a systematic process of collaboration designed with this in mind. This would have involved perhaps six months to a year of preparatory work in partnership with colleagues in the link institutions, and the provision of funds for exploratory work in advance of a joint proposal. This strategy may be an option for future research funding. As it was, outline approval for MUSTER was obtained with a list of possible collaborators. Research fellow positions were advertised and the final list of collaborating partners was agreed in consultation. It took more than six months to firm up partnerships, make the necessary appointments, and draw up draft research contracts.

Thus staff at Sussex initiated the project, negotiated the outline proposal, and became the fund holders accountable to DFID for the research products. In practice, this meant that Sussex, together with DFID, agreed a time-table for products in consultation with the researchers, and disbursed funds against the achievement of agreed milestones in the form of research reports. This was judged a more appropriate way to proceed than the alternative of payments linked to detailed accounting of fieldwork activity[10]. The latter would have created a considerable administrative overhead and not necessarily guaranteed timely completion of work.

As a result of its origins, and the arrangements for accountability for funds, there were some perceptions that MUSTER was hierarchically organised from the centre and 'product-driven'. The latter is in part true and is arguably appropriate for commissioned research intended to inform policy and practice within a finite time scale. Products are needed and completion of research reports can be the most problematic and time-consuming element of

---

[9] For example, we held a full team discussion during the July 2000 workshop, which was taped and transcribed; the D.Phil research students invited the Principal researchers to individual semi-structured interviews about their experiences of the project; June George wrote a short article for the issue of Perspectives that Michael Samuel was editing (an example of South-South collaboration).

[10] Local budgets were subject to the accounting rules of the collaborating institutions.

2 Doing The Research

the research process. However, MUSTER was intellectually driven by the research questions agreed at the first joint workshop, and the products arose from exploration of these questions. The administrative organisation of MUSTER was partly shaped by the nature of accountability to DFID. Overall responsibility for delivery rested with Sussex and through the project co-ordinators with the sub-contracted research groups. This meant that the co-ordinators, without the help of paid support staff, had to become managers and administrators of the project as well as undertaking the research. At times this resulted in considerable stress.

Other approaches are conceivable, and might be considered in future. They would have to satisfy needs to maintain accountability, manage the quality and timely delivery of products, and be administratively efficient. MUSTER researchers did recognise that the structure of the project had some advantages. Thus one comment was that 'the project structure pushed us to draw on our reserves and make that extra effort' in meeting agreed deadlines. Perhaps a less structured approach would have resulted in more slippage in the completion of the various sub-studies.

MUSTER established an email network for communication early in its life. At first communications developed with most information flowing outwards from the centre. This generated a reciprocal flow of responses back to the centre. News from the remote sites was passed on to other sites, with limited communication along the 'rim' of the network. The notable exceptions occurred at the annual workshops where face-to-face interaction was possible. To enhance the flow of ideas among the researchers, drafts from the different sites were made available electronically, and each site was provided with a laptop computer. Facility with new technology varied, as did infrastructure and back-up services, with the result that sometimes communication failed for significant periods. It also became clear that the volume of work produced across the five sites was such that there were problems in simply keeping up to date with developments in all the sites. Sometimes it seemed that there was not enough time to download and read all the material available. Later on, as a result of the experience of the team meetings, and in particular the dissemination workshops, there was more sharing, and mutual learning grew. If funds had permitted it would have been desirable to rotate meetings around all the five sites.

A steering committee was set up which included a 'critical friend' who was invited to comment periodically on the progress of the research. This proved very helpful and various suggestions were taken on board. DFID advisors were also kept in the picture about emerging work and were invited to comment on drafts and attend workshops. This proved useful throughout MUSTER.

2 Doing The Research

2.4.2 Research design and building research capacity

MUSTER experienced some tensions from the outset that are common to many multi-site research projects. One the one hand there was a firm commitment to be responsive to the research interests and enthusiasms of the principal researchers and their teams. Context and priorities differed, as did the history, content, and process of teacher education. It would have been ill-advised if not impossible to ignore this in designing the research in detail. On the other hand, there was an ambition to address common issues to highlight aspects of practice, policy, and possibilities that would not necessarily appear from single country studies. Not least there was an aspiration to address teacher education issues at the international level, and develop dialogue with those working in development agencies and governments on externally assisted Education for All programmes.

At the first workshop it proved possible to identify common questions and approaches to data collection for parts of MUSTER. As a result some sub-studies followed similar pathways for data collection and analysis. Alongside this other sub-studies were devised which were specific to particular sites. Adopting this approach was one of the factors that led to MUSTER growing in scope. Had it elected to focus only on the national without regard to cross-national perspectives, or alternatively adopted a single standard set of questions and research instruments, it would have been less complex. But neither of these options seemed appropriate since either alone would overlook what were generally agreed to be important perspectives, not least because of the interactions between national and international aspects of teacher education curriculum, policy and practice.

The discussions around the development of the research framework encouraged researchers to use a range of data collection and analysis techniques that included those with both qualitative and quantitative characteristics. This meant that to different degrees the researchers had to use methods they were already familiar with and to acquire understanding and skill with those that were new to them. Support for this was provided from Sussex through in-country visits, email, and the opportunities that arose for researchers to spend periods of time at Sussex. The researchers also shared experiences with colleagues in-country and across the MUSTER team. Technical advice was provided from Sussex when unavailable locally.

Developing higher level research skills is time-consuming. Intuitively such skills are best developed with a mixture of systematic study and involvement in the real world of application. MUSTER attempted in some measure to both undertake high quality research, and to develop skills in the process. It has succeeded to a degree evident in the various outcomes and considerable volume of publications by a wide range of authors. In an ideal world many facilitating factors would have been present – a supportive national environment for research, a critical mass of researchers at PhD level, adequate technical support in-country, release time for researchers, substantial infrastructure to underpin national level data analysis, interpretation, and the production of high quality draft research reports. In the nature of the project not all these things were present at each site. The MUSTER infrastructure helped partly compensate for this and generated solutions to many of the problems that arose. It also drew attention to the implications of adopting approaches to policy that are more, rather than less, evidence-based. The reality is that the collection of robust evidence rigorously collated is often a time-consuming and skill-intensive activity. Though the costs can be high, they remain small in relation to the costs of misguided policy founded on assumption and casual empiricism.

2.4.3 Resources

MUSTER supported a wide range of research activity across six sites for four years. Though the funding made available was substantial, it was nevertheless very modest when compared to the resources currently allocated to teacher education in each country and to the size of external support for Education for All programmes. These of course depend at least in part on adequate teacher supply and teacher quality for their success. More could have been well spent. Lessons can also be learned from how the project resources might be utilised more effectively in future.

The MUSTER contracts were largely made with the institutions, not with individuals. The funds provided were intended to include payment for the time of lead researchers and team members, and to cover direct costs of fieldwork, data analysis, report production etc. As a principal researcher noted 'One of the difficulties in doing research in a setting that doesn't have a rich culture of research is finding appropriate blocks of time in which to do the work'. Key individuals often carried heavy teaching and/or administrative loads and responsibilities for other projects. Most of the collaborating institutions did not have formal arrangements for release time for research projects though funding was provided for this purpose. Where they did, norms and practice varied widely. This created difficulties both for principal researchers, and for team members, when the time needed was not necessarily forthcoming.

It was assumed that all the participating institutions would contribute some 'institutional' time and other resources to the enterprise, since the research would benefit the institutions and their staff in terms of capacity building and research profile. All in fact did this in different ways, but there was general agreement among all the researchers, including those at Sussex, that 'the amount of time that was funded was nothing like the amount of time that was put into it'. The project's success was due to the great efforts that everyone made well over and above the personal and institutional contributions originally envisaged. Without these non-costed contributions the MUSTER project would have been compromised.

2 Doing The Research

The institutions all had different ways of handling research money. These sometimes clashed with the project framework established. Thus in general resources were provided against the completion of agreed products e.g. the baselines studies, drafts of sub-study reports, and the full country reports. Internal accounting systems often refused to advance money for research expenses until funds had been transferred notwithstanding the existence of a contract. In spite of some degree of flexibility, in one case it was said the Institution 'lost money through MUSTER though it gained in reputation'. Sussex itself waived research student tuition fees and thereby supported MUSTER research financially. Our experience draws attention to the need to share expertise in research management, not least the fact that accounting systems designed primarily to handle university general business (e.g. student fees, government subsidies, staff salaries etc.) can be dysfunctional for research contracts.

2.4.4 Benefits and burdens

There was no doubt that the project constituted a steep learning curve for all involved, from which everyone gained in terms of professional development. Some of the benefits mentioned frequently by the researchers were:

-    skills in managing research projects
-    working with other academics, sharing ideas, getting feedback
-    gains in academic confidence, especially in writing skills
-    a broadening, or refocusing, of research and career interests

There were many indications that the associated institutions had gained in terms of:

-    enhanced local and international reputation
-    research publications, especially where Discussion Papers, or articles based on them, were made available locally
-    expanding the numbers involved in research to include new and inexperienced researchers

For the research students based at Sussex, being part of a larger project removed some of the isolation of doctoral research, and working in collaboration with a local institute and its staff during fieldwork enriched both their data and the personal experience. The 'hidden costs' to the local institution for hosting such students were, however, considerable, and while many were generously absorbed in a spirit of collaborative activity, in future such costs should be recognised and factored in.

Not surprisingly, given the scope of MUSTER and the dynamic ways in which its emphases changed, some reflections suggested that the project became too ambitious and covered too much ground. The initial enthusiasm generated research agendas that were sometimes out

2 Doing The Research

of proportion to the resources and time available. Everyone mentioned experiencing periods of pressure and stress, especially as deadlines for workshops approached. It was generally recognised that much had been learned and that there were many benefits both individually and to the institutions, though the personal costs in terms of tension and overload had at times been substantial.

2.4.5 Some suggestions for the future

From all this, certain lessons can be learnt. Certain aspects worked well and can be recommended. For example:

- A sequential development of publications, from Baseline Studies to Discussion Papers, and the setting of milestone targets, linked to sub-studies which can be written up for articles and integrated into the final reports.
- An overall research design flexible enough to guide the studies and frame the broad research questions, which also allows more precise and context-specific questions to be identified.
- A Steering Committee, which can serve many purposes, particularly that of providing feedback and suggestions at a distance from the day to day management of the research.

Some suggestions for those undertaking similar projects include:

- Recognising the need to involve Principal Researchers in the design of the research at the earliest possible stage and if financially possible hold full team meetings at all the research sites.
- Trying to ensure that there is at least one full-time researcher at each site for most, if not all, of the research period, whether this is the Principal Researcher or a member of one of the research teams.
- Accepting that if there is an explicit commitment to build research capacity in a sustainable way, additional time and resources are required to guide and support inexperienced researchers as they learn on the job; this needs to be incorporated into the budget.
- Matching funding arrangements to take into account the financial regulations and norms of the receiving institutions, to the extent these are consistent with sponsors' requirements and the progress of the research.
- Negotiating clear and transparent agreements about the contributions of partners, that recognise what they can realistically do with the resources available.

| Chapter Three | **3 The MUSTER Project: Context and Emerging Issues** |

3.1 Introduction

This chapter presents background information needed to set the MUSTER research in context. The teacher education systems in the MUSTER countries differ for complex historical, political, cultural and demographic reasons. All share influences that arise from the activities of missionaries and colonial governments in the formative stages of teacher education in each country. In all cases the systems are now government-controlled, with varying degrees of residual relationships with groups who played a role in the founding of different training colleges. The training institutions exist within different policy and curriculum regimes, and have been subject to more or less developmental support since being assimilated into state education systems. It is the national contexts that determine the level of supply and demand for new teachers, and the nature of new entrants recruited into training. The characteristics of the different training systems are explored in a series of baseline studies (Ghana - Akyeampong and Furlong, 2000; Lesotho – Lefoka, Jobo, Khiba et al, 2000; Malawi - Kunje and Chimombo, 1999; Trinidad and Tobago - Quamina-Aiyejina et al, 1999) and in other MUSTER discussion papers.

The first section describes the current system of training primary teachers, gives contextual information on relevant aspects of the school systems, and notes some of the concerns identified in the Baseline Studies. The second section describes some of the features of the colleges where the training takes place. These include their historical origins, aspects of governance and control; and some of the physical and environmental features that can have an impact on teaching and learning. The final section identifies some key issues that shaped the MUSTER research.

3.2 Overview of the Teacher Education Systems

The training systems in Ghana, Lesotho, Malawi and Trinidad and Tobago vary in terms of the entry level qualifications required, the length and location of training, the type of certification, and the mode of delivery. Figure 2 shows the contrasting patterns. Figure 3 illustrates graphically the length of training and the division of time between college and school-based activity.

3 The MUSTER Project: Context and Emerging Issues

Figure 2: **Forms of teacher training programmes in four countries**

Country	Ghana	Lesotho	Malawi	Trinidad & Tobago
Entry level	5 O level credits	4 COSC credits	JC or MSCE + 2 yrs work	5 CXC passes, On Job Training + 2yrs work
Length	3 years[11]	3 1/2 years	2 years	2 –5 years
Location of Training	Teacher T. College	Teacher T. College	TTC + schools	Teacher T. College
Qualification	Certificate	Diploma	Certificate	Certificate
Awarded by	MOE	NTTC	MOE	MOE
Mode of training	Pre-service, Residential	Pre-service, Residential	In-service, Mixed	In-service.

Figure 3: **Length of college and school-based training in four countries (2000)**

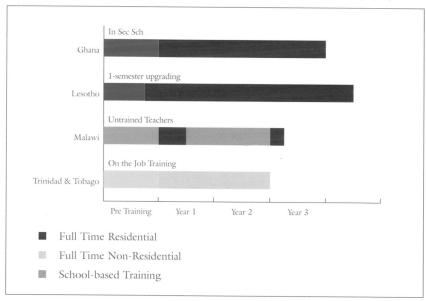

3.2.1 **Ghana**

Ghana has only one mode of initial teacher education. Thirty-eight[12] colleges (seven male, one female, and the rest mixed) provide three-year full-time post-secondary training. All the colleges except one are residential and all prepare teachers for primary and junior secondary level with options to specialise. Since 1993 the number of trainees has increased by over 50% and in 1998 20,400 were enrolled, of whom 38% were female. Average enrolment in colleges was about 500 students, covering a range from 240 to 910. About 1,050 college

---

[11] After the research started Ghana shifted to an In-In-Out system of two years in College and one year in school based training.
[12] There are thirty eight state-run colleges and three private colleges.

3 The MUSTER Project: Context and Emerging Issues

staff are employed, giving an average staff-student ratio of 20:1. Two thirds of staff are graduates and over 80% are male. Formal entrance requirements for training are: a minimum qualification (Ghana GCE 'O'Level – 5 Grade Es or better; Senior Secondary Certificate – 4 Credits and one other pass), an interview, and a common college entrance examination. Some trainees with the minimum requirements may enter college via 'protocol' arrangements that may circumvent normal entrance requirements. A recent reform (2001) of the teacher education system has introduced an 'In-In-Out' system whereby the third year of training will be located in schools rather than in the Colleges. This is in the early stages of implementation.

Ghana is committed to universalising primary education and enrolments have been increasing. Primary gross enrolment rates appear to be around 79%. The proportion of untrained teachers has been falling to below 20%, with large regional variations. There is widespread concern with low levels of pupil achievement that are partly attributed to the poor quality of teacher education. Expenditure on teacher education has been rising and now accounts for about 6% of total recurrent expenditure on education which itself is about 35% of all government spending. The cost per trained teacher is about five times GNP per capita.

There is an on-going debate in Ghana about the most suitable course structure and curriculum for preparing teachers for primary schools, and in particular how such schools can be used as training sites. There are also concerns about the colleges and the professional development of their staff. Currently the large classes, heavy staff workloads, and traditional practices of the colleges seem to militate against innovations aimed at raising the quality of training.

3.2.2 Lesotho

The National Teacher Training College (NTTC) is the only teacher education college in Lesotho. It trains primary and junior secondary level teachers on different courses. Initial training has evolved through a variety of programmes but is being consolidated into a three and a half year residential programme, the Diploma in Education, Primary (DEP). Total college enrolment has been maintained at about 800[13] on various programmes including those for in-service and post-service up-grading. The total numbers enrolled in initial training for primary have fluctuated between 300 and 400 in the recent past. Typically, over 70% of trainees are female. The effective staff-student ratio is about 1:14 on primary programmes. More than 95% of the 44 College staff in the Primary Division hold degrees and about two-thirds were female in 1998. Selection onto the DEP requires a minimum of four credits (one of which must be in English) and a pass in Cambridge Overseas School Certificate. NTTC also interviews some candidates.

---

[13] This includes part time students and is therefore not a full time equivalent figure.

3 The MUSTER Project: Context and Emerging Issues

Gross enrolment rates at primary level are over 100% and are greater for girls than boys. The proportion of untrained teachers in primary schools has remained around 25% over the last five years. The college output of less than 150 new teachers a year has been insufficient to reduce this proportion. The introduction of free primary schooling from 2000 is increasing enrolments thereby increasing demand for teachers. Lesotho allocates between 2% and 3% of the recurrent education budget to NTTC and commits over 30% of government resources to education as a whole. The cost per trained teacher is over ten times GNP per capita.

Major issues in Lesotho concern the status and characteristics of the NTTC as the only teaching training college, how the college curriculum can be rationalised and upgraded, how teacher quality can be enhanced, and how output can be increased.

3.2.3 Malawi

Since 1997 pre-service college-based training for primary level in Malawi has been suspended to allow for large numbers of untrained teachers to be trained through the Malawi Integrated Teacher Education Programme (MIITEP). This system provides for one term in College, four terms in supervised teaching practice, and most of a term in College preparing for and taking final examinations. The programme is run in all six primary colleges (two are single sex) which together enrol cohorts of about 2,500 students at a time, three times a year when fully operating. Six cohorts were enrolled between 1997 and 1999 with each college taking between about 400 and 600 students per cohort three times a year. About 42% of MIITEP trainees are female. Nominal staff-student ratios vary between 1:11 and 1:21. About a quarter of staff appear to be graduates and about 35% are female. MIITEP trainees are drawn from the ranks of untrained teachers who constitute perhaps half of all teachers. Most of those enrolled (65%) have been Junior Certificate of Education (JCE) holders (two years secondary schooling), though the stated policy is to recruit those with the Malawi Secondary Certificate of Education (MSCE) (four years secondary). Candidates are selected from the MIITEP database and are not interviewed or tested. The MIITEP programme was suspended in 1999 for nearly two years whilst negotiations took place concerning continued external support.

Malawi implemented Free Primary Education (FPE) in 1994 resulting in an increase in enrolments from about 1.8 million to 3 million primary pupils. Currently Malawi allocates about 4% of its educational expenditure to teacher education and about 30% to education as a whole. The cost per trained teacher in MIITEP is about three times the GNP per capita.

Important issues in Malawi are concerned with training and upgrading enough teachers to meet the needs created by FPE for more teachers. The MIITEP school-based system seeks to share training between the colleges and the schools but this is problematic given the poor

3 The MUSTER Project: Context and Emerging Issues

infrastructure, stringent resource constraints, and volume of demand. Challenges for training include the extent to which it can prepare trainees for very large classes which can exceed 100 in the lower grades of primary schools, and whether the MIITEP system can be refined to make it more efficient and effective at sustainable levels of cost.

3.2.4 Trinidad and Tobago

Trinidad and Tobago has two government colleges where most primary initial teacher education takes place. The Teacher's Diploma is awarded after two years full-time study (39 weeks) including periods of teaching practice. Total enrolments average between 700 and 800, split evenly between the colleges. About 30% of trainees are male. Staff-student ratios are about 1:13 and 55% of the tutors are female. Selection into the colleges is made from untrained teachers who have been working in schools for two to five years, most of entered teaching via the 'On the Job Training' apprenticeship programme. Students are employees of the Ministry of Education and receive full scholarships. Entrants to the teaching service must have 5 CXC (Caribbean Examinations Council) passes or the equivalent 'O' Levels.

Trinidad and Tobago has achieved close to universal enrolment at primary level. The number of primary students is projected to fall from 188,000 in 1995 to 163,000 by 2005. Overall demand for teachers is therefore falling. However over 20% were untrained in 1997, and opportunities exist to lower further the teacher-pupil ratio in primary schools from its existing level of about 24:1. Teacher training accounts for somewhat less than 2% of the recurrent education budget which is 13% of total government expenditure. The cost of a trained teacher is about three times GNP per capita.

There are concerns in Trinidad and Tobago that the college curriculum is outdated and overloaded, and that it may not be effective in preparing teachers for the practical skills of teaching. Entrants to college enter with experience, but this is not linked to the selection procedure nor to the college curriculum Further, little is known about how the novice teachers utilize their training or what impact they have on the schools

3 The MUSTER Project: Context and Emerging Issues

3.2.5 Some cross-site comparisons

Cross-country comparisons of factors which shape the teacher education systems are shown in Figure 4.

Figure 4: Factors shaping teacher education systems

Country	Ghana	Lesotho	Malawi	Trinidad and Tobago
Population	18.7 million	2 million	10.1 million	1.3 ,million
GNP per Capita	US$390	US$570	US$200	US$4250
Claimed Gross Enrolment Rate at Primary	79%	108%	130%	99%
Rate of Growth of Primary Age Cohort	4% possible falling to 3%	Declining 0 to –1.5%	+2% but may be falling	Declining –2% to –3%
Primary Enrolments	2,290,000	370,000	2,800,000	171,000
Primary Teachers	63700	8100	43400	7311
Pupil-teacher Ratio in Primary	36:1	45:1	65:1	23:1
% Untrained teachers	13.5%	23%	40%-50%	23%
Primary Teacher Attrition Rate	5%	5%-10%	10%-15%	3%
Number of Primary Teacher Education Colleges	38 (includes J.Sec)	1 (includes some Sec.)	6	2
Current Enrolments	20,400 (1998) Full time	900 including secondary and part time students	2500 per cohort, 3 cohorts/year when fully operating	791 (1999) Full time
Lecturers	1044	43 (primary)	150	60
Student-staff Ratio in College	19.5:1	14:1 in primary division	15:1	13:1
Annual Output of New Primary Teachers	6000	150	7000 when fully operating	400
Ratio of Total Number of Primary Teachers to Annual Output	10.6	54:1	6.2	18.2

Ghana and Malawi have relatively large populations and teacher education systems compared to Lesotho and Trinidad and Tobago. The latter is a middle-income country whereas the others are much poorer in terms of GNP per capita. Demand for new teachers is high in three of the countries, but for different reasons. In Ghana the GER at primary is still well below 100% and more teachers are needed to achieve Education for All (EFA) targets for universal enrolment. It also has a high rate of growth in the school age cohort, and teacher output must grow at least at this rate to maintain the current pupil-teacher

3 The MUSTER Project: Context and Emerging Issues

ratio, and more if untrained teachers are to be trained. In Malawi demand arises mostly from the growth in primary numbers, the need to reduce very high pupil-teacher ratios and proportions of untrained teachers, and the very high rates of teacher attrition. During the four years MITTEP was in progress, the ratio of teachers in post to newly trained teachers was low (6.2:1) indicating a high level of effort in training.

Lesotho is different. It has high enrolment rates and low or negative cohort growth. Its primary pupil-teacher ratio is high, but not excessive, and about a quarter of teachers are untrained. The main factor creating demand for new teachers appears to be the very low output of the training system. The ratio of 65:1 teachers in post to output is insufficient to maintain the pupil-teacher ratio at current levels, and replace teachers who leave. This situation is deteriorating as enrolments increase and drop out declines as a result of FPE. Trinidad and Tobago also has a negative rate of growth in the school age cohort. In this case pupil-teacher ratios and teacher attrition are low, and the output ratio of the teacher education system is more than sufficient to maintain enrolment rates at current pupil-teacher ratios.

3.3 The College Context.

Primary teacher training in anglophone Africa and the Caribbean mostly takes place in Teacher Training Colleges (TTCs), while most secondary teacher education is in University Departments of Education (UDEs). In Africa, colleges usually grew out of missionary-run education, though generally with national independence they came under government control. These colleges usually occupy an intermediate position between schools and higher education. They are often more like 'glorified high schools' than universities in their organisation, teaching environment and culture. Their physical location, layout and buildings place constraints on their operation and the opportunities to innovate. Colleges are mostly residential and are often situated away from towns. As a result there may be few schools nearby which can be used for teaching practice. These teacher education institutions have their own history, culture, ethos, practices, etc. and any programme of change must recognise these as a starting point.

3.3.1 Ghana

The first TTC in Ghana was founded in 1848 by the Basel Mission and many of the colleges still have church affiliations. Others grew out of secondary schools; all are now government-funded and have a common curriculum. Training colleges in Ghana have the appearance of traditional secondary schools from the way they were built and their way of operating. Many of them were started as missionary institutions to train ministers, catechists and later teachers. Some of them were built as traditional secondary schools and were later converted into colleges for training teachers. Their characteristic features include residential boarding

3 The MUSTER Project: Context and Emerging Issues

facilities, a dining hall, a daily timetable divided into periods of 40 minutes, classrooms with seats arranged in rows and columns facing a chalkboard (seating between 40-50 students), a small library, staff bungalows, an administrative block and playing grounds for sports activities. Those with strong missionary roots have a chapel. Classrooms have no visual aids or storage facilities for keeping teaching and learning materials. Their science laboratories appear to be poorly equipped and are too small. In one of the colleges studied, there was only one laboratory for practical work in physics, chemistry and biology which could only seat about fifty students. College libraries tended to be small and in one college it was estimated that it could seat about 30 students at a time. In the case-study colleges, the libraries' newest collections appeared to be books donated under recent British aid programmes. Most of the books looked old and unused (Akyeampong 2001).

In the colleges there is an emphasis on discipline and moral training, often with daily worship. Students have to undertake manual labour, such as weeding or sweeping the compound. The strict rules and regulations, sometimes verging on the militaristic, are felt by some trainees to be demeaning. 'We are treated like primary pupils' one said. This could conflict with an aim of producing teachers ready to take responsibility and to make professional judgements.

The curriculum is developed and assessed by the Institute of Education at the University of Cape Coast, under direction from the Teacher Education Directorate of the Ministry of Education. College lecturers are involved to the extent that they sit on subject panels and help mark the exams, but otherwise exercise little control, and are reported to see their role simply as teaching what they are given.

3.3.2 Lesotho

The three main churches in Lesotho – Evangelical, Anglican and Catholic – all developed their own TTCs for primary teachers which were located around the country. This continued until 1975 when all primary and junior secondary training was centralised in a new, secular, National Teacher Training College (NTTC) in Maseru. The NTTC aims were, inter alia, to enhance national unity, modernise the curriculum and effect economies of scale in training. The college was set up as with UNDP support and an American Director. The decision to have an all-graduate staff had several implications: few lecturers could be taken over from the old church colleges, so there was a sharp break with the past; expatriates staffed the college until Basotho were trained; and from the start the college aspired to tertiary status.

After the UNDP project ended financial control was taken over by the MOE, while for academic purposes the college became loosely affiliated to the National University of Lesotho (NUL). The college controls its own curriculum and assessment, though final

3 The MUSTER Project: Context and Emerging Issues

results have to be agreed by the university senate. Negotiations have been under way for some years to give the institution financial autonomy as the 'Lesotho College of Education' but this is yet to become a reality.

Most of the teaching facilities date from the 1970s. The timetable is divided into one- and two-hour slots, and teaching takes place in a lecture theatre or classrooms which have tables and chairs rather than desks. The library has recently been improved, but laboratories are inadequate for hands-on scientific experiments. Most students board, and until recently hostel accommodation was a limit to enrolment.

Throughout its 25 years of existence, the college has depended greatly on foreign aid, first mainly American, and then Irish. The original Primary Teacher Certificate curriculum was heavily influenced by the American educational thinking of the time, which emphasized skills development, micro-teaching, and behavioural objectives. The development of the new Diploma programme took place under Irish advice. The University of Bath had a recent link for upgrading tutors to Masters degree level through a distance programme.

3.3.3 Malawi

In Malawi a number of small TTCs were also originally established by the missionaries. The first government college was established in 1962; this became Blantyre TTC. After 1973 the government took control over teacher education and through a process of amalgamation 13 colleges were reduced to six, of which two are still owned by the Catholic Church. The two colleges selected for MUSTER case-studies present both contrasts and similarities. St. Joseph's, an all-female Catholic-run college, stands 15 km. from a small town, in a rural landscape. It is one of the four colleges which in the late 1980s were substantially rebuilt with World Bank support and has impressive, spacious buildings, including halls, labs and library, but is very poorly equipped with books and materials. Blantyre Teachers' College (BTC) is government-run, mixed sex, and is on the outskirts of the industrial area of Blantyre. Its one-storey buildings, laid out in quadrangles, are 40 years old, the library is small and understocked, there is no staff common room, the labs and technical workshop areas are inadequate; the hostels are grossly over-crowded and have poor sanitary facilities. At one time during the research the water supply failed and the college had to be closed, a not uncommon event.

The teaching day is divided into six one-hour periods, with study time in the evenings, though lack of electricity in BTC prevented students from doing this. In both colleges, classrooms typically are set out in traditional style, with heavy wooden seat-desks that are difficult to move. The few displays were tatty, with no evidence of student work. The total absence of equipment and consumables made the labs inoperable.

3 The MUSTER Project: Context and Emerging Issues

The teacher education curriculum is laid down by the Malawi Institute of Education, which is a part of the Ministry. Examinations are set and marked by the Malawi National Examination Board, with the college tutors acting as markers. The MIITEP curriculum resonates with that of previous full-time residential programmes and dates back to reforms carried out in the 1980s with only minor adjustments to the aims to reflect recent social changes. It is skills-based, aiming to produce teachers who can deliver the curriculum effectively and obtain high levels of examination achievement from pupils.

3.3.4 Trinidad and Tobago

Primary Teacher Education in Trinidad and Tobago started with government and charitable initiatives dating back to the nineteenth century which first set up 'normal' schools and then a government teacher training college (TTC). Later denominational TTCs were set up, but the colonial government retained a measure of control. Alongside the colleges, for nearly 100 years (1870-1963) there was a system of school-based apprenticeship training, by which pupil-teachers gradually acquired qualifications while teaching (Quamina-Aiyejima et al 1999)

In the 1970s all the old TTCs were replaced with two government non-residential colleges, one in the north of the island and the other in the south. The campuses are spacious, with adequate buildings and reasonable resources, though the time-table and organisation are similar to those of a high school, with seven 45-minute periods per day and little free study time. The Board of Teacher Training is responsible for the curriculum, sets the exams in consultation with the college tutors, and moderates the results; there is, strangely, no link with the University of the West Indies. The college tutors, many of whom hold Masters degrees from the UWI, have been active in gradually altering and adapting the curriculum to suit new circumstances.

3.4 Some Key Issues

From the information presented and other insights from the MUSTER data collection a number of key issues can be identified which help frame subsequent discussion. In summary these are:

1. Fundamental structural characteristics are important in determining key issues and future possibilities. Demographics shape teacher demand, and existing institutions determine current capacity. National indicators and targets (e.g. current and targeted GERs, pupil-teacher ratios, % untrained teachers) and national wealth, (current and projected growth in GNP per capita and national resource allocation to education) circumscribe what is needed and what is financially sustainable. Thus, simply speaking, Trinidad and Tobago has minor problems in matching supply and demand and can

3 The MUSTER Project: Context and Emerging Issues

afford to do so. Ghana would need to train many more teachers if it were to raise its primary GER and not see pupil-teacher ratios deteriorate. Malawi has very high teacher attrition rates which create a large demand which, it appears, can only be satisfied by a large scale, mixed-mode teacher education programme based in schools rather than colleges for much of the training period. Lesotho trains small numbers of teachers at relatively high costs which would be difficult to sustain if the current system were expanded to meet projected demand.

2. Two of the countries (Lesotho and Trinidad and Tobago) have very small teacher education systems concentrated in one or two institutions. In principle this makes the systems easier to research, and might make it easier to design and implement reforms to improve quality. Ghana has a large system with considerable variation, and MUSTER therefore could only research specific aspects in an illustrative way. The Malawi case stands in the middle with a single system across 6 institutions, and a radically different pattern of curriculum organisation.

3. As systemic conditions have changed, so have the characteristics of those entering teacher training (Chapter 4 elaborates on this). The teaching profession no longer enjoys the status it once had, salaries are relatively low, and conditions of service perceived as poor. Young people apply to training colleges often as a last resort, lacking the academic qualifications for university, and perhaps seeing it as a stepping stone to other careers. Their characteristics, and the interaction between them and the training process, are core concerns for the reform of teacher education systems. They are a reminder of starting points for more effective training, building from the qualities, perceptions and commitment of those available and willing to train as teachers. Once training has been successfully completed NQTs acquire teaching jobs through a variety of mechanisms which range from being posted (Ghana, Malawi), to applying according to preference to schools or in response to advertised vacancies (Trinidad and Tobago). In Lesotho much recruitment is through the Education Secretariats of the various churches. In all cases colleges appear to have little influence over the first appointment and little systematic knowledge of where their graduates teach.

4. Various changes, notably greatly increased enrolments in most of the countries as a result of Education for All commitments, and curriculum reform at school level to develop improved materials and promote more effective teaching methods, have created new challenges for teacher education. Teacher education curricula have been much slower to change than school curricula. Key questions revolve around the structure and content of the curricula, their appropriateness to new purposes and new audiences, and the quality of their implementation. There are also questions about the relationships between theory and practice, where and how practical skills are best developed, and about the epistemological and professional theories that underpin the curricula.

3 The MUSTER Project: Context and Emerging Issues

5.   College-based systems predominate across the MUSTER countries. History, both colonial and post-colonial, has shaped the institutions that provide teacher education, leaving them poised somewhat anomalously between the secondary and higher education sectors. These institutions have normative characteristics derived from their past and mediated by established working practices. The college sector, often isolated both professionally and geographically from other parts of the system, has been neglected, and teacher educators have generally not been recognised as a separate group in need of professional development. Practice has changed, or persisted, through interactions between piecemeal government policy initiatives, institutional traditions, and the qualities and motivation of teacher trainers.

6.   The content, quality and outcomes of teacher education are in significant part determined by the resources that can be mobilised. There are wide variations across the countries in the levels of allocation to teacher education. Though some of the reasons reflect underlying structural differences, others are not so easily explained. There may be scope for increases in efficiency and effectiveness that make it easier to sustain teacher education systems which more closely approach satisfying demand for new teachers than is the case in several of the countries. Where demand greatly outstrips supply it may be that more radical alternatives to conventional college-based programmes have to be considered.

Chapter Four   **4 Who Becomes a Primary Teacher?**

4.0   Summary

This chapter presents data on the characteristics of trainee teachers, explores some of their perceptions and aspirations, and provides some insights into their self-image and sense of role identity. The main questions guiding these parts of the research were:

➢   Who becomes a teacher and what are their academic qualifications?
➢   What do they bring in terms of images, expectations and experiences?
➢   How are these related to the cultural context?

4.0.1 **Summary of findings**

A survey of entering students across Ghana, Lesotho, Malawi and Trinidad and Tobago produced the following picture:

•   In Ghana and Lesotho trainees are recruited soon after leaving high school, aged between 20-22; some may have taught for a year or two. In Malawi and Trinidad and Tobago all have taught for at least two years and are in their mid-twenties.

•   Primary trainees are predominantly male in Ghana and Malawi, and predominantly female in Lesotho and Trinidad and Tobago

•   In all the sites most teachers claim affiliation to a Christian denomination; Muslims seem under represented in Ghana and Malawi.

•   In multi-ethnic and multi-lingual societies, trainees come from different tribes speaking different mother-tongues, which may not match those of the children they teach.

•   Typically trainees have left school with relatively low academic grades, including poor achievement in English.

•   Family background data suggest that the majority are upwardly mobile, often being the first generation to enter post-secondary education. In Africa, many of the parents work outside the modern sector. A substantial minority, however, have parents and other family members who are teachers.

•   Their attitudes to teaching as revealed by Likert items vary somewhat with the country. While no clear overall trends could be ascertained, some of the responses are out of line with college aims and expectations.

Complementary qualitative data suggest that:

•   Students have powerful memories of their own schooling. Positive aspects include academic success, sports and friendships, as well as teachers who helped them. Negative memories overwhelmingly focus on corporal punishment, to which they now have an ambivalent attitude.

•   Teachers are usually described in terms of personal characteristics, often using images of parent or counsellor, rather than in terms of cognitive or pedagogic skills.

4 Who Becomes a Primary Teacher?

- Trainees are ready to model themselves on memories of their own teachers, without being able to analyse clearly what made their methods successful.
- Studies in Trinidad and Tobago and Ghana indicate socio-cultural metaphors and myths about the role of the teacher, which students may incorporate into their self-image.

4.1   Introduction and Overview

Any effective system of teacher education has to recognise and build on the characteristics and motivations that trainees bring to the profession when they enter training programmes. Understanding what these characteristics are provides a basis for the development of curricula that address trainees' needs and capabilities. It is also a reminder to teacher trainers that the backgrounds and aspirations of those entering training now may not be the same as in the past. Where this is so it invites consideration of how training content and methods should change to reflect new realities.

This chapter exemplifies how different methodological frameworks were used within MUSTER. The questionnaires administered to entering students provided some systematic comparative data on age, sex, religion, ethnicity, prior experience, home background and academic achievement. The Likert items and open-ended sections of the questionnaires provided further insights to complement and deepen this information. Other methods - semi-structured interviews, focus groups and autobiographical essays – were used to try to understand some of the ways in which early experiences of schooling might influence the ways trainees perceived themselves as teachers. The more qualitative studies were designed and implemented in different ways by the different researchers, and the interpretations were site-specific, the intention being to gain insights rather than draw comparisons. Chapter 2 has given more details of the methods and samples used.

The Chapter is organised in four parts. First, the characteristics of trainee teachers in four countries are outlined from the survey data. Second, the perceptions of trainees of teaching and the teaching profession are discussed using data from Likert items in the Entry questionnaire. Third, insights are drawn from qualitative data to illuminate some of the experiences and images of schools and teaching students bring to their training. The last section attempts to bring together insights from all the data sets to point up the implications for policy and action.

4.2   Characteristics of the Student Teachers Entering College

4.2.1 Age

The average age of entrants to teacher education in the samples vary. Ghana (21 years) and Lesotho (22.2 years) have the youngest entrants; Malawi (25.9) and Trinidad and Tobago

4 Who Becomes a Primary Teacher?

(26.1) have the oldest. The most obvious explanation for this is that in the former cases most entrants are admitted directly from the school secondary system. In the latter most entrants acquire teaching experience as untrained teachers before being accepted for training. Figure 5 and Table 1 show the age profiles.

Figure 5: **Age profiles of teacher trainees by country**

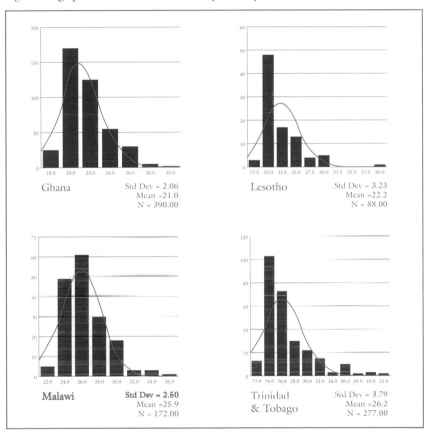

Overall between 70% and 75% of teachers are between 19 and 22 years old in Ghana and Lesotho, and the same proportions are between 23 and 27 years in Malawi and Trinidad and Tobago.

Age may be significant for training in a number of ways. First, older trainees are more likely to likely to have some formal or informal experience of teaching, whether or not this is required for entry. Second, they are more likely to be married, or marry during training and have direct or indirect experience of child-raising. Third, older trainees are more obviously adult learners rather than young students arriving directly from school. Fourth, older

4 Who Becomes a Primary Teacher?

trainees may be more fixed in their views about teaching and teachers, and clearer about their commitment to teaching as a career.

4.2.2 Gender

The proportion of male and female student teachers in the samples in each country is shown in Table 1. Over two-thirds of the student teachers surveyed were female in both Lesotho (71%) and Trinidad and Tobago (67%). The reverse was the case in Ghana, where only one-third of the student teachers were female. These figures are broadly in line with national totals. The Malawi sample also had a very high proportion of female student teachers (84%), but this was due to the inclusion of an all-female college; overall only 28% of MIITEP trainees have been women. Worldwide, the trend has been for primary teaching to become largely feminised; it is interesting that in Ghana and Malawi this has not yet happened.

Table 1: **Characteristics of student teacher samples in the four countries.**

Country	Male (%)	Female (%)	Total	Mean Age	Std Dev
Ghana	265 (66.25)	135 (33.75)	400	21	2.06
Lesotho	26 (28.9)	64 (71.1)	90	22.2	3.23
Malawi	29 (16.5)	147 (67.2)	176	25.9	2.5
Trinidad	98 (32.8)	201 (63.6)	299	26.2	3.8

4.2.3 Religious Affiliation

All the teacher education systems have been influenced by institutions originally established by Christian denominations. Religious affiliation plays an important role in defining identity in each country. In Ghana some colleges, particularly the most prestigious ones like Presbyterian Training College and Wesley, retain strong religious affiliations, though the system of 38 colleges is formally under the control of the Ministry of Education. Religiously-based training colleges were amalgamated into a single secular institution in Lesotho in 1975. Two of the six colleges in Malawi remain affiliated to the Catholic church, though formal control over the Colleges was taken by the government in 1973. In Trinidad and Tobago most of the denominational institutions closed from the 1960s onward, while the government established Corinth and Valsayn Colleges on a secular basis.

The religious affiliation of Ghanaian student teachers in the sample was predominately Christian with 36% Catholic, 16% Methodist, 15% other named denominations and 24% who just classified themselves as 'Christian'. Muslims accounted for 4% of the student teachers, significantly less than their percentage of the population, perhaps reflecting the fact that colleges in the sample were selected from the predominantly Christian South. In Lesotho, the majority of Basotho student teachers were either Catholic (37%) or Lesotho Evangelical Church (33%). About 16% were Anglican and a further 14% 'other'. In Malawi

4 Who Becomes a Primary Teacher?

41% were members of the Church of Central Africa and 29% were Catholic. About 15% were Seventh Day Adventists, and 3% Muslim. Again this is significantly less than the national proportion of Muslims, which may reflect different attitudes to education. In Trinidad and Tobago 22% were Catholic, 19% Hindu, 16% Presbyterian, and 30% were distributed across various other Christian denominations; 6% were Muslim.

The religious affiliation of student teachers, and the denominational history of many of the training institutions, carries implications for the training process. These are not simple to unravel, but are likely to have some influence on student teachers' attitudes towards learning, and their role as teachers.

4.2.4 Ethnic Group or Tribe and Language Spoken at Home

In three of the countries ethnic group is a signifier of difference. The exception is Lesotho which is ethnically (Basotho) and linguistically (Sesotho) homogenous. Ghana is the most ethnically diverse of the countries with 26 groups represented in the sample. The largest groups in the sample were Ashanti (51%), Fante (11%) and other Akan-speaking groups (12%). The remaining 26% were distributed relatively evenly across the 20 other ethnic groups. The language spoken at home in the Ghanaian sample was predominately one of the Akan languages. Twi accounted for 47%, other Akan languages 22%, and Fante 15%. The remaining 16% were distributed across 21 other languages.

Akyeampong and Furlong (2000) draw attention to the significance of language in teacher education. They note that the first language spoken is not a criterion for admission and no consideration is given to the native language of students during posting. Trained primary teachers are expected to use the local language of pupils in grade 1 to 3. The great majority of students sampled speak the Akan family of languages. However, there are four regions in Ghana (and other areas within regions) where the vast majority of grade 1-3 pupils speak little Akan (Volta, Northern Upper West and Upper East regions). If Akan speakers are posted to these areas they will have to use English as a medium of instruction in contradiction to the language policy of Ghana Education Service.

The student teachers in Malawi belonged to one of 9 tribes. The greatest numbers were Chewa (28%), Ngoni (27%), Lomwe (22%), and the Tumbuka (18%). The language spoken at home was predominately Chichewa (83%) even though only 28% of student teachers are Chewa. The majority of Lomwe and Ngoni student teachers appear to speak Chichewa at home. Chichewa and English are the two languages used in the school curriculum. As in Ghana, there is an issue about the posting of teachers to areas which speak a language different to the mother tongue of student teachers, since the policy is that the first three years of primary should be taught in the mother tongue of pupils.

4 Who Becomes a Primary Teacher?

Trinidad and Tobago classifies its population into one of five groupings, each of which has much diversity. The majority of students in the sample were East Indian (56%), African (24%), or mixed (17%). The school system is in English and all students are required to speak it, though they may speak an English Creole at home.

4.2.5 Home Background

The cultural capital that new entrants to teaching bring with them to the teaching profession is broadly influenced by home background and the educational attainment of parents. There is a wide range in the occupations[14] given for the fathers of Ghanaian student teachers. The majority indicated that their father was a teacher (21%), a farmer (18%), or a trader (14%). The other most frequently mentioned occupations were civil servant, accountant, driver, and minister in the Church. The range of occupations given for mothers was smaller. The largest numbers of those responding (52%) indicated that their mother was a trader. About 14% of mothers were teachers, and 13% farmers. The remaining 21% of respondents indicated that their mothers were nurses, seamstresses, housewives, and secretaries.

About 40% of the Ghanaian student teachers claimed their fathers had a post-secondary qualification, of which 15% had degree level qualifications; and 21% said their fathers had a secondary secondary school certificate (O or A Level). This compares to only about 10% of the population who have similar qualifications. Most of the remainder had some secondary schooling, and a small minority had only completed primary schooling or less. In contrast, only 24% of their mothers had a post-secondary qualification, and fewer than 2% were graduates. About 13% had a secondary school certificate; about 35% had some secondary schooling. The remainder had primary schooling or less. It is reasonable to conclude that many beginning student teachers come from families with relatively well-educated parents, though a significant minority do not.

In Lesotho half of the student teachers did not respond to the question about their father's occupation and one-third did not respond concerning their mother's occupation[15]. The fathers of the other student teachers were farmers (21%), miners (9%), and civil servants (3%). Smaller proportions were teachers, drivers, skilled or unskilled workers and a few were listed as not working. The most frequently mentioned occupation for mothers was either housewife (21%) or teacher (18%). The remaining third were fairly evenly distributed across a range of other occupations: hawkers, shopkeepers, civil servants, business people, secretaries and farmers.

---

[14] Occupational classification was problematic in all countries – labour markets and terminology differ and respondents may not be consistent in the use of particular categories. The data reported reflect judgements made in consultation with principal researchers based on answers to open ended questions.
[15] An unknown combination of unwillingness to respond, and lack of knowledge of their father or his occupation, possibly related to historically high rates of male migration to work in South Africa.

4 Who Becomes a Primary Teacher?

About 3% of the fathers of the Basotho student teachers had a degree level qualification. About 17% had fathers with a Cambridge Overseas School Certificate (COSC) or a Junior Certificate, a quarter had a primary leaving certificate and under a quarter had no qualifications. More of the mothers than fathers were qualified above secondary school level, although none of the mothers had a university degree. Over a third of the mothers had a primary leaving certificate, and 17% had no qualifications.

In Malawi about 19% did not respond to the questions about parental occupation. A further third of the student teachers indicated that their father was a farmer (38%), a teacher (12%), or a businessperson (10%). Others were clerical workers, drivers, field health assistants, church ministers, clinical officers, nurse, engineers, a tailor, and a carpenter. There were fewer occupations listed for the mothers than the fathers. The majority of their mothers were either farmers (33%) or housewives (30%). About 6% had mothers who were teachers and 6% businesspersons.

About 11% of the fathers of the Malawian student teachers had a higher education qualification. Nearly a third had a secondary school certificate and a quarter had a primary leaving certificate. A further 21% did not have any qualifications. Very few of the mothers had a higher education qualification, and far fewer mothers than fathers had a secondary school certificate. Over a third of the mothers had a primary leaving certificate and 39% had no educational qualifications.

In Trinidad and Tobago the occupations of the fathers and mothers of the student teachers were broadly categorised and ranged from higher professional to unskilled persons. Approximately 16% did not respond to the question about their parents' occupations. The majority of the fathers were lower professional and managerial (15%), skilled workers (24%), and semi-skilled workers (12%). The remainder were fairly evenly distributed between those who were unskilled workers, unemployed, retired or deceased. Half of the mothers were housepersons. A further 14% were lower professional or managerial (this category included teachers), and a few were skilled, unskilled, retired, unemployed, or deceased.

A sixth of the fathers and the mothers had a higher education qualification. Just over a third of the fathers and slightly more of the mothers had CXC/GCE[16], a further sixth of both parents of the student teachers had a primary school-leaving certificate, but more fathers than mothers had no qualifications. About 15% of the student teachers in Trinidad and Tobago did not respond to the question about their parents' educational qualifications.

Thus the data suggests that about half of parents have no more than primary education in Lesotho and Malawi. Ghana, and Trinidad and Tobago have higher proportions with secondary and above. The gender differences are consistent with known patterns of male

---

[16] Caribbean Examinations Council certificate, equivalent to former General Certificate of Education at Ordinary Level

4 Who Becomes a Primary Teacher?

and female educational achievement in these countries. Table 2 summarises the educational qualifications of student teachers' parents in the four countries.

Table 2: **Educational qualifications of parents of student teachers**

	Father %				Mother %			
	Ghana	Lesotho	Malawi	Trinidad and Tobago	Ghana	Lesotho	Malawi	Trinidad and Tobago
Post Secondary	40.1[17]	6.6	11.4	16.1	23.8	15.6	1.7	16.1
Secondary School	47.6	16.7	31.8	35.5	48.8	18.9	9.7	40.1
Primary	3.0	25.6	24.4	16.4	7.5	36.7	38.6	15.1
None	8.0	22.2	20.5	16.1	18.0	16.7	39.2	12.0
No Response	2.0	28.9	11.9	16.0	2.0	12.1	10.8	16.7

It is clearly difficult to draw simple conclusions from these patterns. However, we can note that in Ghana, Malawi and Lesotho large proportions of student trainees originate from families where fathers and mothers are working in livelihoods outside the modern sector of regular wage employment. The largest proportions of those who are in the modern sector are usually in teaching (Table 3). In Lesotho mothers are in general better educated, and many are teachers, reflecting patterns of male employment and migration associated with the mining industry. In Trinidad and Tobago much higher proportions are in skilled wage employment than in the other countries, reflecting the different structure of the economy.

Table 3: **Percentage of student teachers whose father/mother is a teacher**

Country	% Father	% Mother
Ghana	20.8	14
Lesotho	2.2	17.8
Malawi	11.9	6.3
Trinidad	n.a	n.a.

4.2.6 Educational Qualifications of Student Teachers

It is difficult to present the diversity of the educational experience and qualifications of the student teachers in the four different countries. The examinations in the different countries are often not equivalent and the levels of attainment differ across the sites. However it is possible to make some general statements about the educational qualifications of the student teachers on entry.

---

[17] These apparently high proportions result from the Ghanaian sample responding in terms of any post – O level secondary qualification including 'A' level, whereas the other samples responded in terms of further and higher education.

DFID

4 Who Becomes a Primary Teacher?

In Ghana the majority of student teachers only achieved an E grade in SSCE[18] English, representing a bare pass. About 40% achieved a grade above E in GCE[19] or SSCE. The results for mathematics were slightly more varied than the results for English, but again the majority had low grades for either SSCE or GCE. The range of grades for science examination results was greater than for English or mathematics. Some (9%) student teachers did not have a science qualification, and others had low grades i.e. F or 9. In Lesotho, none of the student teachers achieved an A grade at COSC[20] in any of three core subject areas, and few received B or C grades. Most achieved E grades or lower (62% in English, 66% in maths, and 39% in science). Most of the student teachers in Malawi had passed their English and mathematics at JCE[21] but very few (less than a third) had taken MSCE[22] in English and out of these only a quarter had gained a grade 6 or higher. Approximately a fifth of the Malawian student teachers had taken mathematics and science MSCE, with a sixth in mathematics and a third in science gaining a grade 6 or higher. No student teacher in the Trinidad and Tobago cohort achieved less than a grade 3 in English CXC, with the majority achieving either a grade 1 or 2. The pattern of results was similar for grades achieved in mathematics and science. A third of the student teachers also had A-level qualifications. Overall, the student teachers in Trinidad had substantially higher educational qualifications than the student teachers in the other three countries.

There was very little difference between the achievement of the male and female student teachers in Trinidad. In Ghana, the women had achieved similar results in English, whilst the men achieved better results in mathematics and science. The male and female student teachers in Lesotho achieved similar results in English at COSC, but men did better than women in both mathematics and science at this level. A similar pattern was found in the grades achieved by the Malawian trainees, with men having higher grades than women at MSCE.

The overall picture is that most trainee teachers achieved relatively low results at the end of their secondary school career, leaving them underqualified for higher education. Teacher training colleges, it seems, take the next tranche down from the universities.

4.2.7 School Experience of the Student Teachers

The training programmes are for serving teachers in Trinidad and Tobago and Malawi so all the respondents had taught before. In contrast, in Lesotho and Ghana few had any teaching experience and were direct entrants from schools (Table 4).

---

[18] Senior School Certificate of Education
[19] General Certificate of Education, regarded as equivalent to SSCE
[20] Cambridge Overseas School Certificate
[21] Junior School Certificate after two years secondary. Over 80% of all candidates pass this examination.
[22] Malawi School Certificate of Education

4 Who Becomes a Primary Teacher?

Table 4: **Teaching experience of student teachers for each country**

Country	Never Taught	Less than one year	Between 1 and 2 years	Between 2 and 3 years	More than three years
Ghana	77.5%	14.4%	6.5%	1%	< 1%
Lesotho	70%	16%	11.6%	2%	/
Malawi	1.7%	/	18.2%	15%	66.5%
Trinidad	/	< 1%	< 1%	60%	39%

These profiles highlight radical differences in the experiential base that student teachers bring to training. Though in all cases the trainees are on initial training courses leading to a first professional qualification, in Malawi and Trinidad and Tobago most are experienced but untrained teachers. Other MUSTER studies (e.g. Quamina-Aiyejina et al, 1999; Stuart and Kunje, 2000; Stuart, 1999) indicate that recognition of prior experience is not a prominent feature of course design, and is often not recognised in the structuring of college-based work. Nor is it used systematically as a criterion for selection, except in the sense of requiring a minimum period as an untrained teacher which is not assessed.

This section has given an overview of some of the characteristics of those currently in training in four of the MUSTER countries. It draws attention both to what these are and to some of the similarities and differences found between the groups in different countries. These provide a reminder for subsequent discussions and analysis that contexts do differ, and that the age, gender, religious affiliation, home background, prior educational qualification, and amount of teaching experience of new trainees vary widely. These characteristics are often very different from those manifested by trainee teachers in the UK and USA, where much of the theorising and advice on teacher education reform in anglophone countries originates.

4.3   Trainees' Perceptions of Teaching and the Teaching Profession.

The student teachers' responses to statements about teaching and the teaching profession add another dimension to the biographical information that the students have supplied. The responses give some insight into the attitudes that these trainee teachers bring with them when they enter training. This data is illustrative of how the particular samples responded. Eleven statements were identified which were common across the four country surveys. These are listed below along with their abbreviations.

4 Who Becomes a Primary Teacher?

Common Statements[23] Across Country Samples – Entry Questionnaires

1. The most important thing a teacher can do is teach pupils facts that they need to know (Facts)
2. School pupils learn more from listening to the teacher than from asking questions (Listen)
3. Teachers cannot do much to improve the academic performance of low achieving students (Slow lrn)
4. Children need to be divided into ability groups to be taught well (Grouping)
5. Primary pupils cannot understand English so teachers have to use another language most of the time (Lang)
6. Corporal punishment should be available in schools (Punish)
7. Teachers are born not made (Tchrs born)
8. My friends think I am fortunate to be training to be a school teacher (Fortune)
9. Teaching is a very difficult job to do well (Difficult)
10. I would rather teach in a secondary school than a primary school (Pref Sec)
11. I would rather have gone to University than Teacher Training College (Pref Uni)

Figure 6 shows the means for responses to these common statements[24]. For all the statements there was an opportunity for the trainees to indicate on a Likert[26] scale whether they strongly agreed (1), agreed (2), disagreed (3) or strongly disagreed (4). In Figure 6 mean scores can very between 1 (everyone strongly agreeing) to 4 (everyone strongly disagreeing). The mid point mean score is therefore 2.5 (as many agreeing as disagreeing[27]). A non-parametric (Kruskall Wallis) test was used to find out whether there was a significant difference in the trainees' responses to the statements between the four countries. The results were significant for all eleven statements at the $p<0.001$ level indicating that the overall patterns of response between countries were different[28]. The following discussion draws attention to the directions of some of the simple differences in the samples that can be used to generate hypotheses and reflect on possible implications for teacher education curricula.

---

[23] These statements were developed in MUSTER workshops and tested for construct validity etc. as far as possible through pilot studies.

[24] See Akyeampong & Lewin (2002) for further details.

[26] As noted earlier other more qualitative data was collected and is reported elsewhere. The limitations of this approach to attitude measurement are well known. They include assumptions about construct validity across respondents, the possibility of biases arising from the form of the instrument, and imply association between responses to written Likert attitude items and attitudes manifest through behaviour. Nevertheless this approach is an accepted way of gaining some insight into attitudes of respondents.

[27] Assuming a symmetrical distribution.

[28] For example, the statement *'School pupils learn more from listening to the teacher than from asking questions'* produced a highly significant difference in response (chi-square = 190.231, df = 3, p<0.001) across the four countries and *'My friends think I am fortunate to be training to be a school teacher'* produced a significant result (chi-square = 18.457, df = 3, p<0.001). This indicates that the differences between samples in response are unlikely to occur by chance; it does not imply that differences between any one sample and any other particular sample are necessarily significant.

4 Who Becomes a Primary Teacher?

Figure 6: **Trainees' Perceptions Measured by 11 Survey Items**

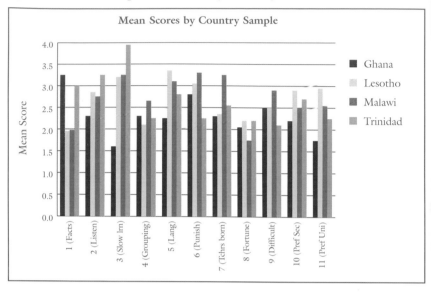

4.3.1 Attitudes to Teaching and Learning

Statements 1, 2, 3, 4, and 5 are items that have a direct reference to the trainee teachers' attitudes to learning and teaching. The Malawian and Basotho trainees agreed more with the statement (1)*'The most important thing a teacher can do is teach pupils facts that they need to know'* than the trainee teachers from Ghana and Trinidad and Tobago. Those who believe this might be considered more likely to hold views of learning that stressed the acquisition and recall of knowledge. The pattern was different in relation to (2) *'School pupils learn more from listening to the teacher than from asking questions'*. In this case the trainee teachers from Lesotho, Malawi, and Trinidad and Tobago disagreed more with the statement than did the Ghanaian trainee teachers. Ghanaian trainee teachers may have more sympathy with didactic approaches to teaching than in the other countries.

Ghanaian trainee teachers were much more likely than others to agree that (3) *'Teachers cannot do much to improve the academic performance of low achieving students'* with over 80% strongly agreeing or agreeing. These trainees appear not to have high expectations of their ability to improve children's capabilities. For statement (4) *'Children need to be divided into ability groups to be taught well'* there was general agreement across the samples except in Malawi, where less than 50% agreed. This would seem to reflect some consensus, if not a very strong one, that ability grouping was preferable to mixed ability classes. The final statement in this section (5) *'Primary pupils cannot understand English so teachers have to use another language most of the time'* elicited disagreement from a large number of the trainees, except in Ghana. Support for this view was strongest in Lesotho, and weakest in Ghana.

4 Who Becomes a Primary Teacher?

Language issues are well established as a problem in all the African countries in the sample. Surprisingly, teacher education curricula seem to give little emphasis to it in the training process (Stuart, 1999).

4.3.2 Attitudes to Discipline

Corporal punishment in schools in all the countries is controversial. It is formally discouraged or proscribed, but still practised with varying degrees of frequency. Trainee teachers' autobiographies (e.g. Akyeampong and Stephens, 2000), indicate ambivalent attitudes and a division of opinions amongst trainees. The responses to the statement (6) '*Corporal punishment should be available in schools*' amongst entering trainees indicate disagreement in three of the countries, which is strongest in Malawi, where only 13% agreed with the statement. Two-thirds of the trainees in Trinidad and Tobago appeared to be in favour of some corporal punishment.

4.3.3 Attitudes to Teaching as a Profession

Some attitudes to becoming a teacher were addressed in statements 7, 8, 9, 10 and 11. The statement (7)'*Teachers are born not made*' produced similar responses across three of the countries of weak agreement, suggesting the samples were evenly split. In Trinidad there was a small level of overall disagreement. It might be thought that those in training would disagree more strongly if they believed in the efficacy of the training process. Responses to (8)'*My friends think I am fortunate to be training to be a school teacher*' gave some indication of the trainees' perception of the status of the teaching profession. There was general agreement with this statement, with more Malawian trainees agreeing than in the other countries, perhaps reflecting the relative scarcity of alternative opportunities. Statement (9) '*Teaching is a very difficult job to do well*' also gives some indication of how entering trainees perceive their intended profession. There was little agreement from the Malawian trainees, implying that most thought teaching was easy, whilst a majority of the Trinidadian trainees felt teaching was difficult. Some more interpretive data[29] suggests that it may be that Malawian trainees are anxious not to be seen as having difficulties since all have been teaching as untrained teachers for several years before entering MIITEP. In Trinidad trainees have also been teaching prior to enrolling on the training programme and they are better qualified. It may be that they regard teaching as more difficult because expectations of them are high, but this possible explanation remains at the level of a speculation.

An aspect of trainees' career preferences are partly indicated by responses to statement (10) '*I would rather teach in a secondary school than a primary school*'. All the student teachers in the four countries are training to be primary school teachers. A majority of Ghanaian trainees agreed with this statement, possibly reflecting the fact that primary teachers become

---

[29] Perspective of D Kunje, Malawian principal researcher, based on data from MUSTER data collection.

4 Who Becomes a Primary Teacher?

qualified for upgrading training and study leave after a few years teaching in primary schools (Hedges, 2000, 2002b; Mereku, 2000). This is not such an established pattern in the other countries. Three-quarters of Basotho trainees disagreed with this statement, with a strong difference between males and females, suggesting females were more enthusiastic about remaining as primary school teachers.

There was a mixed response to (11) *'I would rather have gone to University than Teacher Training College'* across the four countries. Overall the great majority of Ghanaian trainees agreed with this, as did a small preponderance of those in Trinidad. About a quarter of those in Lesotho agreed and the Malawi sample was evenly split. This may partly reflect the chances of trainees actually getting into university – opportunities appear very limited in Lesotho.

These results are not easy to interpret, but they suggest that many trainees enter college with ambivalent attitudes to the profession and that they may be confused about some of the key pedagogic concepts. Teacher educators need to be aware of such views and inconsistencies so that they can deal constructively with them. Chapter 7 reports some further data of this kind showing how such attitudes may change during and after training (see also Coultas & Lewin 2002 for a more detailed account).

4.4   Images, Experiences and Role Identity

Michael Samuel puts forward what he terms a 'force field' model of teacher development, suggesting that 'student teachers develop conceptions of themselves, their roles and their identities in relation to three main forces:

> **Inertial forces**, emanating from their own biographical experiences of teaching and learning [..] constructed during their own home and schooling environments
> **Programmatic forces**, which emanate from the teacher education institution's curriculum and program, including the practicum
> **Contextual forces**, which derive from the macro-educational environment of ....
> policy and the micro-educational environment of ...school culture'
> (Samuel and Stephens 2000: 489)

Though constructed to describe what is happening in South Africa, where there are particularly strong forces for change, it seems useful in more stable environments as well. In particular it reminds us to look more closely at what trainees bring with them, and how they develop a sense of professional identity.

More than two decades ago Lortie pointed to the long - and unique - 'apprenticeship of observation' that trainee teachers have served during their own schooling (Lortie 1975). Bullough, Knowles and Crow (1997) postulate that such experience provides beginning

4 Who Becomes a Primary Teacher?

teachers with a 'schema' which constitutes ' … a model of what the individual believes that teaching is 'supposed' to be' (p.10). Wideen et al (1998), reviewing a large number of studies of the effects of initial teacher training programmes on student teachers' attitudes and beliefs, show how persistent these are, and how difficult it is for training programmes to shift them.

The idea that such deeply held attitudes and beliefs may well be bound up with a teacher's own sense of self has led to a growing interest in research into 'teachers' role identity'. As Ball and Goodson point out, 'the ways in which teachers achieve, maintain and develop their identity, their sense of self, in and through a career, are of vital significance in understanding the actions and commitments of teachers in their work' (1985: 18). This in turn has stimulated the use of life history methods to enquire into such patterns, as exemplified in the work of Goodson (1992) and Osler (1997).

Samuel and Stephens (2000) foreground two key relationships: firstly the relationship between the 'substantive' or core self, and the situational self that adapts to various roles, such as that of teacher; secondly the relationship between the cultural context of the trainees' home, and the professional environment which they enter.

So far no such studies have been carried out among teachers in low income countries and it was part of MUSTER's original intention to explore this area. The difficulties of finding appropriate methods within the given time constraints and changes in research personnel, meant that these studies were not fully carried out in all the sites. However, much useful data was collected and analysed, some of which has been reported in Akyeampong & Stephens (2002) and George, Mohammed et al (2001). This summary will look first at some of the more general findings and then focus on specific studies in different sites.

4.4.1 Memories of schooling

The open-ended section of the entry questionnaire asked for best and worst memories of schooling, which makes it possible to note some similarities and differences across the sites. 'Good memories' appeared to be much more idiosyncratic and varied than bad ones, but even so a broad difference appeared between the Caribbean and the African responses. The Trinidadian students wrote mainly about positive and caring relationships, and recalled a lot of 'fun', often linked to sports and activities outside formal learning. Little emphasis was put on learning, though the bad memories included pressure of work and academic failure. By contrast, while some African trainees also recalled sports and friendships, in all three countries school seemed a more serious place, and the most common positive memories concerned academic success and achievement within the classroom, along with teachers who helped and encouraged.

4 Who Becomes a Primary Teacher?

There was, however, a remarkable uniformity among the 'worst' memories of schooling across all four sites, which all focussed overwhelmingly on the use of harsh and humiliating punishment, usually some form of beating. Caning was meted out for poor academic performance as well as for misbehaviour, and students remembered many teachers as using it to excess, as in this not untypical account from Lesotho:

> *When the students got wrong, she used stick....When she whipped the students, she told them to put hand above the head. If the student ... removed his hand ... she whipped him/she (sic) on the head.*

The most common effect, often vividly described, was to make pupils afraid and to want to leave school. 'Our brains diminished and we could not think', wrote one, and another said: 'He made us freeze.' Students would fail, or come to dislike the subject. A few, however, thought that caning had made them work harder.

Negative memories of schooling in the African countries often reflect the level of economic development: problems of finding money for fees or uniform, the poor conditions of the schools, with few resources and lack of staff, the long walks to school. Other themes are fear, frustration, and incomprehension, and in Malawi a couple of women remember gender discrimination. From the autobiographies, it is clear that a number of students had had to overcome many problems in their childhood, often related to poverty, unemployment or death of a parent. In these conditions, teachers were often remembered with gratitude for their moral or practical support and in many cases may have influenced students' decision to enter training.

4.4.2 Images of teachers

There are again many similarities across the countries. In Lesotho, the essay guidelines explicitly asked trainees to write about their best and worst teachers, and to describe the kind of teacher they would like to be, so details from that country study will be used to exemplify some common themes.

What emerges strongly from the data is that teachers are perceived and evaluated as much in terms of personal characteristics as in terms of professional knowledge and skills; the affective domain appears just as important if not more so than the cognitive. Among the 'personal' characteristics there are strong images of the 'teacher as parent', the teacher as 'social role model', and, combining elements of both these, the 'teacher as counsellor'.

Some used the term 'parent' explicitly and others described teachers as being caring, patient, kind and helpful, but exercising firm discipline. One wrote: 'He was very strict punishing us, but we were enjoying [it] ...I think it was because he did it through parental love'. By

4 Who Becomes a Primary Teacher?

contrast, bad teachers are unfair, harsh and unfeeling.

The 'social role model' included both norms and ethics. Good teachers set an example by adhering to appropriate conventions of manners and dress, and also through their moral attitudes and behaviour. Male teachers were criticised for drinking and dishonesty as well as for poor levels of personal appearance and hygiene; women teachers were, however, more likely to be criticised for over-dressing and wearing jewellery – an interesting gender contrast.

Two key themes about teachers' professional skills, which reappeared constantly through the data, were the ability to explain clearly enough for all to understand, and giving attention to individuals, especially slow learners.

> *She could explain a lesson until everyone heard and understood it*
> *He was always ready to offer help to every child, either in academic problems or personal problems*

Good teachers are remembered for helping pupils pass exams, but also for their ability to encourage and inspire:

> *[ ] was the first teacher in my life who ever made me realise my abilities as far as my studies were concerned.*

Descriptions of bad teachers point up the same themes from the opposite direction:

> *I did not understand his teaching method. The worst thing was that I could not have a chance to tell what I did not understand because always when he entered the class he used to say: if you do not know what you're here for, it's up to you. Others who were slow learners like me were bored.*

But few of these student teachers could describe just how good teachers made things clear to them. Mentions of actual teaching strategies were few and often vague, such as 'she used many methods'; 'we had games and songs'; 'work was marked regularly'. Apparently at this stage in their training they were not yet able to analyse their memories from a professional point of view. However, they remembered that good teachers 'allowed us to ask questions', and identified the importance of encouragement and motivation. Box 4.1 is a student's description of an admired teacher, which covers many of the above points

4 Who Becomes a Primary Teacher?

Box 4.1: **The Good Teacher**

> *He was very punctual to the class every morning… all the lessons he taught were very challenging, [and] he taught clearly. He was very intelligent in …. explanations. He was having a parental love to each and every student in his class. He knew how to treat both fast learners, medium-learners as well as slow learners. He knew how to influence his students to perform very well … he succeeded in making every pupil to obtain better pass-marks….[male student, 27 years old]*

Views from Malawi and Ghana are broadly similar, though interestingly there is rather less emphasis on the nurturing role. This may be related to the fact that primary teaching in these two countries is much less heavily feminised than in Lesotho. But there is the same emphasis on personality – the ability to encourage and inspire - and on commitment – patient, hardworking, ready to help individuals – rather than on professional skills. In Ghana the emphasis on the teacher as social role model extends beyond the individual to the community. (Trinidad and Tobago is discussed below).

In Lesotho, the student views of the ideal teacher – the kind of teacher they would like to be – provide support for the thesis that students model themselves on their own teachers. Eight (out of 27) explicitly said they wanted to be like the good teacher they had described earlier, and several more, either consciously or unconsciously, used the same words, phrases or examples of behaviour in both paragraphs, such as to be a parent, to reconcile students, to explain clearly to slow learners, or to give sweets as a reward.

Some were beginning to use professional terms – not always accurately! – but few mentioned any specific teaching strategies or techniques they would use. There seemed a widespread intention to be less authoritarian: nearly half wrote that students should 'feel free', implying that students could approach the teacher with personal and social problems as well as academic ones, but in general there was no clear vision of learner-centred teaching.

This is hardly surprising. In none of these countries did student teachers have the experience of the kinds of 'progressive', interactive and participatory learning approaches recommended in some of the curricular materials and espoused by some of the college tutors. As the Basotho examples suggest, these student teachers commonly aspire to do better what they remember their own teachers doing: transmit knowledge clearly and effectively, while being patient and kind.

4 Who Becomes a Primary Teacher?

4.4.3 Metaphors and cultural myths

In Trinidad and Tobago the images of the good teacher that emerged from the open-ended survey questions were not dissimilar to those found elsewhere: caring, helpful, encouraging, maternal and dedicated. Again there was little mention of cognitive or pedagogic skills, though a strong theme emerged, different from the African sites, about 'making learning fun'. The survey was followed up by a longitudinal study with a group of 16 trainees, using educational autobiographies, focus group discussions, and individual interviews over 18 months of the 2-year course (George, Mohammed et al 2001), and from this richer data four strong metaphors emerged:

Teacher as nurturer: First and foremost a good teacher must be able to establish caring relationships, understand the children's needs, act as an exemplar, be patient but firm – in other words, taking on a parental role. Many of these qualities are felt to be innate.

Teacher as expert: However, professional and pedagogic skills are also necessary, and the good teacher has to be trained, so they can work effectively in the classroom. After a year, most of the respondents felt they had gained useful knowledge about handling children and delivering lessons, though they still held ambivalent views on corporal punishment.

Teacher as responsible for everything; A primary teacher has to be an 'all-rounder', capable of doing everything on their own. This seems to emphasise the burden on the individual, rather than a collective responsibility.

Teaching as martyrdom. Teachers have to make sacrifices, taking a job with relatively low professional status and poor salaries, while being expected to perform a multi-faceted role in the classroom. (George, Mohammed et al 2001).

George et al conclude that underlying these images and metaphors are powerful cultural myths about being a teacher in Trinidad and Tobago, which have their roots far back in the society's historical experiences. Such myths describe teachers as engaged in self-sacrificing work which they do because of a love of children and a sense of altruism. On the one hand teachers are seen as powerful individuals capable of effecting change through love and selfless dedication, and earning respect; on the other hand they have to forego high salaries and status.

They conclude that this produces great tensions for individual teachers as they start their careers. Both college curriculum and the myth project a certain desired scenario, while trainees experience something much less rewarding. While the substantive self embraces the cultural myth, the situated self has difficulties with the low status and rewards. The college

4 Who Becomes a Primary Teacher?

should, rather, help trainees to explore their images and the cultural myth, and interrogate what it means to become a teacher in Trinidad and Tobago today.

Although this seems very country-specific, it may be that similar studies elsewhere would produce similar results, with the cultural myths varying according to the context. Box 4.2 illustrates some of phrases used newly qualified teachers in Ghana in describing their roles and their work. These suggest similar tensions and contradictions.

Box 4.2: **Perceptions of Ghanaian NQTs**

Teacher as a:

- role model in the community
- self-reliant and independent individual
- 'ne'er do weel' and a drain on the community

Teaching as:

- a stepping stone to better jobs
- duty to family
- a moral or religious ideal of service
- isolation and fear of becoming 'a village man'
- an opportunity for strong friendships
- 'government work'
- an opportunity to pursue other interests like farming and business

(adapted from Hedges, 2000a)

4.4.4 Motivations for teaching

Unsurprisingly, students gave a mixture of motives for wanting to train as a teacher. In the survey many highlighted instrumental reasons such as job security, or the chances to study further. Many, especially in Africa, also mentioned general altruistic reasons such as 'to impart knowledge', to 'bring light' and 'raise the standard of education in the country'. Some of these ideas seemed linked to the Christian traditions of both students and colleges, others to development discourses. A few students expressed an intrinsic interest in working with children, or wanted to win respect from the community as a role model. The qualitative studies confirm these broad patterns, but show more clearly how their idealistic and altruistic motives conflict with their realistic assessment of difficult conditions in the schools and the low status of primary teachers. Students' ideals need to be nurtured and rewarded if they are to act as lifelong motivators.

4 Who Becomes a Primary Teacher?

4.5   Concluding Discussion

Policy makers and course designers need to take seriously the biographies and experiences of entering students, since these will partly determine how the students interact with the course, the kind of teacher they might become, and what career decisions they will make afterwards. Training programmes should adapt to the starting points of the students as they currently are, not as they were in the past or in the minds of curriculum developers.

Students come with different kinds of hopes and expectations, and many are ambivalent about training. Some are following role models, either from family or from their own teachers; these may be inspiring but also perhaps outmoded. Some have altruistic motives and a genuine love of children. Others have sought other options and see teaching as a career of last resort.

Academically, entering students come with both weaknesses and strengths. Many did poorly at high school and identify with slow learners. This may make them patient and successful teachers, but their own knowledge, skills and self-esteem need building up. Others just missed university and still have ambitions for further study; unless these can be later met within the primary career structure the individuals may move on into secondary schools. Where colleges recruit serving teachers, these will be adult learners, often with children of their own. They will need help to readjust to studying, but potentially they have much useful experience to draw on.

Low academic achievement in the main medium of instruction (in all cases English) is worrying. On the other hand, in the African sites students are drawn from many different ethnic groups and may speak more than one local language that is used for the early primary grades. These linguistic skills could be developed and used, particularly if they are willing to return to schools in relevant areas. However, those raised in urban areas, as many of the Ghanaian students were, may be less ready to work in rural villages.

The data shows that trainees come to the college bringing with them much baggage from the past in the form of memories of schooling and beliefs about teaching. This includes well developed images of the good teacher which focus particularly on the personal and affective aspects of the role. Perhaps this emphasis explains why so many students across the sites think teachers are born and not made; they expect college to give them knowledge and skills, rather than developing those most important qualities they believe to be innate.

Typically, students have much vaguer ideas about how good teaching and learning actually occur, modelled on what they have seen their own teachers do. Their ideas about pedagogy are confused at this stage. Most have experienced only transmission methods, though they have picked up some of the child-centred rhetoric and some seem to be groping towards a less authoritarian approach.

4 Who Becomes a Primary Teacher?

The ambivalence around the issue of corporal punishment is a particularly interesting example of the problems in changing their behaviour. Student teachers have strong emotional memories of pain and humiliation, yet many still say the cane should be available, and probably will use it if that is the norm in the school. Elmon Tafa's recent study (Tafa, 2001) showed how widely corporal punishment is (mis)used in junior secondary schools in Botswana, and how NQTs are quickly resocialised into its use. In his view it is a symptom of a widespread authoritarian approach to schooling which the supposedly 'liberal' college regimes do little to challenge.

Indeed, it may not be easy for the college to help students unpack such baggage, analyse and review it critically, discard what is outdated, and remodel valuable ideas into relevant up-to-date practices. In most societies both tutors and students share a wider socio-cultural heritage that may include deep-rooted and powerful myths about the role of the teacher, which trainees may have incorporated into their self-image and role identity. For example, in Trinidad and Tobago George, Worrell et al (2001) suggest that students' prior beliefs and the college curriculum are 'fashioned from the same myth' In such a case it may be difficult for tutors to challenge students interrogate it. Chapters 7 and 8 will take these ideas further.

4.5.1 Key issues for policy and practice

- Many entrants to primary teacher training, particularly in the African sites, have the minimum academic qualifications or below. Ways have to be found of strengthening their academic skills and upgrading their knowledge, especially in the language(s) in which they are to teach.

- By default or by design, 'student teachers' are often adults with previous teaching experience. This has implications for both the content of the curriculum and the way it is taught.

- Primary teacher training is for many an avenue of social mobility. Students who are the first generation in higher education may need support and enrichment programmes.

- The complicated networks of linguistic and ethnic affiliation from which students come could be assets, if their language skills are developed and they are deployed in appropriate areas.

- Student teachers do not come as 'empty vessels' but with powerful memories of their own schooling and of good teachers which may shape their response to training. Teacher educators need to recognise and engage with these, so they can be critically analysed and evaluated during training.

4 Who Becomes a Primary Teacher?

- While motivations are very mixed, many entering students evince a desire to serve, often inspired by religious beliefs, though these values may exist in tension with the realities of a professional career. For others, it is a career of last resort. They are aware of the low status of the profession, and its meagre rewards; if these are not improved, the supply of willing entrants may well decrease.

Chapter Five	**5 The Curriculum of Teacher Education**

5.0   Summary and Overview

A core strand of the MUSTER enquiry was to find out more about 'how new teachers acquire the knowledge, skills and attitudes required to teach in different systems'. We therefore asked such questions as:

➢ How was the college curriculum developed and what influenced it?

➢ What is to be taught, and how?

➢ How is the curriculum delivered, and how far are the stated aims and objectives achieved?

5.0.1 Summary of Findings

The development of the curriculum

- Systematic and consistent curriculum development for initial teacher training programmes is not characteristic of the programmes we researched. The college curricula we examined had traces of missionary origins, signs of post-independence moves to 'modernise' teacher training, and evidence of international borrowing from different periods.

- Much of the curriculum seemed very outdated, and there seemed uncertainty as to whether to try to raise the academic level, or to move towards a more practical orientation

The documented curriculum

- In all the sites the initial training curriculum was linked quite closely to the primary school syllabus and there was little specialisation either by subject or school phase.

- Most time was given to subject knowledge, including subject content and subject methods in different proportions. The time given to professional components varied from 10-30%. Little attention was paid to aspects of general education, such as study skills, or to personal development.

- There were considerable inconsistencies within the curriculum with regard to aims, objectives, pedagogy, teaching-learning materials and assessment.

The curriculum as delivered in action

- Most teaching followed a transmission style, with lecturing and question-and-answer sessions being most common.

- Students were generally assessed by tests, essays and end-of-year exams. Though projects were set, students had little time for independent study; they often lacked the skills, and library resources were seldom adequate.

- Teaching materials were limited, often out of date and culturally unadapted.

- The curriculum appeared very overloaded. Remedial teaching was seldom available, and

5 The Curriculum of Teacher Education

many students struggled with their work. The low failure rate suggests that the standards expected were also low.

This chapter sets the scene by outlining some of the debates in the current theory and practice of Teacher Education. It then gives an overview of the curriculum structure in the research sites. The following sections offer a comparative analysis of the curricula studied, looking at aims, content, teaching and learning materials, pedagogy and assessment. The final part discusses some of the findings and identifies some key issues. For South Africa, the main reference point will be the newly-designed Bachelor of Education degree at the University of Durban-Westville, as it exemplifies a new approach.

5.1 Introduction

Teacher education programmes can only be understood and evaluated within the historical, socio-economic, political and cultural contexts in which they have developed, including the perceived role of the teacher in society, current views of knowledge, and the level of economic development. A further factor is how they are positioned within global educational debates: it is pertinent to ask whether the main influences come as part of an aid package (Malawi), by invitation to selected consultants (Lesotho), through gradual permeation of the discourse (Trinidad and Tobago) or by the deliberately seeking out of new models (South Africa). The following brief discussion of some current international debates indicates the frameworks and terms to be used in analysing the findings of the following chapters.

5.1.1 Theories of teaching and learning

Teacher education programmes, like other curricula, are built up around various theories of learning, though these are not always made explicit (Avalos 1991). Adapting Avalos' ideas, we will here distinguish three broad perspectives: the 'behaviourist', the 'constructivist' and the 'social constructivist'. The behaviourist position, originating with the work of Pavlov and Skinner, emphasises the ways in which the knowledge, communication and practical skills of the teacher brings about learning in terms of observed changes of behaviour in the pupils; teaching is foregrounded.

The constructivist position, drawing from the theories of Piaget and his followers, focusses on how learning takes place when new information and ideas are absorbed by the learner and integrated with previous knowledge and concepts; here the emphasis is on the learner. The more recent school of social constructivism, linked to the ideas of Vygotsky, stresses the way learning is enhanced through interaction with the social environment, highlighting both language and the mediating role of the teacher who has to provide appropriate challenge and support; this shows teacher and learner roles as interdependent (Daniels 1996).

5 The Curriculum of Teacher Education

Avalos comments that 'the dominant theory of teaching [in training colleges] in many developing countries is linked to the behaviourist approach to learning' (Avalos op.cit. p.11). However, in recent years new primary school curricula have been developed in such countries, which are labelled as learner-centred and interactive, and which seem to derive from a broadly constructivist perspective. It seems crucial that pre-service teacher education prepares teachers to understand and if necessary to critique the assumptions underlying the new curricula.

5.1.2 Views of Knowledge

Theories of learning rest on assumptions about the nature of knowledge. For example, the behaviourist psychology had its roots in the positivist epistemology which sees knowledge as objective, existing apart from the individual and social context, and capable of transmission and application in more or less fixed forms. This view underlies what Schon (1983) criticises as the 'technical rationality' model of professional education, where the student acquires discipline-based knowledge and is then expected to apply it routinely to what are often unique and confused situations, that require artistry and individual judgement as well as scientific understanding.

Constructivist learning theories, while not denying the scientific basis of much modern knowledge, stress also its situated and contextual nature, and the way individuals reconstruct what they hear and experience before they can use it effectively. Social constructivists emphasise how the social, cultural and political structures permeate the contexts and affect the way knowledge is acquired and used. Such views suggest putting more emphasis on an extended and supported 'practicum' in professional learning.

5.1.3 The role of the teacher

These debates in teacher education in anglophone countries of the North/West have led to a broad distinction being made between 'teacher as technician' and 'teacher as reflective practitioner'. The technician is seen as having a restricted role, her job being to deliver the curriculum – which is prescribed at a higher level – as effectively as possible, while the reflective practitioner is expected to play a more extended role, that may include developing the curriculum to suit the context, evaluating and trying to improve her own practice, and mentoring new teachers. Such extended professional education tends to be resource- and time-intensive and presupposes certain culturally located assumptions about personal autonomy and responsibility; it also has organisational implications for schools and colleges. However, these are ideal types, perhaps best depicted as two ends of a continuum, and used to analyse trends or compare curriculum goals rather than as prescriptions for practice, as in most situations elements of both can be found, and indeed usefully combined.

5 The Curriculum of Teacher Education

5.1.4 The authoritarian v. the dialogic stance

Another relevant distinction to be made, especially in the African context, is that between the teacher as the unquestioned source of knowledge, and the teacher as co-enquirer. Following Tabulawa (1997), this can be seen to have two aspects, epistemological and social. In many traditional societies knowledge was seen as something fixed, finite and to be handed down, rather than something to be explored, questioned and developed along new lines. The elders were respected because they had this knowledge, and could teach it to the young, whose role was to listen rather than ask questions. Tabulawa argues that these deeply-rooted cultural assumptions have contributed to the resistance to educational change in African classrooms, particularly where this involves the idea of teacher and learner entering into dialogue and pursuing enquiries together. It may well be that under the influence of international discourse such cultural assumptions are breaking down, particularly in urban areas. However, the debate is very pertinent to teacher education. If one accepts Schon's (1983) dictum that the teacher's expertise lies less in routinely applying theoretical knowledge than in framing teaching and learning problems in new ways, carrying out experiments in action, and finding appropriate solutions in unique situations, the roles of both teachers and pupils will have to change.

5.1.5 School-based teacher education

Another international trend is towards bringing theory and practice closer together through campus-school partnerships, using mentor teachers and school internship to complement or even replace the academic studies in university or college. In the UK this has gone so far that graduate teachers may now train entirely on the job, working under supervision and attending seminars in local Teachers' Centres. It seems questionable whether this is a satisfactory way of preparing professionals who have sufficient intellectual grasp of educational issues to ensure their teaching remains dynamic and responsive to social change; it seems more likely to be a recipe for maintaining the status quo. Such training methods also presuppose a high level of both infrastructure and professional development at school level. They are more difficult to introduce into education systems which are poorly resourced and where the teachers in the host schools may themselves not be fully qualified.

5.1.6 Teacher Education and the State

Teacher education is a politically contested area (Stuart and Tatto 2000). Most governments seek to control the teacher education curriculum, either directly by having the colleges under ministerial control, or indirectly through setting centralised standards and guidelines for university departments of education to follow. The state has many, sometimes conflicting, expectations of the teachers. They may be viewed as conservers of traditional values or moral exemplars, and at the same time be expected to act as agents of development

5 The Curriculum of Teacher Education

(Tatto and Dharmadasa 1995) Governments driven by the global imperative to compete successfully in world markets may see teachers as just another set of technicians who are supposed to prepare a skilled and obedient workforce. Where transformation is on the political agenda, teachers are expected to lead the creation of new citizens, having themselves undergone political change. Elliott (1999) discusses how such ideological conflicts are negotiated and played out in different ways in different countries.

5.2   Overview of Curriculum Structures

5.2.1 Approaches to the Curriculum

The term 'curriculum' is here defined as the entire experience throughout the training programme, as taught by college tutors, as organised both on and off campus, and as learnt by trainee teachers. We found the curriculum existed in different forms, viz:

- On paper, as designed and set out in the documents
- In the minds of the tutors
- As experienced by trainees
- As perceived by external observers

Our analysis draws from these different perspectives.

We took as an analytical starting point Frant's (1976) model of curriculum design, which identifies the interrelations between aims, objectives, content, teaching/learning resources, pedagogy, and assessment; this is useful for evaluating how far the programme embodies a consistent and coherent curricular strategy. The actual content of a professional curriculum, however, is more complex than this model allows for, involving a strategic balancing of different academic and practical components, and ways of fitting them into a structure of time and place.

5.2.2 Primary Initial Teacher Education in a state of flux

The last major comparative studies of teacher education curricula in low income countries took place in the 1980's (Dove 1985, Lockheed & Verspoor 1991, Rust and Dalin 1990) and these gave an impression of stasis and neglect. However, recently there has been much talk of change and we found the curriculum in most of our case-study sites in a period of transition. Wideen and Grimmett (1995) distinguish between 'restructuring', where changes are superficial and old practices persist below the surface, and 'reconceptualisation' where thinking changes fundamentally. From the summary below it can be seen that different programmes are going in different directions and there are few common trends. Later analysis will attempt to distinguish how fundamental the changes are.

5 The Curriculum of Teacher Education

Ghana: the 3- year post-secondary certificate course, dating from 1978, has been in a state of flux since 1997. The first major change was to focus Year 1 on upgrading the trainees' subject knowledge; students had to pass exams in all core subjects before they could proceed to Years 2 and 3 where content and methods were taught together as 'curriculum studies'. In 2000 it was decided to implement the 'In-In-Out' model, whereby trainee teachers spend most of Year 3 in school as interns, returning to college only for final exams. The aim was to give trainees more exposure to the realities of classroom teaching, and to emphasise the development of teaching competencies over a longer period of time, as well as to increase output of trained teachers. (Akyeampong 2002).

Lesotho: At the National Teacher Training College (NTTC), a 3 1/2 year Diploma in Education (Primary) (DEP) began in Sept. 1998 to replace the old 3-year Primary Teachers Certificate (PTC). The main changes were higher entry qualifications, a one-semester bridging course in core subjects and study skills, an overall greater emphasis on academic subject content, and a two-stage practicum totalling 15 weeks. The intentions were both to raise the academic levels of primary teachers and to introduce a more reflective orientation, so that they would be capable of taking on a more 'extended' professional role. (Lefoka & Stuart 2001).

Malawi: One- and two-year residential training programmes were replaced in January 1997 by the 2-year mixed-mode Malawi Integrated Inservice Teacher Education Programme (MIITEP), whereby unqualified serving teachers spend 3 months at college followed by 20 months distance learning under supervision in their schools; they return to college for a month's revision and examinations. Graduates receive the same Teachers' Certificate as before. MIITEP is a slimmed-down curriculum, condensed from the old full-time 2-year version; it is largely skills-based, and considered to be the minimum necessary to turn the present unqualified teachers into more 'effective instructors'. (Kunje & Chimombo 1999); Stuart & Kunje 2000; Kunje, Lewin & Stuart, 2002.

South Africa: The entire system of teacher development is being transformed and moved into the Higher Education sector. In this report, we shall refer briefly to the curriculum of the new 4-year Bachelor of General Education and Training (BAGET) degree introduced in January 1999 at the University of Durban-Westville (UDW). This has been designed from scratch, with new ways of linking content and methods, and with a large element of school-based training (Samuel and Pillay, 2002). It is not typical of current South African practice, but will be used as an example of reconceptualisation. It is consistent with the new South African 'Norms and Standards for Educators' which set out the threefold competences – academic, practical and reflexive - needed to enable teachers to take on multiple roles as 'critical professional educators'and contrasts with other longer standing forms of provision (see Samuel 2002; Reddy 2002b, Robinson, Vergani & Sayed, 2002, Lewin, Samuel & Sayed, 2003).

5 The Curriculum of Teacher Education

Trinidad and Tobago: there have been no recent published alterations to the 2-year post-experience Teachers' Diploma programme. However, the curriculum is evolving slowly, mainly through incremental changes brought about by the lecturers themselves, in the direction of more reflective practice. It is hoped to link it more closely to the year-long the 'on-the-job' apprenticeship training given to unqualified entrants to teaching. (Quamina-Aiyejina et al 1999, George & Quamina-Aiyejina, 2002).

5.2.3 Programme structure and location

One obvious difference is between those programmes – Ghana, Lesotho, South Africa - which take candidates straight from school for 3 or 4 years full-time, usually residential, training, and those which offer a two-year course to trainees who already have experience, such as Malawi and Trinidad and Tobago. The latter provide contrasting examples: while Trinidad and Tobago offers on the job training for a whole year, and then a two-year full-time college-based course later on, Malawi offers a very brief orientation, and later a 3-month residential course followed by distance learning, with a short final residential block. The curriculum components are constrained and modified by such structures.

5.2.4 Specialisation by school phase

This important issue does not always receive the attention it deserves. Internationally, it is common for teachers to follow (at least partly) different courses to prepare them for, respectively, Infant/Lower Primary, Upper Primary, and Secondary, on the grounds that different subject content and different methods are appropriate for each phase. In Ghana recent practice has been to have just one programme to prepare teachers for the whole Basic School cycle, comprising both Primary and Junior Secondary Schools (JSS), even though primary schools need class teachers and JSS require specialists. In Malawi and Trinidad and Tobago the programmes train class teachers for the whole of the primary years; in Lesotho there was for a short time an elective course for 'Early Years' which has been dropped in the new Diploma in Education (Primary). In South Africa primary teachers have traditionally been trained as part-specialists, which is reflected in their curricular patterns. We found little discussion of this issue, though in Ghana there were suggestions that colleges might specialise in either Primary or Junior Secondary.

5.3   Aims and Objectives.

There is often a lack of clarity about what the programmes intend to achieve, or think is achievable. Documentation, especially for the older programmes like the Lesotho PTC, was often incomplete, course outlines apparently being handed on from one generation of tutors to another. Where new programmes were being introduced, there were indeed lists of intentions; however, these did not always match the rest of the programme. For example,

5 The Curriculum of Teacher Education

the Lesotho DEP programme aims seem based on the 'reflective practitioner' model of the teacher, who would have high levels of knowledge and skills, but also be expected to use their professional judgement, help develop the curriculum and act as change agent. But the individual subject courses seemed premised on a 'behaviourist' model, giving no space to reflection, self-evaluation or implementing classroom change. Similarly in Malawi, some of the MIITEP documents mention the 'teacher as facilitator and agent of change' while the overall national objectives for teacher training remain unchanged, emphasising the role of the teacher as effective instructor and moral guide.

The curricula in Ghana and Trinidad and Tobago state no overall aims. This leaves the tutors free to develop the curriculum on the one hand, but on the other gives no impetus for change. The BAGET syllabus is a more coherent document; it was to be taught by the same group as developed it, and was planned in the context of a strong government push for transformation (Samuel 2002).

When we probed, through interviews, for tutors' views of the kind of teacher they wanted to produce, two broad themes stood out from the descriptions: someone who knew their subject and could teach it effectively, and someone who related well to children. This is the common ground among the practitioners. But the teachers' role is also related to political, epistemological and ideological perceptions which permeate the education system more generally. The following oversimplified phrases give something of the emphases in different places. The teacher produced by training should be:

➢ In Ghana, a 'technical practitioner'
➢ In Lesotho, well-grounded academically
➢ In Malawi, an efficient instructor
➢ In South Africa, a critical educator
➢ In Trinidad and Tobago, well educated and knowledgeable

5.4 Content

It is generally agreed that the key components of any initial teacher training programme must include:

• **Subject content** : adequate knowledge and understanding of the subject(s) to be taught in school
• **'pedagogic content knowledge'** or **'methods'**: ways of teaching and assessing the subject(s) appropriate to the learners' level (cf. Shulman 1987)
• **education & professional studies**: a basic understanding of how children develop and learn, plus some 'craft knowledge' on how to manage the teaching process
• **a 'practicum'**: opportunities to bring all these together and practise performing the role of teacher.

5 The Curriculum of Teacher Education

Some would add:

- **general education**: courses designed for personal growth and enrichment.

The practicum needs to be analysed separately and is dealt with in Chapter 6.

5.4.1 Subject Content.

Table 5 enables some comparisons to be made regarding the subjects studied: All programmes are closely linked to the primary syllabus. Attempts to prepare primary teachers to teach all subjects often lead to a crammed time-table and superficial coverage. This is only partially mitigated by combining subjects into broad learning areas or offering electives, as shown above. Students and staff alike feel overloaded and worry about 'covering the syllabus', with negative effects on teaching methods, as discussed below.

Table 5: **Proportions of contact time suggested for each subject area**

Subject Area	GHANA*	LESOTHO	MALAWI	T & T	UDW**
Education	14%	10.4%	16.3%	24.1%	30%
Local lang.	6	13.8	8.4	-	5
English	14 + Elec.	13.8	13.9	22.4	15
Maths	8 + Elec.	13.8	12.3	10.3	15
Science	13 + Elec.	13.8	11.2	7.8	15
Social Studies	Cultural Stds. 6 + Elec.	R.E. & Dev. Stds. 10.4	Soc. & Gen. Stds 8.6	Soc. Studs. 6.7	5
Expressive Arts	[extra-curricular]	Art & craft, PE, music, drama 10.4	Music 4 Creative Arts 3.6	one from A & C, music, dance, drama 5.9	5
Technical/ Applied Science	Tech. Skills Voc. Skills [Elec. only]	Agric., Home Econ., Health Ed. 10.4	Agric. 6.3 Home Econ. 6.1	Agric. 2.7	Econ. Ed. 5 ICT 15
Religious/ moral educ.		-	R.E. 4.4	Family Life Educ. 6.7	Life Skills 5
Physical education	4 + Elec.		P.E. 4.6	Physical and Health Ed. 4.4	
Electives	35%	-	-	9%	10%
Study Skills	-	2.7	-	-	

*   *Proposed 2000. Several core courses can also be taken as electives, which form over 1/3 of the course*
** *Students choose between certain core subjects*

Language, maths and science form the core. There are, however, differences in weighting: for example, Lesotho gives considerably more time to maths and science (27%) than does Trinidad and Tobago (18%). In the African countries language content has to include both English and the local language. In such multi-lingual contexts, it is disturbing to find so little attention paid to developing trainees' own language skills, both in English as the main

5 The Curriculum of Teacher Education

medium of instruction, and in other local or national languages needed for teaching in the lower grades. Lesotho's curriculum attempts some remediation in the bridging course and within the English syllabus, but observation revealed an old-fashioned grammar approach which did little to enhance communication (Lefoka and Ntoi 2002, Lefoka, Jobo, Moeti et al 2000). All the evidence from the African sites suggests trainees need to be much more fluent and confident in the relevant language(s) of instruction. This is beginning to be addressed in the South African context, and by the same token, the Trinidadian colleges do put effort into helping trainees acquire 'international standard English' in addition to the local creole.

A major dilemma is whether to give the trainees just the content needed to teach the syllabus, or to teach them the discipline to as high a level as possible. This in turn is constrained by students' entering levels, and by the time available. Most of the students surveyed rated at least some of the core subjects 'difficult', and qualitative studies in Lesotho and Malawi revealed many students were struggling to keep up. Tutors routinely complained about low academic levels. The partial evidence we obtained from exam papers and results suggest that in reality most primary trainees do not make much progress beyond upper secondary school level.

5.4.2 'Pedagogic content knowledge' and subject methods

A related question in designing such curricula is whether subject content and subject methods are taught separately or together, and what balance obtains between them. Close scrutiny of curriculum documents suggest that even when syllabi are supposedly designed to a common pattern, subject teams interpret and teach them differently; often the sciences put more emphasis on content, and teach methods separately, while the humanities more often combine them.

In broad terms, Ghana, Lesotho and Trinidad and Tobago try to teach content and methods separately, while Malawi and UDW try to integrate them. This is related to the question of academic level, but in interesting ways. The MIITEP course mainly teaches subject content and methods together, apart from science, using an approximate balance of 1:2. Thus methods, generally in the form of routine skills and prescriptive advice, predominate. At the other end of the academic scale the UDW team conceptualised 'Science Education', 'Maths Education' and 'Language Education' as disciplines in their own right, and designed the programme around such courses with the explicit intention of developing the students' academic and pedagogical knowledge together.

By contrast, in Ghana the first year is devoted to subject upgrading, and the second to teaching the methods to be used for each subject in the relevant grades of the basic schools, so that the two are roughly balanced in terms of time. Lesotho's new DEP is deliberately

5 The Curriculum of Teacher Education

designed to enhance trainees' academic knowledge, and the desired content to methods ratio was set at 70:30, with separate modules for each. Again, the maths and science are more heavily oriented towards content, with little on the conceptual frameworks related to maths or science 'education'; the science does not seem closely related to the primary school. The English syllabus pays attention to developing the trainees' own knowledge of literature and grammar as well as to theories of teaching reading. Observation confirmed tutors followed these patterns.

The Trinidad and Tobago curriculum is in general heavily oriented towards giving trainees a 'knowledge base', with well over half the modules devoted to content, but the subject approaches vary; in science and maths the modules are set out as separate, while in arts and humanities knowledge and pedagogic aspects are more likely to be treated within the same unit. Classroom observation, however, suggest that experienced tutors interpret the curriculum in their own way, and the most effective integration was observed in a science lesson.

5.4.3 Education and Professional Studies

This component comprises both courses on educational theory and those designed to teach practical, managerial and administrative skills, including preparation for the practicum. As can be seen from Table 5 it is often squeezed into quite a small proportion of the timetable. Box 5.1 gives some details.

5 The Curriculum of Teacher Education

Box 5.1: **Professional and Educational Studies**

> **Lesotho**: the eight 'theory' modules include the traditional 'ologies': psychology, sociology and philosophy of education, together with curriculum studies, guidance and counselling and educational administration. There are also modules on Early Primary and Special Education. The remaining seven 'methodology' modules cover methods, resources, testing, and micro-teaching, ICT and research skills.
>
> **Malawi**: The residential course starts with the technical professional skills of writing lesson plans, formulating objectives, drawing up schemes of work and keeping records, as well as introductions to different kinds of teaching methods and how to improvise and use various kinds of teaching/learning aids. It moves on to child development, theories of learning, and testing. The school-based units focus on management and administration of schools, keeping records, roles of head and PTA, school and community relationships, professional ethics and conditions of service, together with more classroom management skills.
>
> **Trinidad and Tobago**: Professional Studies is divided into three: Education I and II are largely theoretical, and cover the traditional areas of sociology, psychology, social psychology and history of education, with some references to the local context. There are also sections on 'contemporary issues in education' and on gender. Education III is devoted to methods and micro-teaching.
>
> **Ghana**: Education Studies here have a more integrated approach, taking themes from the old 'disciplines' of psychology and sociology of education, setting them in the Ghanaian context - a number of modules are explicitly concerned with local issues - and tying to them to practice via observation of pupils in local schools.
>
> **UDW** has broken with the traditional divisions and topics. BAGET sets out seven modules designed to integrate themes from a range of educational theories and apply them critically to the local context, as the titles show: Teaching and learning, School and Society, Policy and Practice, Identity and Diversity, History and Administration of Education, Concepts, Ideas and Values, Teaching and Assessment. The practical aspects are subsumed under the subject-oriented modules.

  DFID

5 The Curriculum of Teacher Education

From an international perspective, the four college syllabi appear both outdated and conservative, caught in an intellectual time-warp. The old 'foundations of education' or 'ologies' are still apparent. In psychology, behaviourist and Piagetian concepts are taught, but much recent work on cognitive development and on constructivism is missing, and Vygotsky's name appears unknown to the tutors, some of whom are clearly recycling their university notes of years ago. The sociology modules, where they appear, seem to take a functionalist perspective, though Trinidadian tutors have developed new modules.

In spite of the rhetoric, we found little real integration of theory and practice. In general, the educational theories seem to be taught, and learnt, for their own sake, rather than as a means of understanding and enhancing practice. Child development and learning theories are not related to specific subjects, such as language acquisition or misconceptions in science. The general professional and pedagogic skills are taught separately from the theory, and the only opportunity to bring these together, in teaching practice, is seldom exploited for this end.

The educational theories are drawn from Western sources, and not subjected to critique in the light of local culture and norms. This is particularly marked in the African colleges, as an example from Malawi shows.

Box 5.2: **Piaget in a different cultural context**

> The tutor was teaching Piagetian child development to a class of mature students, many with children of their own. The text stated that children aged 2-4 engaged first in 'solitary' and then 'associative' play, but there was no discussion of whether this occurs in a Malawian village, nor what happens when 'the child becomes curious and asks many questions' in a culture where children are not supposed to ask adults questions! (Stuart & Kunje 2000).

Such incidents, and similar ones from Lesotho, suggests there may be two parallel educational discourses going on: a theoretical one largely drawn from Western conceptual frameworks, and a more practical one about the kinds of teaching, learning and socialisation that go on in the real communities, and which students 'know' at a different level. This may be one reason for the particularly strong disjunction between theory and practice found, for example, in the Ghanaian colleges.

The topics, and the way they were taught, suggest an authoritarian, conservative ideology, where debate is not encouraged. This is itself at odds with the espoused principles of participatory, learner-centred and enquiring pedagogy. It was also noticeable that gender issues were seldom foregrounded or discussed.

5 The Curriculum of Teacher Education

5.4.4 General and personal education

Most aspects of this were neglected; the only positive example being in Trinidad and Tobago, where the expressive arts options encourage students to develop their own skills in music, art and drama, and the electives permit them to pursue individual interests to a higher level.

One area of great need is to help students coming from transmission-oriented high schools to adapt to a more independent form of learning. Study skills are given brief attention in Lesotho's bridging course, but students' experience suggest this training should continue throughout the course. In MIITEP, the college-based block could potentially introduce trainees to independent learning – students could read, prepare, take notes, draft reports in the evenings for discussion and feedback next day in class – but this is apparently not done, and they are ill-prepared for the subsequent 20 months of distance learning.

The curricula we studied, both in the colleges and in UDW, are focussed on the cognitive or instrumental aspects of teacher preparation, while the personal and affective aspects are neglected. It is strange that while many of the formal programme aims – and often the espoused aims of the teacher educators – highlight professional attitudes, responsible personal behaviour, and interpersonal skills, there are no specific areas in the curriculum as documented or as delivered where these are discussed or developed. They seem to be left to the 'hidden curriculum'. This may sometimes promote positive attitudes; for example, Malawi students noted the opportunity 'to share ideas, work together and get to know people from other tribes and areas' as one of the best things about college, and Ghanaian students appreciated some of the social and moral aspects of their training. On the other hand, the strict rules and authoritarian attitudes in many African colleges seem unlikely to develop independence, personal and social responsibility, or a sense of professional agency.

5.5   Teaching and Learning Materials and Resources

Our evidence suggests that while resources are often limited, and sometimes outdated or of poor quality, equally important factors are how tutors and students use them, and how far organisation and timetabling facilitate or hinder resource-based learning.

The MIITEP programme was supported by five 'Student Teacher Handbooks', which present an example that might be followed elsewhere. Observations suggest few other resources were used apart from primary school syllabi, textbooks, and teachers' guides. The college libraries were poorly stocked and closed during the evening study periods.

5 The Curriculum of Teacher Education

Box 5.3: **MIITEP Student Teacher Handbooks**

> These were specially written by local teams, and used all tutors and trainees. Effectively they structured the course, setting out both the content and how it should be taught in hour-long units, though there were discrepancies between subjects. The books provided lesson plans for the tutors, and resources for the students in both face-to-face and distance mode. They were much praised, even though to some degree they sent out 'mixed messages', such as inviting students to discuss their own views, and then listing the 'points you should come up with'. There were lively illustrations.

The curriculum documents in the three other sites include prescribed texts as well as books for further reading, but these may not always be appropriate. In Ghana and Lesotho many of the books listed were published before 1990 and very few, apart from the local school textbooks, are by African authors. In Ghana students could buy pamphlets written by tutors, comprising their lecture notes with past exam questions as examples. In Lesotho few textbooks were used in class, the students often working from photocopied handouts. The library at NTTC has been recently restocked and is reportedly heavily used in the limited times when it is open and the students have free time.

No colleges made regular use of AVA equipment such as overhead projectors. In one Malawian college there is one video, lodged in room too small to take a normal teaching group in comfort. One tutor used it while we were observing her. Resources for practical activities in maths and science appeared adequate only in Trinidad and Tobago. In Malawi the colleges had virtually no teaching/learning aids of any kind, and lecturers had to improvise demonstrations with materials brought from home. Even in Lesotho students doing physics practicals used diagrams rather than real equipment.

All this suggests students are being offered limited intellectual horizons, and are not being prepared for resource-based learning. The choice of texts can be criticised from two different directions: they do not have access to the latest Western ideas on teaching and learning; nor are they given opportunities to reflect on how appropriate these might be to the African context. Even when resources are there, the overloaded curriculum and transmission mode of teaching do not permit good use to be made of them, and it seems unlikely the graduates will be able to undertake any form of curriculum development or adaptation in the schools.

5 The Curriculum of Teacher Education

5.6   Pedagogy

The curriculum documents often list a range of student-centred, interactive and participatory methods – demonstrations, group work, role play, fieldtrips, project work – but observations in three of the African sites revealed a predominantly teacher-centred transmission mode. Teaching 'subject content' resembled traditional high school methods: the tutor would present information orally, using the board or textbook, interspersed with (tutor) questions and (student) answers; only occasionally were attempts made to develop a class discussion. The levels of cognitive demand seemed low; in places students' poor language skills inhibited debates. In English and maths students might do individual exercises; in science experiments were usually demonstrated by the tutor, probably because of shortage of both time and equipment. In most places, at least some tutors used group work of some kind, with varied levels of effectiveness, as few tutors were clear about what they wanted to achieve through groups.

What was striking was that quite similar styles of teaching predominated in 'methods' lessons, although there tended to be more student activity, and more group work. But in the main, trainees were **told** about how to handle primary classes, and occasionally **shown**, as when the tutor did a demonstration lesson, or showed a video, but very seldom did they actually **experience** the kind of student-centred methods that were preached. We did see students perform a couple of role-plays about primary teaching, but these reproduced the teacher-led methods of their own experience; they were not opportunities for students to try out new approaches.

Trinidad and Tobago proved a partial exception to the rule, though it should be noted that the lecturers observed were a self-selected group and probably represent the most innovative ones.

5 The Curriculum of Teacher Education

Box 5.4: **Examples of Good practice in Trinidad Colleges**

Literary Studies. Mr. M. said he wanted to make literature relevant to the real life circumstances of the trainees. He gave a university-type lecture to nearly 200 students on a short story by a local writer. His lively, idiosyncratic style encouraged student responses and through a shared exploration of the text he modelled ways of responding to literature. The notes he dictated included observations by students. Only one reference was made to primary school teaching.

Maths. Ms. A. deliberately tried to model teaching strategies she expected her students to use. In a lesson on ratio taught to 35 students, she used a learning cycle approach to concept development, incorporating varied appropriate materials. Strategies included whole group, individual and pair work. Summaries helped pull ideas together and discussion sessions were used for students to clarify concepts. Students were encouraged to analyse the lesson in pedagogic terms and identify the methods used.

Science. Ms. J. taught 44 students a double session on 'Matter'. She used everyday materials in her teaching and tried to provide situations that would help trainees to understand science and to identify their misconceptions. After the tutor had elicited their prior knowledge through discussion, concrete examples and text, students in groups classified substances into solids, liquids and gases, and reported back giving reasons for the classification, which the tutor summarised on the board.
The concept of gas/volume relationships was explored with the help of more concrete examples, backed by probing questions from the tutor. This was reinforced by a 'fun' role play in which the students in 3 groups enacted the different properties of gases, liquids and solids. More groupwork followed on how kinetic theory could explain changes in state caused by temperature, and much discussion ensured before the results were presented. The tutor summarised and discussed some issues still unresolved. This was a highly successful lesson, well-structured in terms of pace and variety of activity, where learning was reinforced by a number of strategies. The methods used were transferable to school classrooms.
(George, Worrell et al, 2000)

It is ironic that the pedagogy of teacher education courses themselves should be so neglected, and that teacher educators so seldom apply their espoused theories to their own

5 The Curriculum of Teacher Education

practice. Several reasons may be adduced for this situation. Firstly, in some places large numbers made interactive work more difficult, but not impossible, as there were isolated examples in both Lesotho and Trinidad and Tobago of tutors handling large groups in participatory ways. Lack of resources was certainly a factor, particularly in Malawi. The exam pressure and the consequent need to cover the syllabus, were clearly important in both Malawi and Ghana. The Ghanaian tutors said that because of the overcrowded syllabus, extra curricular activities and the looming exams, there was simply no time to engage in activities requiring extensive exploratory work by students. In addition, Ghanaian tutors did not set students collaborative work for fear it would lead to 'copying' in the exam (Akyeampong, Ampiah et al 2000).

Our overall evidence, however, suggests deeper elements. In part, there seemed a kind of collusion between tutors and trainees, who knew little else from their schooling, to maintain the transmission mode. The surveys support this, showing students often found project work 'difficult' and groupwork 'less useful' Students reportedly demanded notes, and where books are in short supply, this makes sense both for the exams and for later reference. NQTs said they often relied on college notes in their teaching.

Finally, interviews with tutors reveal that in many cases the transmission mode is the one they feel most comfortable and confident with. Few have fully internalised the constructivist, student-centred approach to learning, and even those who want to move in this direction find themselves constrained by the current college system and ethos. It was notable that in Malawi the Student Teacher Handbooks were used by tutors as adjuncts to a transmission mode rather than starting points for a more learner-centred approach. Most tutors regard the students as 'empty vessels', and do not recognise or value their prior experiences. Insights from theories of adult learning – mentioned in the Malawi Trainers' book - are ignored (Rogers 1996).

5.7 Assessment

All the programmes use a mixture of coursework and exams. Teaching Practice is assessed separately, as described in Chap. 6, and usually constitutes a small part of the overall result. The suggested types of coursework– weighted up to 50% in Trinidad and Lesotho, less elsewhere – are often varied and interesting, but in practice we found very few being used: these were mainly tests, written assignments and occasionally some library-based project work. Tutors felt overburdened, and the organisation, supervision and marking of, say, field-based studies, would have been difficult with such large numbers of students. In Malawi, there was little formative assessment of any kind. Terminal exams everywhere were felt to be important and had a backwash effect on teaching and learning, as described above. Only in Lesotho and UDW do the tutors set and mark the exams; in other places external bodies exercise varying amounts of direct control.

5 The Curriculum of Teacher Education

Detailed analysis of assessment papers in Malawi — set and marked by the Malawi National Examination Board (MANEB) - revealed a number of weaknesses. The exams were poorly designed, did not always match the balance in the syllabus between content and methods, and were couched mainly at recall level, with some simple comprehension or application. Even the school-based assignments and projects tested content knowledge rather than being related to classroom practice and experience.

Apart from some micro-teaching, or the occasional making of a teaching aid, most of the college-based assessment in the sites studied seems only distantly related to the classroom. The ambition of the South African 'Norms and Standards for Educators' – to assess broad holistic teaching competences in authentic situations – is far from being realised.

5.8 Concluding Discussion

History seems to weigh heavily on these curricula, especially in the three small African sites. Innovation has been sporadic, and often lagging behind changes in the school curriculum. There are apparently few mechanisms for regular review and renewal. Typically Ministries of Education work with college staff, sometimes with the aid of external consultants, to reform the existing curriculum rather than to renew it completely. Old ways of thinking and doing persist behind the façade of innovation and change. International borrowing sometimes results in curricular ideas being deposited, one above the other, like geological strata, without any of them being critiqued and adapted in the light of local needs and cultures.

Apart from BAGET, all the programmes are based on a 'behaviourist' rather than a 'constructivist' approach, and seem closer to the 'technical rationality' rather than 'reflective practitioner' model of preparing teachers. While these models may be seen as complementary rather than mutually exclusive, the chosen focus has implications for the kind of teacher produced and their ability to work in an innovative way. Only in South Africa and in Lesotho there were indications that graduates of the programme would be expected to take forward educational changes. This view permeated the UDW programme, but in Lesotho it remained at the level of general aims, without being translated into practice.

The forces of conservatism seem very strong in teacher education generally, especially when directed from a government department. Where good practice was found, as in the new BAGET design and in some Trinidadian classrooms, it was usually as a result of initiatives by the teacher educators concerned, who had acquired new perspectives through formal or informal study, rather than innovations being imposed on the colleges from outside. This issue is taken up again in Chapter 8, but it also raises deeper issues about where and how reform interventions can most effectively be made.

5 The Curriculum of Teacher Education

From what we could glean about the processes of curriculum development, there seems to have been little discussion of what are the essential elements for the new primary teacher to acquire in that particular context during pre-service training, and what can be learnt later, or elsewhere. This reflects, perhaps, a general lack of consensus about what such elements might be. Consequently, there is too much to teach in the given time, leading to overload, stress, a transmission style of teaching, and superficial learning.

One aspect of this is the lack of specialisation. It seems particularly strange in the African sites, where pupils are taught in their mother tongue for the first four grades and in English thereafter, that no distinction is made in training programmes between the lower and upper phases. It may be that age-ranges in primary schools have traditionally been very wide, so methods designed for young children were inappropriate. But with Education for All, it seems time to reassess this policy.

From the curriculum analysis we found a number of inconsistencies, mismatches and dilemmas. For example, the aims are themselves not always clear, or may represent conflicting views of different stakeholders. Some of the espoused aims may be unrealistic within the short term, especially given the qualifications of the entrants and the time available. The overall aims are often inconsistent with the more detailed specific objectives which guide the component courses. A likely explanation is that general aims originate outside the college, and may be influenced by international borrowing of various kinds, while the courses are usually developed by groups that include, or work closely with, college tutors. Often the interpretation and delivery of the curriculum guidelines vary considerably between different subjects.

Primary teachers need to be confident of their subject knowledge, but the academic ambitions of some of the curricula are often mismatched to the students' levels of achievement. In particular, the difficulties of learning in a second language are under-estimated (and under-researched). The pedagogy is ill-matched in several ways: it does not use adult learning methods where appropriate; it seldom practises the kinds of learner-centred methods it preaches; it copies secondary schools, and does not teach trainees to become independent learners. By the same token, the assessment methods reinforce transmission teaching and rote learning rather than problem-solving and independent study.

Some elements of the professional components, especially the introductions to psychology, are found useful by students, while other topics may be less relevant for pre-service and better taught as in-service modules. Certain aspects of educational theory seem culturally remote, and need to be debated in the light of local contexts. Not all courses have kept up with changes in schools and in society, such as universal primary education. Students are not being well prepared for large and/or multi-grade classes, or for dealing with pupils of widely differing ability and achievement levels. Gender issues are seldom highlighted.

5 The Curriculum of Teacher Education

While everyone agrees that the effective teacher needs good interpersonal skills and appropriate attitudes, the formal curriculum neglects these and other aspects of personal development and growth. There are, of course, huge pressures to push through large cohorts of teachers – the MIITEP is one example; classes are also very large in Ghana – but good teachers cannot be 'mass produced', and this contradiction needs to be resolved in some way, at the in-service if not the pre-service level of training.

The curriculum often assumes the trainees enter as 'empty vessels', with little knowledge or experience of teaching, therefore missing opportunities to build on prior learning. In particular, it does not engage with the images, metaphors and myths that students bring with them. Tutors do not seem to be helping them to deconstruct and reconstruct their own ideas of teaching in ways that will enable them to understand and internalise the new approaches, and consequently training does not have the impact that it should. (See Chaps.4 and 7.)

5. 8.1 Key issues for policy and practice

- The overall aims of the curriculum should set out more clearly what sort of teacher is needed for the particular context, and this vision should inform the whole curriculum and the way it is delivered.

- Currently initial training curricula are quite long and heavily overloaded. Ways need to be found to make them more selective, focussing on what trainees need to start teaching, and complementing this by regular continuing professional development at later points in the career. Upgrading in academic subject content might be more effectively done separately, either in a preliminary year or by distance methods.

- The curriculum should be matched more closely to the needs, strengths and weaknesses of the entering students. This may involve helping them find new ways of 'learning to learn'; language and communication skills need particular emphasis. It also means recognising that students do not come as 'empty vessels' but with powerful and affect laden memories of schooling, images of teachers and personal experiences of learning and teaching. These should be discussed and used as starting points for developing professional understanding.

- Professional components need to be overhauled and reworked in the light of new understandings of teaching and learning. At the same time they need to be made more relevant to the local context and culture, so they can prepare students adequately for local classroom realities and problems.

5 The Curriculum of Teacher Education

- College pedagogy seems underdeveloped, often resembling high school teaching. Lecturers need to adopt adult teaching methods, so that student teachers gain a deeper experiential understanding of learner-centred pedagogy.

- A wider range of assessment methods should be used during training, so that relevant levels of knowledge and practical skills are tested in realistic and useful ways. This would have a positive effect on teaching and learning.

- There is an urgent need for practical, up-to-date, locally relevant textbooks for trainee teachers, which could both form the basis for professional studies and subject methods during training, and be a resource for NQTs.

- At present there is little specialisation by phase. In the light of UPE and changing language policies, some teachers could be given special training for the lower primary grades.

- In theory, colleges seem an appropriate place for change to start, but our evidence suggests this rarely happens except in the context of a more general political transformation.

Chapter Six   6 Teaching Practice and School-Based Training

6.0   Summary and Overview

A crucial component of any training is the practicum, variously termed 'teaching practice' or 'school experience'. This chapter therefore focuses on the research questions:

➢ How are the practical elements of the curriculum delivered, and how far are the stated aims and objectives achieved?

➢ How do trainees experience teaching practice and how do they value it?

The MUSTER studies covered two different types of school experience, traditional teaching practice (TP), in Ghana, Lesotho and Trinidad and Tobago, and school-based training in Malawi and in Trinidad and Tobago.

6.0.1   Summary of the Findings

- **Trinidad and Tobago**: The 12 weeks of TP were highly organised into three carefully structured blocks, with regular supervision by college tutors. Trainees found it valuable but stressful, because of the emphasis on assessment. Though schools were co-operative, there was little sense of partnership between them and the college. Supervisors did not all share similar assumptions about the theory-practice interface, resulting in some internal contradictions.

- **Ghana**: The trainees had two 3-4 week blocks of TP, and some received only one or two visits from tutors. Though they valued it highly, the experience came as a 'reality shock', in which they found their 'recipes' for teaching did not always work in real classrooms. The emphasis from tutors on 'doing things right' seemed to conflict with experimenting and learning to deal with the problems they found

- **Lesotho**: Since students chose the school where they would spend the 15-week block, they were scattered over a wide geographical area, and supervision by tutors was uncoordinated, infrequent and rushed. The trainees rated TP as useful, but as the schools seemed unable, or unwilling, to provide much assistance, they were often left to learn what they could on their own. Other evidence from Lesotho suggests that field-based supervision, in liaison with the college and the schools, could offer more effective support and training.

- **Malawi**: During MIITEP training the teachers spent 20 months in full-time work, following a distance learning course and attending zonal workshops. The first cohorts of trainees received insufficient support and supervision, study facilities were non-existent, and most schools lacked basic resources. Shortages of time and money prevented college tutors from making visits, and few of the district advisors and head

6 Teaching Practice and School-Based Training

teachers had yet received appropriate training. Alison Croft's (Croft 2002a) complementary in-depth study shows, however, that pockets of good practice do exist which can be built on to develop culturally relevant models from which new teachers could learn.

- **'On the Job Training' in Trinidad and Tobago**: This offered a year-long part-time apprenticeship to would-be teachers, combining a small amount of supervised teaching with weekend and vacation courses. It proved potentially useful, but the curriculum was lacking in coherence, and there were no links to the initial training courses offered at the colleges.

- All the findings highlight the difficulties of implementing this vital part of the professional training in an efficient and cost-effective way.

This chapter first describes different forms of the practicum and then draws on MUSTER case-studies to outline three examples of traditional teaching practice and two examples of school-based training. The South African scene is briefly commented on. The final section discusses what can be learnt from the case-studies.

6.1   Introduction

Traditionally, initial teacher preparation programmes which are college-based have sent students into schools for various lengths of time, under varying degrees of supervision from visiting tutors and 'co-operating teachers' or 'mentors'. Students commonly report this to be the 'most useful' part of their training; tutors find it exhausting and time-consuming; for the college it is expensive and difficult to organise; schools are often unsure of their role and seldom organise the time to the mutual benefit of trainee and school. At one extreme, staff may take time off, leaving the trainee to sink or swim; at the other the teacher may re-teach each lesson so her class doesn't suffer.

More recently, in high income countries, forms of training have developed which reverse the school-college relationship. The trainees are based in school and go out to a campus for academic and professional training sessions. In the UK, one can now gain 'qualified teacher status' via such a school-based training route, which is seen by some as preferable because of its practical bias and criticised by others as lacking academic rigour. In low income countries, such training 'on the job' is mainly used to upgrade and certify unqualified serving teachers, rather than seen as a respectable pre-service route. There are often problems with providing good distance learning materials and adequate professional support in remote areas, especially where schools are poorly resourced and offer few good models of practice (Perraton 2000).

6 Teaching Practice and School-Based Training

Theorists of professional learning point to the situated, contextual nature of much professional knowledge, and how it can be developed and built up through experience, but stress also the role of public propositional knowledge and the need for support and guidance from more experienced others through several stages (Eraut 1994, Calderhead and Shorrock 1997). This suggests, ideally, that professional learning takes places through alternating periods of input and practice over a considerable period of time.

The MUSTER research provided opportunities for in-depth studies of the practicum in a number of countries. It is interesting that our research found very little curricular documentation to guide or accompany this component; the data comes mainly from observation and interviews. Fig. 7 gives a schematic picture of how time is divided between campus and schools in the case-study locations.

Figure 7: **Structural patterns: the place of the practicum**

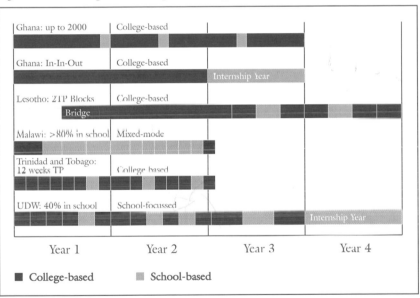

6.2 **Case-studies of Traditional Teaching Practice**

In Ghana, Lesotho and Trinidad and Tobago the research looked at the 'traditional' type of teaching practice (TP), where students go out to schools for one or more 'blocks' of time and are visited by college tutors. In all of these places, the college organises and controls the practice, leaving the schools merely acting as – sometimes reluctant – hosts. Though different messages come from different studies, all provide some form of critique of this pattern, and show how difficult it is to bring theory and practice together in this way.

6 Teaching Practice and School-Based Training

6.2.1 **Trinidad and Tobago: contradictions in the technical rationality model**

The Trinidadian colleges have a highly organised system of teaching practice (TP)[30]. Although structured slightly differently at the two colleges, TP takes up 12 weeks, arranged roughly in three block periods over the two years. Trainees have a 120-hour programme of preparation for TP; they visit the schools (selected by the college but as close as possible to their homes) and prepare all lesson plans and units of work prior to each block. Trainees are supposed to teach only four lessons a day, but some do more. All tutors participate in supervising, each having 7-8 students in 2-3 schools, whom they visit regularly to observe lessons and discuss them afterwards. A grade is awarded at the end of each block, and during the final TP a sample of trainees is seen by external examiners for moderation. The assessment instrument lists 16 discrete skills or competences, each marked out of 10.

Because this is in many ways a very well organised example of 'traditional' TP, it is possible to see more clearly some of the underlying assumptions, strengths and weaknesses of this model.

The system is dominated by the college tutors; the role of the co-operating teachers is not laid down, and they interpret it in different ways – as nurturer, facilitator, or observer, but hardly ever as a partner in training. The school principals act as hosts, but otherwise have no clearly defined task. Since the whole process is assessment-driven, trainees are also highly dependent on the tutors; they see themselves as having to satisfy each supervisor's – often different – expectations in order to pass, and they develop coping strategies to this end. Trainees found it all very stressful.

Conditions in the schools are not always conducive to interactive and participatory teaching. Though classes seldom have more than 30 pupils, they are furnished with rows of heavy desks crowded together, and partitions between rooms are thin or non-existent. Trainees have to provide their own instructional aids.

The integration of theory and practice does not seem to take place as it is supposed to do (George, Worrell, Rampersad 2002). Analysis of post-lesson conferences showed that formal theory was seldom mentioned. The styles of supervising tutors varied: for many good teaching seemed to be equated with being able to perform well a number of discrete behaviours, which include planning lessons, delivering them through specific kinds of skills

---

[30] The researchers carried out a study into two separate blocks of TP in 1999. They analysed documents, observed 96 lessons, audiotaping the post-lesson conferences of 8 supervisors with 73 trainees, as well as interviewing the supervisors, trainees, 39 cooperating teachers and 8 principals. This analysis draws closely on the full report in George et al (2000) and on George et al (2002).

6 Teaching Practice and School-Based Training

– motivating, questioning, grouping, closing – managing the class, using instructional aids and assessing the pupils. Only a few supervisors used a more holistic approach, encouraging the trainees to respond in a dynamic and creative way to the specific needs of the learners in that class. Even in these cases, the conversations would involve personal theories and experiences, rather than the theory taught in college.

There are contradictory assumptions operating here. The college curriculum is premised on the idea that after acquiring a corpus of knowledge, trainees will be able to apply this to their teaching. Yet supervising tutors talk about practice and experience, and implicitly suggest the need for personal theories developed over time which can use and apply situated knowledge. This suggests an altogether different model of learning to teach, one that focuses on the trainee's own developing understanding of what she is doing in the light of knowledge and of reflection on experience. The study seems to expose clearly one of the contradictions that lies at the heart of the technical rationality model, as Donald Schon (1983) pointed out: trainees expected success would come by applying what they had been taught in college, yet in practice they found they had to reflect and make their own judgements – something college had given much less emphasis to.

6.2.2 Ghana: Reality Shock v. Doing it Right

The case-study data in Ghana clearly shows up some further problems and short-comings of the 'technical rationality' approach to teacher training, and illustrates how difficult it is to bring theory and practice together in the traditional college course[31].

At the time of the study, trainees had an observation period in schools at the end of Year 1, during the long vacation, and a 3-4 week block TP during each of the two subsequent years, making a total of 12 weeks in all. Schools were approved by the District, and 4-5 tutors would be allocated to a cluster of schools; under this arrangement most trainees got supervised at least twice. Sometimes more than one student would have to teach the same class during supervision, so that the exercise became rather artificial. There was apparently a good deal of preparation in college, including micro-teaching, and afterwards some follow-up activities in methods classes.

However, most trainees saw this as inadequate, and interviews revealed just how unprepared they felt for the reality of Ghanaian classrooms. The methods classes in college had presented them with certain standardised and approved ways of teaching the syllabus, topic by topic, for each grade. When they got to class, they found they could not apply these in a textbook way; they found problems of learning unreadiness and absenteeism, they had to deal with children of varying abilities, or with poor English language; resources were scarce, and they did not know what to do.

---

[31] A fuller account is given in Akyeampong et al (2000)

6 Teaching Practice and School-Based Training

When the tutors came to supervise, the trainees felt they were being judged not on their ability to adjust their methods to the needs of the pupils or how to adapt to each situation, but on whether their lesson plan was 'correct' and whether they had 'got things right'. There was apparently little dialogue with supervisors about how to solve the problems they were encountering. When class teachers or the principal observed them, there was a similar emphasis on the lesson plan or scheme, but often the advice was conflicting, which simply confused them further.

In spite of all this, the trainees felt that TP was the most valuable part of the course as it made them realise 'what the job was really about'. The proposed reforms in Ghana are to replace block practice with internship through most of the final year. No details were available about how trainees will be supported and supervised during that time, but such support and guidance will be crucial to its effectiveness.

6.2.3 Lesotho: learning on one's own

The Lesotho TP study reveals starkly how in Southern Africa geography and economics together constrain the possibilities of school experience, though the problems may be compounded by poor administration, lack of determination to make TP a priority, and failure to bring schools on board.[32]

The study was carried out by surveying 120 Primary Teachers' Certificate (PTC) students recently returned from TP, and interviewing some of the staff involved. The system had already been the subject of earlier critical reports, and the MUSTER study confirmed that little had been done to implement the recommended changes.

In the PTC programme, school experience occurred in Year 2. During the first semester, as part of Teaching Practice Preparation (TPP), groups of students plus a lecturer visited local schools to observe and to teach one or two lessons each. The second semester – 15 weeks – was spent entirely in a school chosen by the student, provided it lay within reach of the tarred roads in the lowland areas. Students were supposed to be visited four times, the first three for formative feedback and the last for assessment, though reports from earlier visits and from the Principal would be taken into account. The original 'pass/fail' was being changed to a five-point grading scale, with an elaborate system of reports from tutors and heads inviting comments on a number of aspects of teaching.

Students said they found the block practice valuable - they seemed less enthusiastic about TPP - and about the right length. They stressed how they were able to develop the professional and personal skills needed to manage classes and deal with children, as well as learning to operate as a member of the school and community. In addition, they felt more

---

[32] This account is based on Lefoka, Jobo and Moeti 2001

6 Teaching Practice and School-Based Training

confident in carrying out administrative and technical tasks like planning, recording, setting and marking tests. Little mention was made of actual teaching and learning methods. They admitted finding the large classes, shortages of materials and slow learners particularly difficult to cope with.

Whatever they learnt, they seemed to have picked up mostly on their own. Less than half thought the school had given them enough help, and many complained about teachers' negative attitudes towards them. Supervision by college tutors was uncoordinated, infrequent and rushed. Only 15% of students were seen four times, with most getting just 2-3 visits, often from different tutors, particularly in the remoter areas. While the majority got some written feedback, only half thought they had been given a grade, and some just got verbal comments. As almost all students pass provided their attendance and behaviour are satisfactory, there seems no real assessment of their performance and abilities. Nor does such a system help the students to overcome weaknesses and develop their strengths in a coordinated and targeted way.

Certainly there are difficulties inherent in the situation. There is no money for student accommodation on TP, so they must go to a school near home or friends, which makes it difficult for the college to select the best schools, or those nearest to the college. Tutors have to fit visits around other teaching commitments. Again, there is limited money for travel and overnight allowances, distances are long, and vehicles in short supply even when tutors go in groups or use their own cars.

What alternatives might exist? Lesotho's experiences both past and present suggest there are workable possibilities using field-based staff. For example, when the PTC had internship during the whole of Year 2, supervisors were based in the regions and trained to guide, support and help assess the interns. This scheme, running well for over a decade, apparently foundered on a combination of expense and the reluctance of tutors to live in remote rural areas

The District Resource Teacher (DRT) scheme, set up as part of INSET provision, has fared better. There are nearly 100 of these peripatetic advisory teachers regularly visiting small, multi-grade schools to help upgrade unqualified teachers. DRTs are drawn from the ranks of ordinary teachers, and may not have high academic qualifications, but they get regular professional development courses. The scheme has been generally accounted a success, and such trainers could be equally well used for PRESET students.

The Hopkin report (1996) already made many suggestions for improvement, including setting up a TP department and building partnerships with selected schools. Joint guidelines and workshops for both tutors and school mentors would be a key component. The National University of Lesotho Faculty of Education has a small-scale mentor programme

6 Teaching Practice and School-Based Training

for beginning teachers in secondary schools, which might be useful as a prototype. The reason why so few of the recommendations have been implemented is not clear: perhaps college management has not made TP a priority; perhaps tutors are reluctant to change old habits; perhaps the college does not want to relinquish any of its power to the schools. The new DEP has split TP into two blocks, which potentially offers more chance for discussion and reflection during the intervening college phase, but the organisation appears to have changed little.

6.3   School-based Teacher Training

The MUSTER research also looked at two very different ways of using the schools as training sites. The Malawi study shows this is no easy option, particularly in resource-constrained conditions. Much infrastructure has to be in place and all the support personnel trained before the schools can deliver effective training. The Trinidadian scheme originated from a concern to guide unemployed youth into teaching. It illustrates ways of providing school experience as an orientation to teaching, and perhaps as a selection mechanism, rather than as part of a formal training programme.

6.3.1 **Malawi: depending on the schools**

The school-based component of the MIITEP scheme is worth studying in detail because it shows the many constraints and problems of trying to upgrade large numbers of teachers 'on the job', as well as offering some pointers to good practice and potential starting points. This account draws both on the main MUSTER study (Kunje and Chirembo 2000) and on the work of Alison Croft (2002a) who studied a small sample of Malawi Standard 1 teachers with the aim of identifying examples of good practice, and of exploring how student teachers develop their own styles of teaching under this system.

As explained in Chapter 3, MIITEP attempted to train 18,000 teachers, in six cohorts, over a total of four years, with each cohort spending five terms in 'school-based training'. The intention was that during this time they would receive support from the school, especially from the headteacher, and from the locally-based Primary Education Advisors (PEAs), who would run periodic zonal seminars. College tutors would make supervisory visits, and mark the 16 assignments to be completed during this period.

MIITEP was a huge, elaborate scheme devised to meet a crisis, without sufficient time to put into place the necessary administrative infrastructures; for example, some trainees' records were incomplete and it was not always known where they were. The disbursement of the external funds on which it depended did not always match the needs and timing of the programme. A key training element - the complementary Malawi Schools Support System Programme (MSSSP) – which was to train headteachers and PEAs in management

6 Teaching Practice and School-Based Training

and supervision, began some time after MIITEP itself. Thus, while detailed criticisms have been made (Kunje and Chirembo 2000) this account will focus on some of the emergent issues, looking at the constraints but also at the potentials, emphasising the prerequisites for such a scheme to work.

The conditions in schools are one major constraint on such training. In Malawi primary schools it is rare for pupils to have desks and chairs; many schools lack classrooms and children have to be taught in the open except when it rains. Since the advent of UPE, classes can range up to 200-300, especially when combined for lack of space or lack of teachers. The blackboard is the main teaching aid, though enterprising teachers collect bottle-tops, stones, etc. for counting. Textbooks, if available, usually have to be shared between several children; some teachers do not have teachers' guides, and there are virtually no other published resources. In the lower grades, many pupils do not even have pencils or exercise books and infant grades sometimes practise writing in the sand. The diversity within one class is enormous, not only children with different abilities and aptitudes, but also of different ages: the range in Std. 1 may often be from 4 -14 years old. Pupil absenteeism is high, and many are ill-nourished. Neither the college classes nor the Handbooks focus on helping students deal with these kinds of conditions, and it is in the schools that they develop strategies for dealing with them.

The head teacher has to coordinate the training, for example pairing the trainees with more experienced teachers – though in over half Malawi primary schools less than 50% of the staff are qualified – organising training sessions, supervising them regularly, and sending in reports. At the time of the research, most head teachers felt unprepared for the role and many thought they should be paid extra. In practice, they checked the trainees' lesson plans daily, but delegated or ignored much of the rest. Pairing seemed ad hoc, and help depended on forming good relationships with co-operating teachers. The trainees did not, on the whole, feel the school had given them much support.

The PEAs were supposed to supervise and report on the trainees regularly, and to run 12 zonal workshops for each cohort, on the top of their other in-service responsibilities. At the time of the study they were newly appointed, had received little training, the Teachers Development Centres (TDCs) were not built, and transport to schools was difficult. It seems most students had only one or two visits. However, one team of PEAs had managed to visit some students several times, giving effective formative feedback before allocating a final grade. Since then, all PEAs have been issued with motorbikes, building is underway, including houses for PEAs in their zone, and they have received training through the MSSSP.

Only 3-4 zonal seminars took place for the first two cohorts because of lack of available funds, but these were rated by both trainees and observers as useful, practical, and

6 Teaching Practice and School-Based Training

participatory; not only did trainees get information and skills that could be immediately applied in their classrooms, but they could share ideas and experiences with each other. This suggests the potential for more locally-based training delivered by PEAs.

College tutors were supposed to visit trainees five times during the 20 months in school. However with the first four cohorts following each other directly into college, and with no funds for travel or subsistence, tutors were not released for this until Cohorts 1 and 2 had been many months in school. Allowed just 4 weeks, with limited vehicles, tutors could only spend a brief time in each school, perhaps seeing only part of a lesson, and having little opportunity to give feedback – yet a grade had to be given. Tutors were not always able to see their own students, and some never got visited at all.

Under such a system, assessment can hardly be more than a ritual. Officially, an assessment form is used setting out 25 behavioural points to be assessed from 1-4, the totals being graded A,B or C. Almost all trainees passed with A or B. If no mark could be reported from the field, the mark given for the one lesson taught by each trainee in the demonstration school during the college period was used. A small study, in which one of the researchers accompanied first tutors and then PEAs when they assessed trainees, suggests that inter-judge reliability may be very poor, and that the standards set by MIITEP are much lower than those that would have been expected by inspectors in the past.

So what did the trainees learn through school-based practice? Evidence from the main study suggests they picked up the more technical and administrative aspects: they knew how to keep records, write lesson plans and schemes of work, and manage a class – though they must have learnt some of this while working as unqualified teachers. They had been inducted into school and community life; they sat on committees and learnt to deal with parents. Unfortunately the assignments set during this time did not ask trainees to develop practical aspects of their teaching, or to provide evidence of what they had learnt other than from the Handbooks.

As far as academic progress was concerned, studying at a distance, especially in rural areas, was difficult, with no easy access to libraries or even Teachers' Centres, and no tutorial support or feedback. Sometimes trainees carried full teaching loads, and conditions were not conducive to studying in the evenings, often in cramped accommodation with no electricity. This may have been particularly hard on female trainees with their multiple roles as wives, mothers, teachers and students (see Croft 2000).

Croft's study (see Croft 2002a,b) offers some insights into what they might be learning less formally if good role models were to hand. She shows how experienced and committed teachers have developed strategies for teaching in the difficult conditions described above. These include for example, singing songs for both learning and classroom management,

6 Teaching Practice and School-Based Training

using older/brighter children as models, monitors and group leaders, allowing younger children to spend the first year just listening to lessons as a way of getting used to a classroom, and giving children with learning difficulties extra help after school. Croft describes some of the whole class teaching as 'children-centred' rather than child-centred, as teachers appear to focus on groups of children rather than on individuals.

Among these experienced teachers, who had been only trained to Certificate level, there was evidence of thoughtfulness, commitment, a deep contextualised understanding of their pupils, and the ability to use their own experience to improve practice. Trainee teachers working alongside such teachers, copy and in some cases develop such practices. Interviews showed that some trainees too were able to articulate, albeit haltingly, rationales for what they were doing.

However, limitations also show up. This programme is like a traditional apprenticeship, with mutual observation but devoid of much intellectual content. The trainee works closely alongside the experienced teachers, often sharing the planning, teaching and marking, and picks up the skills. They observe each other, the teacher gives feedback. But the co-operating teacher has had no training in mentoring, has no extra books or resources, and is not used to explaining the reasons behind her practice to a younger colleague. In addition, teaching in such conditions is very hard work, and there is little time to discuss, or to experiment with new approaches. Neither school nor college have encouraged a questioning or analytical approach.

There are a number of lessons to be learnt from the Malawi experience:

- It is extremely difficult to train new teachers in school conditions where so many basic resources, both human and material, are lacking.

- A locally-based PEA or equivalent, given accommodation, transport, and some resources, can run local workshops/seminars, and supervise and assess trainees in schools. Initial training and follow-up support are of course essential. The Lesotho schemes mentioned above confirm this analysis.

- With such local support in place, college tutors would not need to make so many visits. Their role could become one of moderating school-based assessment through a sample of visits. However, group visits and some teaching in local demonstration schools is valuable for both tutors and students if it can be economically carried out.

6 Teaching Practice and School-Based Training

- Distance mode teacher education is known to be problematic (Perraton 2000). Evidence from here and elsewhere highlight the importance of:
  - good preparation in college especially in study skills and language competence
  - well-designed materials, at least some of them context-specific
  - professional assignments which force trainees to develop, examine and reflect on their own practice
  - some regular face-to-face contact, either through PEAs or perhaps a small cadre of peripatetic tutors who are released from regular teaching in the colleges

- The headteachers and schools need to organise support, through appropriate pairing, training activities, and supervision that includes formative feedback.

- In schools there are experienced teachers who have devised contextually useful strategies, which facilitate pupil learning, that could become starting points for working out improved methods that draw on international theories of learning but which are also culturally and economically appropriate.

6.3.2 **Trinidad and Tobago: On the Job Training (OJT) – a partial apprenticeship**

In Trinidad and Tobago, where there is no pre-service training, some potential teachers undergo a year's apprenticeship in schools while being paid a small stipend[33]. It was devised by the Ministry of Education (MOE) in 1993, as part of a wider national initiative for unemployed youth, to attract potential teachers and to act as a filter for unsuitable ones. The current programme includes:

- a 3-week induction course covering professional and curriculum studies, which are continued in Saturday classes; these are taught by curriculum support staff from MOE.
- Two terms placement in schools, organised by the principal, who selects an experienced teacher as mentor to instruct them in practical classroom skills; the apprentices are allowed to teach only two maths and English lessons per week.
- Vacation school in the Arts
- Evening classes for computer literacy

Although theory and some content are included, the emphasis is on practical skills rather than on academic knowledge, along with personal aspects concerning attitudes and conduct. The programme is assessed by portfolios, written exams, attendance and classroom performance as evaluated by the school. About three-quarters pass.

---

[33] See George et al (2000) for more details

6 Teaching Practice and School-Based Training

The OJT graduates who went later to college valued particularly the practical aspects, such as lesson planning, which they found very useful for their first teaching practice. Some found the limited amount of teaching frustrating, and all agreed a good relationship with the mentor was a crucial element for success (George, Fournillier, and Brown 2000).

The main weakness was the lack of coherence within the course; there was no standard curriculum and no links between the theory classes and the practical training in school. Neither were there any links to the college curriculum. Mentors were not trained or supervised. Plans were in train, however, to develop a more coherent and better monitored system.

However, such an orientation course provides an interesting model that might be adapted elsewhere, perhaps in condensed form. The key elements are:
- the participation of the school principal and mentor in the training
- learning practical elements in the classroom, supported by more theoretical elements at induction, in vacations, evenings and weekends
- a phased introduction to teaching, through observation and team teaching before taking over the class
- an introduction which offers basic skills, strategies and confidence-building, which can be complemented later by more substantial academic and professional training.

6.3.3 A Note on South African Experience

The MUSTER studies in South Africa did not examine any aspects of the practicum in detail. The new national guidelines – the Norms and Standards for Teacher Education (NSE 2000) – emphasise that a qualified teacher should be able to integrate academic, practical and reflexive aspects of teaching, and demonstrate their competence to do so in an 'authentic setting' i.e. the classroom. All training courses are therefore likely to involve a substantial practicum. The BAGET design gives an example of how an urban-based programme might develop. As Fig.7 above shows, there are four short periods of practice teaching – one of which being in a teaching workplace other than a formal school, such as early childhood education, adult training, or community development - and the fourth year is a internship. Peripatetic lecturers would work in partnership with teachers in the schools to supervise the interns. Such a pattern would be difficult in rural areas.

As a result of the policy changes in South Africa, currently there is little development of pre-service courses, and much emphasis on in-service and upgrading of underqualified teachers on the job. This will hopefully enhance the ability of the schools in future to play a more significant role in initial training. Further details can be found in Lewin, Samuel & Sayed (2003).

6 Teaching Practice and School-Based Training

6.4 Concluding Discussion

The practicum ought to be at the heart of the curriculum but more often it is like an appendix. In places TP seems to be little more than a ritual. It is interesting that in Trinidad and Tobago trainees became as stressed about their TP as any novice, even though they had already taught for several years. It is as though the college were expecting some different kind of performance from 'normal' teaching. Perhaps this is one facet of the wide gap between colleges and schools that was apparent everywhere; nowhere did they work in partnership.

The studies show up some of the weaknesses of the 'technical rationality' model, which assumes that theory can be learnt separately from practice and that knowledge acquired on campus can be applied easily in the classroom. A more useful model seems to be one that includes the importance of contextual and situated knowledge, as well as propositional knowledge, and highlights ways in which beginning teachers need to bring these together, through support and guidance from trainers and through learning to use their own experience thoughtfully.

Such a model requires some kind of extended and supervised practicum as an essential component of learning to teach. If this is not provided – if trainees get only a short period of practice, or if there is inadequate support and direction, or inappropriate emphases on assessment and the 'right way' – they will learn to cope, but the standard of teaching may be low, and it is unlikely that methods will change. Yet a fully supervised practicum has considerable resource implications.

The assessment of such a practicum has to match its aims. Current TP assessment often focuses on discrete skills, assumed to be 'measurable' in some meaningful way. Some methods need to be developed whereby higher level, more holistic competences can be evaluated, which might indicate how far the new teacher will be able to continue to develop and improve in the coming years. This is a challenge to teacher educators, since assessment of this kind requires considerable professional experience and judgement.

Our studies also reveal the logistic and administrative problems in providing appropriate practical experience. The block practice system can work reasonably well in a small densely populated area with developed transport, such as Trinidad and Tobago, or the urban areas of South Africa. It is much more difficult where schools and people are scattered and communications are poor. In addition, it is very expensive and may not be giving good value for money. And yet, if the college tutors do not visit, they have no feedback on how well their students are performing, and they can become out of touch with real classroom conditions.

6 Teaching Practice and School-Based Training

One alternative, glimpsed in Malawi's demonstration schools, is to encourage 'Professional Development Schools' close to the college, where students can go regularly to observe selected teachers in action and get some classroom experience supervised by their own tutors. It is difficult, however, to provide enough practice for large cohorts of trainees in this way. Often such schools are better resourced and untypical of conditions elsewhere.

The internship year is another way of using schools. Placing it in the middle of a 3-year course provides more chances for post-experience reflection and focussed study on returning to college, but Zimbabwe's experience suggests a year is too long (Chakanyuka, personal communication). Placing it at the end – as in the new Ghana scheme - means students are better prepared, and it provides a bridge into work (see Chapter 7) but allows no opportunities for further studying. The costs vary: if trainees work as real albeit part-time teachers, they can be paid a salary; if they are supernumerary, they still have to get enough to live on, which means extra costs to the government.

Such constraints suggest some form of school-based training might be better, but this is also problematic where the schools are poorly resourced and where many of the staff are not fully qualified. In such conditions, training reverts to mere apprenticeship, where students learn to survive by copying the strategies used around them. An entirely school-based course, especially in low income countries, is unlikely to provide enough academic content, intellectual challenge or professional vision for training good teachers. Our studies show that residential periods of training, especially after some field experience, are much valued by students. At best, they can provide opportunities not only for intensive academic study, but also for personal development through reflection on experience and sharing ideas with others.

There remains the problem of supervision in school-based training. Where most serving teachers are already professionally qualified, mentors can be selected and trained for this, as some Zimbabwean colleges are trying to do (Chakanyuka 2002). Where most teachers are themselves under-trained, one option is to invest in well-prepared cadres of mobile trainers, like the DRTs in Lesotho and the PEAs in Malawi, based in regions, districts or even selected schools. Their work could include running local workshops and seminars, setting and marking practical assignments, supervising and assessing classroom performance, and training school mentors.

If training becomes largely or even partly school-based, colleges have to find a new role. At the very least, they have to work in partnership with schools, giving up some of their control and authority. At best, they could become centres for innovation, research and development, training the trainers and moderating standards, but as Chaps. 5 and 8 shows, their track record is poor and there are many barriers to change. Potentially, regular interchanges of

6 Teaching Practice and School-Based Training

ideas and personnel between colleges and schools could help improve the schools through providing INSET for teachers alongside induction for new teachers.

The Trinidadian OJT scheme suggests how school-based orientation can precede and be complemented by college programmes. Equally, though this was not part of our research, there is need for further school-based training to follow on as part of continuing professional development.

6.4.1 Key Issues for policy and practice

- The practicum is central to learning to teach. Ideally it should alternate with campus-based learning. However, it is difficult to organise and expensive to run. One solution is an 'internship year' in the middle or at the end of the course.

- The practicum needs supervision by some type of trainer. Using college tutors can only be cost-effective within small geographic areas. Alternatives might be:
    - Peripatetic or zonal-based trainers
    - Professional development schools attached to colleges
    - Training selected teachers in the practice schools as mentors responsible for supervision and assessment

- Much assessment of practical teaching is ritualised and neither valid nor reliable. New ways of assessing practical teaching need to be developed that emphasise a students' ability to solve problems in real classes and to learn from their own experience.

- School-based training can be cost-effective in that trainees are also teaching, but it needs to be complemented by sufficient external input, such as residential periods, local workshops and distance learning. This also requires considerable infrastructure and organisation to ensure the components are integrated.

- Schools undertaking training need substantial support in terms of professional development and basic resources.

- In many low income countries, good practice does exist in local schools, where experienced teachers have developed their own ways of dealing with large classes and few resources. Such practice should be recognised, used in training, and developed so that innovations and reforms are built around what is possible.

- Some kind of orientation is essential before untrained recruits start teaching. A period of supervised on-the-job training can be used both as a filter and as a preparation for subsequent college-based courses, but there needs to be coherence between the two.

Chapter Seven

7 What Happens After Training?: Induction and Beyond

7.0 Summary and Overview

This chapter brings together the evidence related to Arena 3 (see Chap.1) in answer to the research questions:

➣ What are the competences, in terms of knowledge, skills and attitudes, of the graduating NQTs?
➣ How have their attitudes and career intentions changed during training?
➣ How do they value their training in retrospect?
➣ What happens in their first years of teaching in terms of utilisation or washout of the course?

7.0.1 Summary of findings

- In Malawi and Ghana NQTs are 'posted' by central agencies to their schools, while in Lesotho individuals apply to schools for jobs. The latter process appears linked to a stronger sense of professionalism.
- In Ghana the process of posting is complex, ineffective and has pernicious effects on new teachers' morale. Many manage to subvert the system so that rural schools remain understaffed.
- None of the countries have a formal system of induction or probation for NQTs. Some support is given by heads, and in places by zonal or regional officers. Most advice appears to focus on management and administration rather than on developing instructional skills.
- NQTs apparently value their training as interesting and useful, but they wanted more time given to practical teaching methods. Many, especially in Ghana, felt college had not prepared them adequately for classroom realities. In school they rely heavily on notes and materials brought from college.
- Head teachers were also ambivalent about training. NQTs were generally seen as a source of fresh ideas and materials, and some were felt to be competent. But many heads thought NQTs were under-prepared, and others complained about their attitudes.
- Small scale observations comparing NQTs with untrained teachers suggest training does make NQTs more aware of their professional roles, and enables them to work more effectively within given norms and practices. But there is little evidence they contribute to change.
- Cross-sectional studies of attitude change suggest that dispositions and expectations of trainees do not change very much over the training period, and sometimes the changes are in an unlooked-for direction.

7 What Happens After Training?: Induction and Beyond

- In general NQTs did not perceive primary teaching as a desirable career. Only in Lesotho were a majority expecting to stay on at that level; elsewhere most wanted to move into secondary schools or further. Status, pay and conditions of service, and opportunities to study further seem important contextual factors.

In this chapter we present the evidence and discuss the issues under five headings:

1. How NQTs are deployed after graduation and how they are inducted into their work
2. How they value and use their training as they look back after 2-3 years
3. How others evaluate the NQTs' performance in schools
4. Evidence for attitude change
5. Career ambitions and intentions after training

Finally we discuss the issues raised by the findings.

7.1   Introduction

The questions explored in this chapter are among the most important for policy-makers: much money is spent on training, but many people question whether it makes any difference. These aspects are also the most difficult aspects to research, for both practical and conceptual reasons. Firstly, it was difficult to contact the newly qualified teachers, now widely dispersed into schools. Secondly, there is little agreement on what constitutes 'good teaching' and even if we were able to define and measure it, many factors intervene between the training and the way the NQTs perform in the classroom, most obviously the quality of the schools, the pupils, and the support they are receiving.

Studies on the effectiveness of training in low income countries have produced ambiguous results (e.g. Tatto et al 1991, Lockheed & Verspoor 1991, Dove 1985, Avalos and Haddad 1981, World Bank 1978). As noted earlier MUSTER did not set out to replicate such studies, but to develop new perspectives and grounded data. In relation to the effectiveness of training it sought to explore in specific systems and in some depth, the experiences of NQTs and the perceptions of different stakeholders about the usefulness of training.

As the most detailed evidence comes from Ghana, drawing both on the MUSTER team's work and on John Hedges' doctoral study into NQTs (Hedges 2002a), the Ghanaian case will be taken as the exemplar, with additional evidence from other sites as appropriate. As was described in Chap. 2, NQTs were surveyed in Ghana, Lesotho and Malawi, and in all four countries some observations were made of small samples of NQTs in their classrooms, albeit in different ways, and heads were interviewed.

7 What Happens After Training?: Induction and Beyond

7.2 What Happens to NQTs after Leaving College

7.2.1 Getting off to a good start; how teachers are deployed and settle in

The actual process of getting a job in a school differs widely between countries: in some the teachers apply, while in others they are 'posted' to vacancies. The system of deployment has wide implications for how the newly trained teachers are, or can be, utilised most effectively and encouraged to stay in the profession.

Hedges (2002b) argues that in Ghana the process of posting, together with the late payment of salaries, has a significant effect on the morale and effectiveness of NQTs. In a complex process, final year students state their preferences in terms of region and religion, and then they are assigned to schools by the Ghanaian Education Service (GES) in consultation with regional and district offices, and in some cases with religious educational units. As most students prefer the urban or developed regions where they grew up, when they are posted to the rural areas they try, sometimes by underhand means, to get a transfer.

The NQTs identified many practical concerns, such as poor accommodation, the lack of amenities such as transport, piped water and electricity, but they also highlighted cultural aspects, such as the different social values and norms of village life, and the ambivalent attitude of some rural parents towards education. One said he feared to become 'a village man' if he remained in the rural areas; this suggests that many young teachers perceive such postings as a threat to their very identity, and therefore will leave, by one means or another. Women face additional problems, such as intrusive scrutiny and gossip, and for this reason among others are seldom posted to villages, although their presence would provide good role models for girls.

Such conditions would seem to call for a comprehensive support system, but Hedges shows how the GES bureaucracy can make life even more difficult. Salaries can be up to nine months late, the posting system is seen as unfair, and little professional support is available locally. Thus new teachers find it difficult to settle down and feel comfortable in their posts and even those who do report for duty often manage to transfer within a couple of years, being replaced once more by untrained teachers. Those who stay on mention a number of altruistic and intrinsic reasons, but many also indicate they intend taking study leave once their stipulated three years' service is over, and moving out of primary teaching.

In Malawi teachers are also 'posted' to schools, and report similar practical difficulties; almost all had experienced late payment of salaries, and the majority also mentioned accommodation, food and transport, but they seem to have fewer problems with community relations, perhaps because they already knew the area. All teachers in MIITEP had already been posted to schools when they were first recruited, and most returned to the school

7 What Happens After Training?: Induction and Beyond

where they had previously taught, though some were posted to secondary schools and one became a head teacher!

By contrast, in Lesotho graduating teachers apply directly to a school, or through the Church Secretariats who own most of the schools. This 'market system' probably means that rural schools get the least effective teachers, but the evidence suggests most teachers felt more satisfied and in control of their lives. The NQT survey here revealed far fewer practical problems – only transport was sometimes difficult – and focussed more on professional and personal issues such as coping with large classes, teaching all subjects, and dealing with colleagues

7.3   Induction

In none of the countries studied was there a formal system of induction or probation for NQTs, and in most places it was left to the headteacher, with other teachers and local education officers sometimes playing a minor role. Most of the help concerned the managerial aspects; we found little evidence that NQTs were helped to develop their teaching and learning strategies. The Ghanaian studies (see Box 7.1) provide some interesting insights, showing how even well-meaning efforts by the bureaucracy do not meet all the needs of NQTs, especially in rural areas, and how the school does not give enough assistance in the classroom.

7 What Happens After Training?: Induction and Beyond

Box 7.1: **Induction in Ghana**

For the Ghanaian teachers there was some minimal briefing at college, and the Districts were supposed to provide some orientation, including visiting NQTs during their first term. One pro-active district organised a one-day workshop for NQTs, to tell them about:

Schemes of work; lesson planning; recording and reporting; current educational policies; classroom management; assessment of pupil learning.

These clearly reflect a bureaucratic approach, and while the NQTs found it useful, a focus group session produced a rather different list of their most pressing needs:

- Orientation to the school and local educational bureaucracy;
- Survival information: what to do about finance, accommodation, transport and health
- 'enlightenment about the customs, norms and values of the communities';
- teaching methods from experienced teachers
- GES code of conduct and the expectations of a teacher.

This district gave the DOs each three schools to contact regularly. However, further investigation showed that DOs were reluctant to visit rural schools and that often their 'supervision' was limited to ritual checking of lesson plans. The heads, therefore, become pivotal figures in the first teaching post, mediating for the NQTs between the communities, the bureaucracy and the classroom, but the evidence suggests this varied greatly in type and effectiveness. Heads seem to emphasise mainly issues such as: discipline, the teachers' role as carer and moral exemplar, and relations with the community. Notably they seemed to have given little help to NQTs in their instructional role, except to insist on punctuality and to look at their daily lesson notes. One of the NQTs' greatest difficulties was to adapt the curriculum to the needs of the children, but here they seem to have received little advice.

[adapted from Hedges, 2002a]

In Lesotho teachers have to rely entirely on the school for orientation, and less than half of our sample reported any induction at all, most of it brief and scanty. In Malawi many NQTs seem to have slotted into the ongoing Malawi School Support System Programme, and to have received help from PEAs alongside other staff. This shows how useful an integrated system of induction and in-service could be.

We found little evidence that other experienced teachers were used to support probationers. In Trinidad and Tobago a few senior teachers were given a more explicit mentoring role, though again no training is offered. In Lesotho a pilot mentoring scheme for beginning

7 What Happens After Training?: Induction and Beyond

teachers was set up in some secondary schools, but has not yet been extended to primary.

It seem strange that after so much money has been spent on the training, so little attention or funding is given to supporting the NQTs in their first years of teaching. Though some teachers were observed occasionally by district officers or inspectors, nowhere was there any sustained external assistance during the first two years, in the form of regular supervision, workshops, or INSET. It is unrealistic to expect the headteachers to take on this burden, but it is also difficult to organise regular visits by external trainers, especially in underdeveloped rural areas. Given that TP is often so short and so problematic, it seems obvious that NQTs are going to need help in their first year. This is a problem that seems to have received too little attention.

7.4   How NQTs Value their Course

In general, NQTs say they value their training highly. Survey respondents assert that everything was very useful to them, and in interviews comments like: 'it enabled me to function as a teacher' and 'it opens your mind' testify to the potential for empowering and illuminating. It can be noted that the language used by the NQTs to talk about teaching had changed; they had been inducted into a new discourse. However, there were also ambivalent voices, varying with the contexts, and in places the data was contradictory.

One clear and almost unanimous message from the survey in three sites was that the balance between content and methods should be tipped further towards methods, and in balancing theory and practice, there should be more weight given to practical activities. While many, particularly in Malawi, also rated the subject content as very important – particularly those with only JC - the most popular item everywhere for 'improving the course' was 'more methods'. Professional Studies / Education was often singled out in interviews as being the most interesting and useful. Teaching Practice was seen as extremely valuable, particularly in Ghana, where it was felt to be much too short. By contrast most NQTs in Lesotho thought that four months was enough, and did not, in retrospect, rate it so highly – possibly because it was so badly organised. Nowhere did micro-teaching find much support.

Another general finding was that all NQTs rely heavily on their college materials – notes, books, teaching aids – when they go into schools. In resource-constrained systems, this may be an important input; by the same token it may mean that these are then used year after year, with little innovation or improvement.

It is difficult to estimate how competent and confident NQTs actually were. Survey respondents tended to assert they felt well-prepared for teaching and had settled in, but they also reveal many concerns, most often over classroom management, assessment and dealing with individuals, as well as problems with parents and colleagues.

7 What Happens After Training?: Induction and Beyond

The small-scale in-depth study of NQTs in Trinidad and Tobago interestingly showed a wide divergence of opinion. Of the eight interviewees, three felt very positive about their training, two said it had made little difference to their teaching, and three had mixed feelings. Most found the education courses, both theory and practice, very useful, even though not all the methods worked in class, but several criticised the subject content as irrelevant to the primary curriculum (Morris and Joseph 2000).

The MIITEP graduates were unanimous that the taught part of their course was too short, too rushed, and too crammed. They wanted more of everything, in particular content, and although some claimed teaching was easy if one had resources, they did not seem very confident about anything.

The Ghanaian teachers had a number of criticisms. The main one was that the colleges were out of touch with the reality of the schools, and they had not been taught strategies for coping with such things as the pupils' very low levels of achievement, their poor English, and the frequent absenteeism. Some felt the college curriculum was overly academic, especially in preparing Primary teachers. The policy of training teachers for both primary and JSS together appears misconceived; the two kinds of school have different curricula and require different approaches, and the NQTs found they were not properly prepared for either. On the other hand, they valued the extra-curricular activities – drama, sport, regular worship, the social life – and several felt the collegial life had been personally enriching. This view seemed peculiar to Ghana, and did not figure strongly elsewhere.

In some ways the Lesotho and Malawi courses seemed more closely attuned to the schools, with an apparent consensus between the tutors and teachers about what constituted appropriate teaching. Survey respondents in those countries claimed to teach in ways similar to those taught by the college, particularly in areas such as content, planning, assessment and methods. They noted more divergence in those areas which have to be learnt by individuals on the job, such as handling discipline, and responding to individual needs in large heterogeneous groups. The Ghanaian NQTs experienced much more of a culture shock, especially in rural areas, and felt in particular they were not prepared for the real problems in the primary schools.

Insofar as we can generalise from very different contexts, the message from the NQTs seems to be: while much of the training was interesting and useful, it did not give them enough of the practical skills they needed. Those who had taught before went back to a familiar world somewhat better equipped, but many novices felt unprepared for the problems of real classrooms.

7 What Happens After Training?: Induction and Beyond

7.5   How Others Evaluate the NQTS

7.5.1 Views of Head Teachers.

In Ghana, Lesotho and Trinidad and Tobago the researchers interviewed small numbers of head teachers on the effectiveness of the training. In Ghana, most – though not all – the heads thought the quality of NQTs was declining, and did not put a particularly high value on the training. Their main criticism seemed to focus on attitude and commitment, saying many were 'not serious' and that they would leave for further study at the first opportunity. By contrast the local untrained teachers, were perceived as more hard-working and committed.

With respect to classroom performance – although it is unclear how much they had observed them teaching – the heads hoped that NQTs would bring in new ideas, but although some proved competent, others performed below expectations. In some cases NQTs' subject content knowledge was said to be inadequate, especially in maths and science. But the chief criticism was their tendency to 'teach above the pupils' level', which suggests the real deficiency was in their 'pedagogic content knowledge'; they did not have the skills to diagnose the pupils' problems and adapt their teaching accordingly.

In Lesotho the heads interviewed seemed much more reluctant to criticise the NQTs - perhaps because the researcher was a member of the college staff – and their glowing reports about NQTs 'knowing their subjects' well, and 'bringing in new methods' contradicted the impressions of the rather traditional and occasionally inaccurate lessons observed. However, here too the heads highlighted problems of professional attitudes, mentioning poor time-keeping, too much use of the cane, and lack of commitment (Sebatane & Lefoka 2001).

The Trinidadian heads were able to compare teachers, in general, before and after their training and on the whole took a more positive view. Though they thought the college put too much emphasis on content at the expense of methods – a view shared by the NQTs – the heads felt that after training they did bring in 'a positive attitude to work, a good relationship with the children, and some use of new methods'. (Morris & Joseph 2000: 4).

From the heads' perspective, then, college training does make a difference, and NQTs can enrich the schools by bringing in up-to-date ideas and materials and providing new energy. But other factors, such as personal characteristics, and the school or community environment, are just as important. In certain cases untrained teachers are considered more reliable and to teach nearly as well.

7 What Happens After Training?: Induction and Beyond

7.5.2 External observers.

We can add to the heads' views with some evidence from observations of the classroom performance of NQTs, and to some degree compare them with that of untrained teachers (UTs). The samples are small, and can only offer indications of what might be found if further research were carried out in this area.

In Ghana seven NQTs and four untrained teachers were each observed in 2 or 3 lessons, mainly maths and English, but also some science, social studies and Ghanaian language. Though the differences between the two groups were not very striking, the NQTs were judged to be more competent in the areas of curriculum content knowledge, a wider repertoire of methods, classroom management, and planning. The UTs were more likely to use 'chorus reading', and some of their lessons lacked structure or became disorganised. Most notably, the NQTs usually produced written lesson plans, even though some were rather sketchy or incomplete, while three out of the four UTs showed no evidence of lesson planning. Both groups, however, demonstrated equally cordial and relaxed relations with pupils. Neither group evaluated pupil learning satisfactorily, or took remedial action where it was clear that pupils had not achieved the intended results. This overall picture is confirmed quite independently by interviews with heads, where they too said untrained teachers, however willing and committed, had patchy subject knowledge, used a limited range of methods, and did not know how to make plans. (Akyeampong, Ampiah et al 2000).

John Hedges, after observing and interviewing four of his sample of NQTs, takes the analysis somewhat further. He found the lessons to be fairly traditional and teacher-centred, where the teacher would present and explain topics, engage pupils in question and answer sessions, make them read aloud, or give them exercises to do. Although NQTs could give reasons for some of their teaching strategies in terms of college discourse, or quote things taught there, Hedges suggests that their training has not enabled them to think through and evaluate traditional, ritualised classroom practices – caning, clapping, chorusing, individual counselling, question and answer sessions – in the light of modern teaching/learning theories, in ways that would help them distinguish what is useful, or what could be adapted, from what is ineffective.(Hedges 2002a).

All the evidence in Ghana points to the wide gap between the college rhetoric and the classroom reality. The primary curriculum which the NQTs had been carefully trained to teach often seemed inappropriate in these rural schools, with large classes, fluctuating attendance, and lack of resources. They were particularly concerned with the language issue: pupils' English was so poor that teachers had to spend disproportionate amounts of time on remedial English, something they had not been prepared for.

7 What Happens After Training?: Induction and Beyond

In Ghana it seems then, at one level, training is valued, and seen as useful. It boosts NQTs' confidence and helps them to function as a teacher. They know how to carry out the administrative tasks to the head's satisfaction, planning lessons, keeping records, managing a class. At a deeper level, what is taught at the college does not connect directly to the classroom; NQTs are not prepared for the conditions they will meet, or for diagnosing and solving children's learning problems.

Evidence from Lesotho points in similar directions. With one or two exceptions, the six NQTs observed had adequate knowledge of the curriculum, and managed their classrooms confidently, but on the whole their lessons followed a traditional pattern of teacher talk, interspersed with question and answer sessions, which allowed only limited pupil participation. Chorus answers were common, and evaluation of individual student learning was erratic. Again, a relaxed and friendly atmosphere appeared the norm, though in some classes pupils appeared very passive.

The phenomenon of 'training washout' was exemplified in Lesotho. Noticeably, there was little evidence that these NQTs had attempted to implement the learner-centred strategies taught in college, such as displaying pupils' work, setting up activity corners, or providing materials for them to handle as opposed to look at. Untrained teachers interviewed in two of these schools claimed to be impressed by the NQTs, and to have learnt from them, but the evidence here suggests that training helps you do better what you are already familiar with, rather than introducing new ideas or encouraging creativity (Sebatane & Lefoka 2001).

The evaluation in Malawi took a different form, using the standard observation form for assessing TP. A small sample (17) of MIITEP trainees were observed just before their training began, and again nine months later during their school-based practice; a further small sample (12) from a different cohort were observed just after completing the whole programme. Numerical scores were given, and the group means computed. According to these results, the overall changes in teaching performance were positive but small. The mean scores of the group in training had improved by 3 percentage points, and the post-training group scored on average a couple of points higher.

These figures need to be treated with caution. Firstly, the instrument used attempted to measure a limited number of skills and behaviours, rather than high level competence. Secondly, although all these observations were done by two researchers sitting together, other evidence showed that inter-judge reliability was weak, and different observers might have come to different conclusions. Certainly the results, though not statistically significant, are in the right direction, but they do not, in themselves, suggest what has made the difference, or how the programme could be improved.

7 What Happens After Training?: Induction and Beyond

Croft's classroom studies including three student teachers suggest that MIITEP did have traceable effects. Students in talking about their practice, could give examples of what they had learnt both from the college and from working alongside experienced classroom teachers. How far these actually made an impact, depended, as always, on their own tenacity and commitment, and on the pupils and schools they worked with.(Croft 2002a)

The Trinidadian researchers who observed eight NQTs using a more qualitative approach concluded that training did produce, overall, real benefits to the schools. In general the NQTs demonstrated a concern for proper lesson planning, systematic development of the curriculum, a heightened awareness of individual differences among students, leading to concern for their varying learning styles, and the need for different forms of assessment. (Morris & Joseph 2000). While a minority of NQTs were unimpressed by the training, and taught much as they had done before, the majority were seen to be implementing many of the methods and techniques suggested. Coming to college with so much classroom experience may have made them more receptive.

This limited evidence suggests that training does have some impact, in that it makes NQTs more aware of professional responsibilities and enables them to work somewhat more effectively within the given norms and practices of the schools. It does not seem to equip them as agents of change. Further studies would be needed to evaluate whether, over the longer term, they continue to improve and teach better than untrained colleagues.

7.6 Evidence of Attitude Changes

The survey administered to three groups of students – at entry, at exit, and after two-three years of teaching – included a section of Likert-type items, inviting respondents to agree or disagree on a four-point scale. The items were chosen to reflect important topics and issues relevant to teacher education, and the teaching profession; they were discussed by the whole MUSTER team, and adapted for the different sites. (See Chapter 4.3 for a list of items[34]). There are well-known problems with such instruments, including whether the respondents interpreted the language of the statements in the same ways as the researchers, but some of the findings are disquieting, and all suggest avenues for further enquiry.

The evidence below is based on those items common across the surveys and across more than one country. This allowed cross-sectional comparisons, but not longitudinal ones. The data is therefore suggestive of changes that might be occurring, but not sufficient to draw firm conclusions without more detailed attention to sampling. Figures 8 and 9 show changes in mean scores between entry, exit and NQTs in Lesotho and Malawi[35].

---

[34] Item 5 was not used across the entry, exit and NQT samples and has been deleted from the analysis which follows.
[35] More details can be found in Coultas & Lewin (2002).

7 What Happens After Training?: Induction and Beyond

7.6.1 Lesotho and Malawi

The mean responses across entry, exit and NQT samples in the two countries did not vary greatly. Typically the range in mean score was 0.5 or less between the greatest and least. In Lesotho, samples on three items (3, 9 and 11) showed a consistent direction of difference between entry, exit and NQT. In Malawi there were seven items (1, 12, 3, 4, 8, 10, 11) which had a consistent trend. Depending on the item, it might be expected that attitudes would continue to change in the same direction over time as training and experience had a cumulative effect. But equally, since the experience of passing through a training programme, and the experience of induction are different and may not in reality be much of a continuum, a change in direction of the mean response might be consistent with realities actually experienced.

Figure 8: **Entry, Exit and NQT Perceptions - Lesotho**

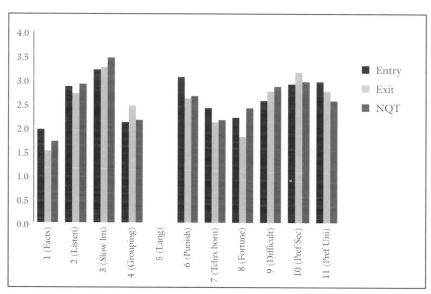

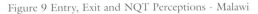

7 What Happens After Training?: Induction and Beyond

Figure 9 Entry, Exit and NQT Perceptions - Malawi

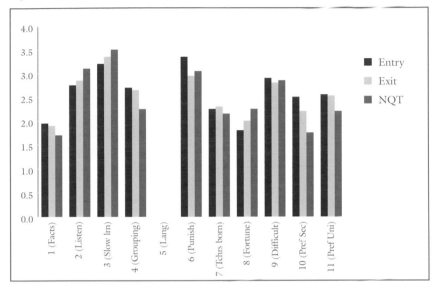

For this preliminary discussion we can just note some possible interpretations that suggest further analysis is needed. In the Lesotho data set NQTs are significantly more likely[36] to wish they had gone to university for training* (11). Exiting trainees are significantly more likely to think they are fortunate to be teachers* (8) and entering trainees seem most likely to disagree with the use of corporal punishment* (6)

In Malawi NQTs and exiting trainees appear more likely to believe teachers should stress facts (1), more likely to disagree with the statement that pupils learn most from listening to teachers** (2) and to disagree with the statement that slow learners cannot be helped much by teachers** (3). They also agree more with grouping by ability. NQTs disagree significantly less with the use of corporal punishment**(6) and are significantly less likely to think themselves fortunate to be teachers** (8). They are much more likely to want to teach at secondary level** (10), and to wish they had gone to university** (11).

In both country data sets student teachers who have completed training seem more likely to feel they can benefit slow learners (3), to agree with the use of corporal punishment (6), and to wish they had gone to the university for training (11) though these changes are not significant at the 0.05 level.

These data sets from Lesotho and Malawi begin to suggest areas for deeper enquiry and possible reasons for the changes observed. At another level, taking the data at face value, it is not immediately clear that training programmes and the experience of being an NQT,

[36] Chi square where * = p<0.05, ** = p<0.001

7 What Happens After Training?: Induction and Beyond

have dramatically transformed the responses trainees give to the items selected. Whatever effects training is having they are apparently not sufficient to cause large shifts in perspective across the groups. This might be considered disappointing, or perhaps an indication that the task teacher educators have is a very difficult one. It may also suggest that the perceptions represented by the items are deeply entrenched, and/or that they are strongly influenced by factors exogenous to the training process.

7.6.2 Ghana

The results of the Ghana study, which was the most extensive and used a total sample of 834 students, are discussed fully in Akyeampong and Lewin (2002) and the findings are only summarised here.

The data suggest that:

- Attitudes to teaching as a profession deteriorated over the training period; whilst a majority of beginning teachers held a positive view, the majority of NQTs did not. Whether this was due to peer influence, to disappointment with training, or with classroom experience, is unclear.
- Views on corporal punishment became more authoritarian; it may be that although the college preached against the cane, trainees were not given alternative strategies of classroom management.
- Those with more training and experience are more likely to believe that teachers are born and not made, and they also tend to agree more strongly that teaching is more difficult than many other jobs. This suggests they do not hold training in great esteem.

On the more positive side:

- All the groups indicate a sense of agency, in that they feel they can improve the performance of slow learners, and bring about changes in schools
- In the area of pedagogy, all the groups strongly support group work, and their enthusiasm for 'teaching facts' diminishes with time and training.

The conclusions seem to be that training does not seem to change attitudes, as expressed in answers to these items, by very much. Those changes that do show up are not very encouraging: that they are less positive about teaching as a profession, that they find it more difficult, and that good teachers have to be born that way. Their sense of agency and their use of progressive discourse seem to predate the training, and not to translate into practice; if they revert to using the cane this shows the effects of training may be cancelled out by other factors. Classroom observations did not confirm the apparent trends towards more learner-centred pedagogy, and it may be an example of learning a discourse rather than a fundamental shift in belief.

7 What Happens After Training?: Induction and Beyond

7.7   Career Ambitions

Whether or not the NQTs intend to stay in the profession seems to have little to do with the mode of training or its curriculum, though phase-specific training may be a factor. Much more influential are the conditions of service, the status of the profession, and the availability of other more attractive options. We found some significant differences between sites, suggesting that policy needs to be very context-specific.

In Ghana the MOE's policy is to allow college-trained teachers to apply, after three years service, for a fully-funded degree course. So those who failed to enter university the first time round can use teacher training as a 'stepping stone' to better paid and more prestigious jobs, rather than as induction into a career as a basic school teacher. Virtually all the NQTs hoped in five years' time to have moved on, either into study or into a different job. It is noteworthy that being trained for both primary and JSS raised their expectations, and those posted to primary schools had a sense of disappointment. Such a training, in conditions of teacher scarcity, also means they can move more easily into senior secondary schools. Some intend to leave education altogether.

By contrast, in Lesotho few of those surveyed wanted to move into secondary schools or to leave teaching. Nearly three-quarters said they hoped to 'further their studies', but since there are few funded opportunities for this in Lesotho, even through distance education, by default most of them will remain in the primary schools. Realistically there are few jobs in Lesotho offering similar security, albeit at a relatively low salary. Our data, from several different sources, seems to confirm that young teachers do have a sense of identity as primary teachers, and feel it is a worthwhile profession; this is noticeably different from the other sites.

In Malawi salaried employment opportunities are few, and nearly all the respondents thought they would still be teaching in five years' time, though 10% indicated they would prefer something else. The majority said they hoped to be in secondary schools rather than primary, which is understandable given the difficult conditions in primary classes and the higher salary paid to secondary teachers. It is also realistic in that the secondary system is expanding and MIITEP graduates, despite their lack of subject-specific training, are likely to be transferred to the new secondary schools.

In Trinidad and Tobago it seems that that the NQTs' experience of teaching so far had shown them it involved hard work and self-sacrifice with few social or financial rewards. Though less than 10% wanted to leave education altogether, most of those surveyed on entry planned to study further so they could move out of primary school teaching into secondary or other education-related jobs. To some degree, they also saw their training as a stepping stone to better things.

7 What Happens After Training?: Induction and Beyond

7.8 Concluding Discussion

The evidence so far presents a very complex picture from which it is difficult to draw general conclusions, and still less does it suggest clear-cut policy recommendations. All we can say with confidence is that teacher training does have more of an impact than some of its critics claim, but that its effects are less than its proponents desire.

On the positive side, most NQTs value their training. It boosts their confidence, raises their awareness, and provides them with a new discourse – they can 'talk the talk' of teachers. Whether they can 'walk the walk' is another matter. Evidence suggests they have gained some knowledge of curriculum content, and of a wider range of methods. They have been alerted to new aspects of psychology and child development. They have acquired a number of managerial skills – lesson planning, record keeping, managing children and resources in a classroom, keeping time – which enable them to please heads and work with colleagues; they can fulfil bureaucratic requirements. Importantly, they have been provided with resource materials in the form of notes, books and aids, which they will use in resource-poor schools. Heads believe, on the whole, that they bring a slow but steady stream of new information and practice into schools. In sum, training has laid a foundation.

On the other hand, training does not appear to have had a dramatic effect on NQTs' behaviour, attitudes or understanding. NQTs seem to teach rather more competently than untrained ones, but not very differently. Their attitudes towards the profession, and towards teaching itself change only marginally through their college years, and not always in the hoped-for direction. There is little evidence from the programmes studied here that they have gained deep insights into teaching and learning processes that would enable them to continue to develop and improve their own practice, though this may happen with some students in Trinidad. It seems clear that initial training courses cannot themselves be used as engines of change, as MIITEP shows only too clearly.

There are certainly elements within the programmes which seem to work against effectiveness. Some have been identified in earlier chapters, such as the contradictions within the curriculum and the mismatches to student needs (Chap. 5) and the shortcomings of school experience (Chap. 6). Most obviously the gap between colleges and schools, so clearly shown in Ghana, means that students are not properly prepared to deal with the actual problems of teaching and learning in the classroom. It may be that training focuses more on the appearance of teaching than on the realities; it provides certification, it enables NQTs to 'feel like a teacher'; in some ways it may function as a symbolic 'rite of passage', while the real learning occurs on the job.

However, there is no-one available or trained to guide the NQTs' learning during those crucial first years. Heads are overburdened, DEOs visit infrequently, and teachers have

7 What Happens After Training?: Induction and Beyond

neither the time nor the skills. The internship year proposed in Ghana and by UDW may offer a useful bridge; it will be interesting to see how interns are supported during this time. Evidence from Malawi suggests there is potential for experienced teachers to act as mentors, but they will need to be given appropriate professional development and rewards. All this suggests moving resources from the colleges to the schools. This would be consistent with policies for Whole School Development, whereby selected schools become environments conducive to training in good practice; adequate resources, supportive heads and colleagues, and good school management would enable NQTS to utilise their training more effectively.

However, this chapter also highlights the importance of other factors external to the training programmes. In Ghana the 'further study' policy encourages trainees to think of the college as a springboard to 'better' careers, rather than as a place for learning to teach. In Trinidad and Tobago primary teachers feel their hard work is neither recognised nor rewarded adequately. It is clear that if other conditions and policies are not conducive to keeping teachers in the schools, the colleges are working in vain, no matter how good the training.

Teacher training is part of a much wider cultural system, and only one stage in a cycle in which trainees come from schools where they were socialised into certain attitudes, values and practices, enter college where these are only challenged superficially, if at all (cf. Tafa 2001), and move back into similar schools; it is not surprising that attitudes are deeply rooted, and change little over three years. Much more time and effort will be needed.

This analysis leads us to consider fundamental issues about how far along the 'path to competence' pre-service training can be expected to take new teachers. In particular, what can the college realistically contribute to learning to teach, and what has, inevitably, to be learnt on the job in the first 2-3 years? Should the college try to do less, and if so, how can new teachers' continuing development be better supported in the schools? At present, there is so little effective induction and inservice available that if training is not given at the start, it may be left out altogether. A paradigm shift in policy and resourcing would be required to put the focus on regular continual professional development rather than on pre-service courses.

7.8.1 Some Key issues for Policy and practice

- Some basic initial training for intending teachers is essential but the traditional three-year pre-service college-based course does not seem to achieve its aims effectively and alternatives need to be explored.

- The lack of support everywhere in the first years of teaching is a serious deficiency, which contributes both to lower morale and to 'washout' of training. Systematic school-focused induction and on-the-job support from trained mentors and/or advisors could

---

7 What Happens After Training?: Induction and Beyond

make a substantial difference. There could be useful ways of integrating induction and in-service with Whole School Development strategies.

- The system of deploying NQTs affects their morale and sense of professional identity. If it is centralised, then practical, logistical and financial arrangements for settling in need to be given high priority by educational management systems. Where there is a significant urban-rural divide, those sent to rural schools may need specific moral and social support.

- Entrants to primary training often see this as a stepping stone to other jobs with higher status and rewards. Improvements in pay and conditions of service for primary teachers, as well as less tangible rewards such as social respect and sense of self-esteem, are needed to retain those trained.

- Many attitudes and perceptions of trainees seem to persist despite their initial training, and colleges seem to do little to break the traditional patterns of thought and behaviour. Tutors and trainers need to engage with and challenge students' ideas more constructively.

Chapter Eight   **8 Teacher Educators in Colleges**

8.0   Summary and Overview

This chapter[37] focuses on the college teaching staff, and provides some answers to the questions:

➢ Who becomes a college tutor, how and why?
➢ What induction and professional development programmes are available for them?
➢ How do they perceive their work, with particular reference to their views on how young teachers acquire the knowledge, skills and attitudes they need?
➢ What needs should be prioritised for staff development?

8.0.1 **Summary of findings**

Characteristics and career patterns of college staff

• We found no clear career path for tutors, and most joined the college as a promotion from school teaching rather than out of an intrinsic interest in training. Consequently most were middle-aged or older and the gender balance reflected that of the local teaching force. Many primary tutors were themselves secondary-trained, and this trend was more marked among the younger recruits. Qualifications varied, often in line with the country's wealth, so that in Malawi and Ghana some had only Teaching Diplomas, while in Trinidad and Tobago many had Masters degrees.

Professional Development

• Very few tutors received specific training for their role, even when this involved a reorientation to primary education. No college studied had either formal induction or professional development policies in place. Some departments had informal support programmes for new colleagues. In-service mainly consisted of workshops organised by Ministries of Education wishing to disseminate innovations, though in some systems individuals had found opportunities for short courses or degree-level study. In general, tutors trained as they had themselves been trained.

Perspectives on their work

• While perspectives differed between countries, and between individuals, particularly among the most qualified, we found also many similar themes. In general, neither individual tutors nor the colleges as institutions had very clear conceptual models of how students learn to teach. Generally, training teachers was seen in terms of transmitting knowledge and skills, which the trainees would then apply uniformly. Tutors' views of the 'good' primary teacher, especially in the African sites, stressed personal and affective characteristics rather than cognitive and instructional abilities. They saw themselves as producing teachers who would deliver the curriculum effectively, rather than as developing professionals who would use their own judgement to solve problems. In line

---

[37] An earlier version of this chapter is published in Stuart 2002

8 Teacher Educators in Colleges

with this view, trainees were often treated like high school pupils rather than tertiary-level students.

- The intellectual horizons of many college staff seemed narrowly embedded in the local world-view. Though the discourse often showed borrowing of ideas from high income countries, there was little evidence that new concepts were being thoughtfully adapted to the local context and used to develop more effective ways of training.

- However, in spite of perceived heavy workloads and poor conditions of service, we found many hardworking and committed individuals, some of whom had developed their own ideas about teacher training, and who found intrinsic satisfaction in the job. There appeared to be neglected potential for development at both the individual and college levels.

This chapter begins with an introduction highlighting the dearth of studies in this area, and details how the data was collected. The following sections describe first the characteristics and career paths of the tutors, and second their views and perspectives on their jobs. The data is drawn from the four smaller sites only, as in South Africa the MUSTER research was carried out in University Departments of Education.

8. 1 Introduction

Teacher educators all over the world are an underdeveloped group. In few countries are there specific career paths or professional courses for them. From an academic point of view, little research has been carried out in this field and the available literature, even in the West, is very sparse. One exception comes from a group of (mainly) North American university teacher educators, working in the 'reflective practitioner' mode, who used self-study and action research approaches to theorise about their own professional learning and how to improve their practice (Russell and Korthagen 1995).

Reports from high income countries suggest that most cadres of teacher educators tend towards a conservative ideology rather than a radical or transformative one. This is perhaps to be expected when they have themselves usually come up through the same system. Yet it seems obvious that if educational change is to take place, those who prepare the next generation of teachers must play a key role in innovation. Writing about educational development in general, Beeby pointed out the self-perpetuating nature of educational systems and the problem of where to break the cycle:

> Teacher trainers in low income countries who do try to break with the old pattern
> usually get their ideas from travel in rich countries, or from books written there, and
> often hand them on, in the form of indigestible theory, to teachers who need practical

8 Teacher Educators in Colleges

guidance to take even simpler steps forward. The reformer's most puzzling question frequently is: 'Who is to re-train the teacher trainers?' (Beeby 1980: 465-6)

In many low income countries today this question is still very pertinent, and there are only a few reports of relevant research or action. One describes the concerted efforts made for colleges in Papua New Guinea (Burke 1996, McLaughlin 1996). A useful example comes from Namibia, where teacher education was planned as the spearhead of reform, and all college tutors were invited to take a postgraduate higher diploma in teacher education. The theory and practice of this course were based on the same principles as those underlying the reforms in the rest of the system, so that tutors were better prepared to train future teachers in the new methods (Shilambo and Dahlstrom 1999).

8. 2 Data Sources

The principle sources of data used for this chapter are interviews, questionnaires and observation of teaching in the colleges, but procedures and coverage varied between the sites, with the most detailed studies coming from Lesotho and Malawi (see Stuart, Kunje and Lefoka 2000). A questionnaire was administered to representative samples of tutors in selected teacher training colleges (TTCs): four colleges in Ghana, two in Malawi, and the Lesotho National Teacher Training College (NTTC). This asked for personal data, qualifications and teaching experience; their views on the curriculum and on students; perceptions of the good teacher and of how the college strives to produce them. Most questions were closed, though a few asked for individual views, and respondents were invited to agree or disagree with a number of statements.

In Lesotho and Malawi semi-structured interviews were carried out with a smaller sample of tutors, drawn from the main subject areas and balanced for age, gender and qualifications. These interviews were intended to follow a modified life-history format with multiple meetings (see Kelchtermans 1993), but time and resources did not permit this, so only one hour-long interview was carried out with each subject. In Malawi most of the interviewees (20) were also observed teaching. In Lesotho, observations were separately negotiated with eight tutors. In Trinidad and Tobago eight tutors from the colleges were interviewed about their teaching, some of whom were also observed (George, Worrell et al 2000); in Ghana nine tutors were studied in a similar way (Akyeampong, Ampiah et al, 2000). Other contextual data on the colleges were gathered from documents and from observations during fieldwork, enabling some triangulation of the findings to be carried out.

8. 3 Characteristics of College Staff

Table 6 summarises some of the tutors' backgrounds, career trajectories, and working conditions.

8 Teacher Educators in Colleges

Table 6: **Comparisons of backgrounds of college tutors and career trajectories**

Aspect	LESOTHO	MALAWI	GHANA	*T&T
Personal:				
Gender	Mostly (>2/3) women	Mostly men, just over 1/3 women	Mostly men, (< 1/4 women)	Over half women
Age	26->50, most 36-45	30->50, most over 40	26->50; most 41-50	35-58; most 40-50
Teaching background	Mainly secondary, <50% primary experience	90% originally primary, some topped up with secondary	70% JSS/upper primary, 45% lower primary	Mostly secondary
Qualifications	Graduates, 1/3 with Masters degrees	Mostly Diplomates, 1/3 with degrees, incl a few Masters	3/4 graduates, others Diplomates, 3% Masters	50% with Masters
Becoming a tutor	Applied: change, challenge, further study, for pension/ higher salary	Some applied to do DPTE; otherwise all were 'picked, posted or sent'	Promoted from secondary schools	Applied for intrinsic reasons
Prof. Preparation:				
Specific training	Dip. in Primary Supervision (2/38)	Dip. in Primary Teacher Educ. (9/33)	None	T.Ed. option within M.Ed
Induction	Informal, sparse, given guidelines and books	Informal, collegial, given materials, peer observation and feedback	N/A	Some informal help
INSET received	50%, mostly workshops/short courses, incl. research. A few F/T overseas scholarships, some P/T self-funded	All sent occasionally on 1-2 wk workshops. Very few overseas scholarships to gain degrees	2/3, all short courses, mostly 1-2 wks. No study leave	Some scholarships for post-graduate study
Work context:				
Average workload	8 contact hours p/w; TP supervision	13 contact hours p/w, marking distance assignments	> 20 contact hours p/w	9-10 contact hrs. p/w; TP, counselling
Class sizes	15-200	30-80	Average: 52	Up to 200
Career Aims:				
Current feeling about job	Most: intrinsic satisfaction, some altruism. Frustration with management and conditions of service	Most: low morale, dislike MIITEP; some residual intrinsic satisfaction; frustration with lack of resources and poor conditions of service	N/A	Most: intrinsic satisfaction and job interest. Main concern; being paid same as high school teachers.
Future intentions	50% would stay, others move to NUL or MOE; 13% would leave education	<20% would stay, >20% would leave education, most would go to MOE	<50% would stay, nearly 40% would leave education	N/A

* *College tutors did not respond to questionnaire; information comes from general sources and from the sample interviews.*

8 Teacher Educators in Colleges

8.3.1 Background and training

Almost all primary college tutors have come up through the teaching ranks, but in different ways and from different starting points, so that not all have relevant experience. Most of the older Malawian tutors began as primary teachers, but as nowadays college staff must have degrees, the younger ones are secondary-trained. For similar reasons, in Lesotho less than half the staff have any primary experience and most of those surveyed agreed that 'most tutors do not know much about teaching primary pupils'. In Ghana most have had upper primary or junior secondary experience; fewer have worked in the infant grades. In Trinidad and Tobago most tutors have a secondary school background, again because they are degree-holders while primary teachers are not.

Unsurprisingly, tutors' qualifications vary with the country's wealth and with the opportunities offered for academic and professional development in the education system as a whole. Thus in Trinidad and Tobago half the tutors hold Masters degrees, in Lesotho almost all tutors are graduates, and about a third have Masters degrees, while Ghana about three-quarters hold a B.Ed and very few have Masters. In Malawi the majority of tutors have only diplomas; the rest have Bachelors degrees, with a sprinkling of Masters. While Malawian tutors are expected to be generalists, and may teach two or three subjects, including Education, elsewhere the tutors specialise either in one subject or in Education, though occasionally they may hold degrees in both.

It is notable that few of the qualifications were specifically designed to prepare people to train teachers, though a number of the Malawi tutors went through a 'Diploma in Primary Teacher Education' (DPTE) in the 1980s, and a couple of the Basotho[38] staff had done a Diploma in Supervision. In Ghana, most college tutors had attended either the University of Cape Coast (UCC) or the University College of Winneba but they were not specifically trained as teacher educators since it was assumed that anyone graduating in education would be capable of teaching at a college, even though most of the methods taught were for secondary level. However, in Trinidad and Tobago the UWI offers a teacher education option within the M.Ed., which includes training in supervision, and several tutors had received scholarships to undertake this degree.

The gender balance broadly reflects the more general participation of women in the local teaching force. In Lesotho most of the college staff are women – though the Director has always been a man - and in Trinidad and Tobago just over half the tutors are women, while in Ghana and Malawi they are mostly male. However, Malawi's policy of promoting suitable women is raising the proportion in the colleges, two of which had female principals at the time of the study. (See Croft 2000 for a gender analysis of teacher education in Malawi).

---

[38] In Lesotho, one person is a Mosotho, the plural is Basotho

8 Teacher Educators in Colleges

Thus, while tutors come from the local teaching force and mirror many of its characteristics, this poses a particular problem for countries where primary teachers have low status and minimal training, making it difficult to find people to staff the colleges who have both academic standing and first-hand knowledge of primary schools. The lack of attention paid to specific training for the job is also a widespread phenomenon.

8.3.2 Career Paths for college tutors

As in many other countries, the careers of teacher educators appear haphazard and unsupported (cf Russell & Korthagen 1995). Nowhere did we find a clearly defined career structure, and ways of crossing from the school world to the college world are varied and unpredictable. In Malawi, for example, tutors reported being 'picked' from their schools to fill gaps in the colleges and promotions depend on the MOE. In Trinidad and Tobago, where there were few material incentives to transfer, tutors seem to have applied out of personal interest, or via encouragement by others, some having already proved themselves as advisory teachers. Elsewhere the moves seem to have been more deliberately planned; for example in Lesotho, tutors said they moved to get better conditions of service, less stress, and the opportunities for further study – not all of which actually materialised, since criteria for study leave and promotion were unclear. In Ghana, many teachers begin in the primary schools, further their studies by training as a secondary teacher, and then aspire to become a college tutor. This is seen almost as a 'natural progression' towards better conditions of service and more prestige; it also shows how training colleges in Ghana are regarded 'post-secondary' rather than tertiary or higher educational institutions. In sum, very few people became trainers from an intrinsic interest in improving the preparation of teachers.

8.2.3 Induction and in-service

One of the most troubling findings was the lack of any formal induction for college tutors. There seemed a general assumption that since you were a trained teacher, you would know how to train teachers yourself. The Malawian colleges offered some informal support; newcomers were given books and syllabuses and encouraged to seek advice, to observe others, or to be observed themselves. In Trinidad and Tobago there was a system of informal mentoring where new tutors could 'sit in' on colleagues' lectures, and were paired with experienced tutors on Teaching Practice rounds.

But at the NTTC peer observation was unknown and informal support apparently very sparse. It seemed that most staff had learnt on the job, drawing on memories of their own training. In the English department, tutors with only secondary training were allowed just to teach content at first, picking up the 'methods' courses later on. In the case of Professional Studies, some tutors appeared to have relied largely on what they had been taught at the National University of Lesotho (NUL) in Educational Foundations courses;

8 Teacher Educators in Colleges

this would imply that what is being offered to NTTC students may be 15-20 years out of date.

It was clear that when they had first come to the college many tutors had not known what to do, and relied on serendipitous help. One reported a conversation with a colleague thus:

> *I asked him: 'What kind of things do we do here at NTTC?' And he said: 'just teach as you have always taught, there is nothing new here'[...]. But in the department, there was a lady who was very helpful. I learnt a lot from discussions with her.* (Female tutor)

If this kind of experience is widespread, it begins to be clear why colleges are not centres of innovation. Just as new teachers often teach as they were taught, so college tutors will train others as they were trained, and indeed three Ghanaian tutors explicitly mentioned ways in which they had copied their own tutors.

It is significant that none of the colleges studied had a staff development policy. All tutors expressed the need for refresher courses in both subject and professional areas, but complained that provision was inadequate. In the African countries studied in-service commonly takes the form either of local short courses, or long award-bearing courses that often require foreign travel. In Malawi and Ghana staff are usually sent by the MOE on short workshops to be told about developments in school or teacher education curricula. For example, in Malawi they were all given a two-week orientation to MIITEP, though it was apparent from interviews that this was not sufficient. In Lesotho tutors exercised more personal initiative, but opportunities were sporadic, and the courses usually short. A notable exception was that six staff were trained to run a special programme in Early Learning, through a combination of short courses and regional study tours, which was perceived as very successful.

Many tutors would like to upgrade their academic qualifications for both intrinsic and instrumental reasons, but opportunities are limited by funds and often by the lack of suitable local programmes. While in Trinidad and Tobago tutors could study for an M.Ed. at the local UWI campus, the African colleges were still largely dependent on overseas scholarships. In these countries there were individual tutors who had done post-graduate study in the UK or the USA, and while such courses were stimulating they often found considerable problems in applying the ideas at home. For example, one who studied in the UK said, only half jokingly, that although the course had been an 'eye-opener', he had had to 'reverse what he had learnt' in adapting the ideas to Lesotho because of the lack of resources in schools. In Ghana over a hundred college tutors were trained in British Universities under the Junior Secondary School Teacher Education Project (JUSSTEP), but they were able to make little impact on their return due to the deep-rooted conservatism of the colleges (Akyeampong, Ampiah et al, 2000).

8 Teacher Educators in Colleges

Improvements in the college environment, its leadership and vision, are pre-requisites for change. Even the best in-service is only valuable if the lessons learnt can be applied in one's own classroom, and this depends on a number of other factors, such as basic resources, follow-up support, a critical mass of sympathetic colleagues, supportive management, and a culture conducive to change. Our case studies suggest many of these factors are often missing. But the external environment is also crucial, since colleges are usually part of wider systems, and fall under the Ministries of Education. In both Ghana and Malawi traditional assessment practices, outside as well as inside the colleges, acted as a brake on efforts to change (cf Akyeampong 1997). In Trinidad and Tobago colleges there were both innovative tutors and supportive Principals, but the Board of Teacher Training maintained a conservative grip on the curriculum that the colleges were only just beginning to challenge.

8.4   Tutors' Views and Perspectives

Our research suggests that a lot of confusion surrounds the concepts of teacher education in these sites. Both discourses and practices seem to derive from various sources of training and experience, and often include concepts and models that originated elsewhere, resulting in a lack of any coherent theory about professional training. While this ferment and international borrowing has many positive aspects, it also leads to disjunctions between rhetoric and actual practice. Colleges seem to be grappling with the paradigm shift towards constructivist teaching and learning so they could adapt it to local contexts and to development needs, but the shift comes into conflict with values, attitudes and beliefs about knowledge and schooling held by different stakeholders. There is a need for clearer models of training which incorporate recent developments in our understanding of professional learning, but which also acknowledge local starting points, striking a balance between the old and new.

Tutors' views are here explored from a number of aspects. Some broad patterns can be discerned, but the conclusions drawn can only be very tentative.

8.4.1 **Tutors' perceptions of their own role vis-à-vis the students.**

Interviews and observations revealed some differences which reflect the ambiguous position of teacher education in these countries, and can be related both to tutors' qualifications and to the ethos of the college. Malawian and Ghanaian tutors see their work as similar to high school teaching, and themselves as deliverers of a set curriculum. They regard their students in deficit terms, as empty vessels to be filled with the correct ideas and skills, even though in Malawi most students were in their late twenties and all had taught before. Many of their Basotho and Trinidadian counterparts by contrast feel themselves to be tertiary lecturers, have more control over what and how they teach, and expect more independent learning from their students, though this is not easily developed where the students' curriculum is

---

8 Teacher Educators in Colleges

overloaded, there is little time for personal study, and where students are used to 'transmission' teaching in high school.

One universal complaint from the tutors was the perceived low level of student academic standards. Yet the tutors had not developed pedagogic strategies for dealing with this, such as remedial classes, study skills, or training in independent learning. Lesotho's introductory upgrading semester partly addressed these issues, but the strategies were not continued into the main programme. A truly 'learner-centred' approach would suggest adapting the curriculum to student needs, both in terms of content and of process.

8.4.2 View of the good primary teacher.

The studies explored, in different ways, how tutors perceived good primary teachers, in the hope this would reveal something of their personal views of teacher education. Several themes around the 'ideal' teacher emerged; in many ways these were similar to the images held by entering trainees. (See Chap. 4).

There was a strong personalistic theme: the good primary teacher is committed and caring, plays a nurturing role, and in her exemplary behaviour acts as a role model. This came through particularly strongly in the Malawi and Lesotho case-studies. By contrast, in these countries not much stress was laid on how teachers can enhance pupil learning outcomes or teach for understanding. The teachers' personal characteristics and attitudes were foregrounded rather than their knowledge and cognitive skills.

In general, the teacher's role was seen as 'restricted'. This was particularly evident in Ghana and Malawi, where tutors described the good teacher as one who delivers the curriculum efficiently by using a variety of classroom skills and techniques, that can be listed, learnt and applied. In Lesotho the discourse was more child-centred, stressing that the good teacher responds to individual needs and adjusts her approach. Asked to rank characteristics of 'effective schools' it was noteworthy that the Basotho ranked 'children take responsibility for their own learning' much higher than either Malawian or Ghanaian tutors. Yet few Basotho tutors appeared to put this into practice in their own lecture halls (Ntoi and Lefoka 2002).

The Trinidad and Tobago tutors seemed to expect rather more initiative of their graduates: they should be able to plan classes to meet the specific needs of the pupils in their charge, present interesting and innovative lessons that are mainly student-centred, and which make adequate use of teaching resources, manage their classes well, and administer appropriate evaluation tasks. Though tutors hoped that individuals would keep trying to improve their own skills, there was little emphasis on training graduates to be agents of change in the local school context.

8 Teacher Educators in Colleges

8.4.3 How the college produces such teachers

In general, few tutors have well-developed or clearly articulated strategies for producing these 'good' teachers. In both Ghana and Malawi tutors seemed to have a relatively simple model of training in which both knowledge and skills are transmitted to students who will then be able to apply them routinely. In Malawi this went along the lines of: 'we tell the students what to do, let them practice it, and they should be able to do it'. Similarly, in Ghana tutors seemed to pursue an 'additive' strategy; they thought students would be adequately prepared if they gave them an adequate store of ways of teaching each topic (Akyeampong, Ampiah et al, 2000).

Basotho tutors' views varied more, with some tutors seeing learning to teach as a more complex task. Some key terms used were: 'we discuss, model ways of teaching; bring them to the level of the child; give them content and methods; teach them to behave as teachers.' But when asked directly how well the college achieved its aim, some seem unsure how far the reality matched the rhetoric, as one confessed:

> *I really do not know. I think they are well-prepared for their work. They have been given enough content, they have been given enough resources, they have been given enough practice under supervision, so they should be more or less good teachers. As I said, though, it also depends on their commitment.* [Experienced woman tutor]

Tutors in Trinidad and Tobago seemed much more aware of the contextual nature of good teaching, and stressed the need for students to find their own ways of dealing with the diverse conditions in the schools. Some were quite critical of the college programme, suggesting various changes such as more emphasis on practical training, an extra year, and assessment through performance rather than exams.

In general, tutors everywhere seem ambivalent about the role of the schools in the process of learning to teach. On the one hand, many said that teaching practice was an extremely valuable part of the programme. On the other, most tutors, both in survey responses and interviews, expressed mistrust towards the schools and did not value the teachers' contributions. Overall, there seemed little conception of integrating college and school training as a way of creating 'performance learning' (Calderhead and Shorrock 1997), in which knowledge and skills are integrated and used appropriately in the context of a real classroom. (See Chapter 6)

8.4.4 Views of Knowledge

Epistemological views held by the college tutors interviewed varied sharply between countries. The contrasts probably partly reflect the differences in level of academic

8 Teacher Educators in Colleges

qualifications, but also the different historical and cultural contexts. In Malawi most tutors held a rather closed view of knowledge as something 'out there', fixed and given, which was to be transmitted to students. Public propositional knowledge was given precedence while the student teachers' personal experiential knowledge was devalued. Most strikingly, tutors implied there is 'one right way to teach', which students must learn. In Ghana there was a similar view. Tutors supervising Teaching Practice hoped to find students doing exactly what they had been told or shown in college, rather than responding to the situations and needs found in the classrooms.

In Lesotho tutors held a relatively open view of knowledge, albeit not explicitly 'constructivist'. Although they taught propositional knowledge in the form of theory, and expected students to apply this, at least some also recognised the value of teachers' experiential and situated knowledge. In Trinidad and Tobago some tutors did indeed appear to be aware of the need for students to develop their own understanding of classrooms, and their own 'personal theories' of teaching. However, very little of this openness was apparent – in either country - in the college curriculum documents or in the classrooms observed. It may well be that individual tutors' own 'espoused theories' could not be implemented given the different orientation of the more general educational discourse, ethos and practice. This points to the need for a much deeper epistemological change at the system level.

8 4 5 Tutors' own pedagogy

Tutors everywhere are aware of the recommended shift to 'learner-centred' teaching, on which modern primary curricula are supposedly based. They pay lip-service to this, in that they teach their students about participatory and active learning methods. But very few of them appeared to be able to put these into practice in the college classrooms (see Chap. 5 above). Usually there was much more emphasis on teaching than on learning, with the result that most of the tutors observed were following a transmission style: lecturing interspersed with question-and-answer sessions at a low cognitive level, and the occasional discussion. Where group work was used it was seldom organised so as to enhance student learning. Only in Trinidad and Tobago were some – not all – lecturers able to model effectively the methods they recommended. This ability seemed related to their higher levels of education, to their professional confidence, and to a more supportive atmosphere in the colleges.

There was some evidence in Lesotho from the interviews that tutors working with smaller groups of in-service students did use much more learner-centred, interactive and constructivist approaches. It may be that the 'massification' of initial training programmes militates against what tutors know to be good practice.

Certainly tutors frequently find themselves in a dilemma. They feel they need to cover the syllabus and 'teach' – as they understand it – their subject content, including Education, and

8 Teacher Educators in Colleges

some are also aware that they should be modelling ways of teaching used in the primary school. However, the teacher education curriculum is overloaded, and assessment is mainly by terminal examinations which often drive the teaching and learning. In addition, the trainees expect to be taught by the transmission methods with which they are familiar, and they often resist more student-centred approaches. If new kinds of teacher training are to be developed, these factors have to be taken into account as well.

8.4.6 Overall approaches to Teacher Education

In terms of the framework outlined in Chapter 5, almost all the tutors we studied were working within some form of the 'technical rationality' paradigm, though this varied somewhat with the context. Training teachers is largely seen in terms of transmitting knowledge and skills which trainees will then apply. As one Malawian said: 'When one has enough content plus teaching strategies he can disseminate it.' Academic knowledge was strongly foregrounded in the Trinidad and Tobago curriculum, and in the new Lesotho programme. In Malawi the discourse often seemed derived from a 'behaviourist' approach to teaching, yet paradoxically even the skills element was often taught through tutors telling rather than through students practising and doing. Similar practices were observed in the Ghanaian colleges as well.

In Lesotho much of the discourse – though not the practice – was about 'child-centred pedagogy'. This seems an example of an 'applied theorist' approach, in that students were presented with the concepts as though this model of teaching could be used regardless of context, rather than being presented as a set of guiding principles or hypotheses to be tested, developed and modified in Lesotho classrooms.

There were few suggestions that learning to teach involved learning to solve problems, or to exercise informed judgement in unique, confused and difficult situations (Schon 1983). Reflecting on practice, learning from mistakes, developing one's own personal theory of teaching and repertoires through experimenting both individually and collectively, were seldom part of the discourse. Still less was any notion that teachers might help transform society through their work. There were, in all the countries, individuals who demonstrated a reflective attitude when talking about their practice, and clearly some of them tried to work with their students in inquiry-oriented ways. But because this was not shared by colleagues, and because the whole programme, in both structure and content, was geared toward the transmission of knowledge and skills, their efforts seemed not to reach beyond the limits of their own classroom.

What often seemed missing in these colleges was some shared vision and philosophy of good teacher education, together with ways of implementing it, which could be based on the local cultural context and responsive to local needs. As one Trinidadian tutor put it:

8 Teacher Educators in Colleges

We have a transmission mode of education and we are intent on transmitting certain stuff that is vague to us [and] to the students [...]A lot of the notions were not created in our culture... [and are] presented in a language that is not even ours, in a sense of how we think and how we interact, and all the examples and references.... Some of the terminology is so remote [gives example from Piaget] You have to swallow the terminology first. That's how we have been educated ... swallowing books. [Woman Education lecturer]

To change this, and to develop more appropriate models, a high degree of professionalism is required, together with a real sense of ownership of the programmes that are to be implemented. The 'books' must be created and written, rather than swallowed. It is difficult in the present situation to see where the impetus or the professional knowledge and skills for this might come from.

8.5 Concluding Discussion

8.5.1 The problem of selecting, recruiting and retaining appropriate staff.

As academic standards are raised, tutors need to be university graduates, and so increasingly they come up through secondary school teaching, but such people may have little understanding of, or sympathy for, primary classrooms. It is essential to select suitable primary teachers for professional upgrading so they can take on the role of tutor.

Beyond that, there need to be sufficient avenues of promotion and reward structures, with clear criteria, to attract and retain quality personnel. A key issue in all the countries studied concerned the pay and conditions of service for teacher educators. We found much goodwill and commitment among the tutors, and many individuals described their work as intrinsically rewarding, mentioning, for example, the intellectual challenge, their professional relationships with students, or the sense of doing a worthwhile job. However they often felt undermined by the lack of equivalent monetary rewards and status. This was strongly apparent in Trinidad and Tobago, where the college tutors were classified and compensated on a par with secondary teachers, although they were far better qualified, carried heavier workloads, and felt that they were doing a more difficult and responsible job.

8.5.2 Induction and professional development

It is obvious that all tutors should have a proper induction and orientation when they move from schools to colleges, followed by opportunities for academic upgrading. But in addition they need training in the fields of human development, such as adult learning, counselling and social psychology (Korthagen and Russell, 1995). The key problem is how to introduce new ideas that will both change the discourse and reshape the practice in ways that have an impact on the teachers' performance in schools. The research suggests several ways of doing

8 Teacher Educators in Colleges

this. Probably most useful are opportunities to see and hear about good practice in situations not too unlike one's own; thus well-focussed workshops and short courses (if necessary with external consultants), regional study tours, or part-time study with assignments related to one's own context, should be used where possible. Full-time award-bearing courses overseas may also have a part to play, especially as 'eye-openers' that can stimulate awareness of alternative ideas and practices.

8.5.3 Whole college development

As in all teacher development and INSET work, the new ideas and skills will only be put into practice if there is opportunity and support in the home environment. Just as teacher INSET is moving towards 'whole school development' approaches, so a strategy of 'whole college development' is needed. Such an approach would require a senior management team with a clear vision of change – and a brief from the authorities to carry it out – and groups of tutors prepared to commit themselves to professional improvement. This has implications for the ways in which the colleges are administered and managed, since such things as rigid timetables, heavy teaching loads, examinations system, and bureaucratic regulations constrain the ways in which professional teaching and learning can take place. College management is currently given little training or support for innovations, and the system of financing often adds yet more problems (see Chap. 9). Changes in structures, as well as in the mindset of those who work within them, are equally necessary.

8.5.4 New approaches to teacher education

There is a strong need for new and contextualised models of teacher preparation and development. The current variants of the 'technical rationality' model found in the colleges seem inadequate for preparing teachers to deal with the realities of primary and basic education classes in countries of the South. Developments in our understanding of professional knowledge and learning suggests more interactive and more flexible approaches would be more likely to produce teachers able to deal with the challenge of 21st century classrooms. However, these cannot be borrowed wholesale. One major task for teacher educators in low income countries is to adapt the new approaches to local realities and cultures. Textbook knowledge about teaching – often deriving from very different cultural origins - is often seen as sacrosanct, and local contexts become forced into ideal models of teaching. In effect these theories about learning to teach become the lenses through which teaching is viewed, rather than hypotheses to be tested out in local contexts (Akyeampong 2002).

Part of the way tutors think and act in colleges may be a legacy of the once strongly-promoted behaviourist views about learning and is often consonant with prevailing local cultural discourses about education (Tabulawa 1997). Yet there is another strand in the discourse, one that harks back to missionary days and stresses the personal and 'vocational' nature of teaching. When the tutors emphasise professional attitudes and ethics, when they describe primary teachers in terms of personal characteristics and interpersonal skills rather than knowledge, when they complain they cannot work with such large groups of students, they are implicitly critiquing the 'technical rationality' model that focuses on knowledge and skill rather than on personal development. It seems plausible that this tradition, if linked to a more open and constructivist view of knowledge, would be a good foundation for developing a more reflective and more professional view of teacher education.

The process of change is long and complex. This chapter has explored a few of the issues, focussing more on the people than the institutions, but both are equally important. Though some patterns have emerged, it is clear there can be no 'one size fits all solution', since teacher education institutions and their practices have developed out of their own unique experiences and contexts. Common themes seem to be the isolation of many colleges - both from the world of practice in the schools and the world of intellectual debates - the low status and rewards accorded to the tutors, and the lack of opportunity for professional development. Dealing with these problems should be starting points for any realistic policy.

8.5.5 **Key Issues for policy and practice**

- Teacher educators could be the fulcrum for raising standards among teachers and therefore in schools, but they have been neglected by policy makers. They should be recognised as an important sub-group with particular professional needs. Among these are:
    - Induction and orientation when they move from school to the college
    - A career structure that offers them appropriate status, promotion opportunities and monetary rewards
    - Accelerated academic development programmes for selected primary teachers to enable them to become trainers with equal status to their secondary-trained colleagues
    - Continuing professional development that includes academic upgrading in their specialised area, as well as training in the theory and practice of adult development
    - Opportunities to work closely with schools throughout their careers

- Many colleges have a long and respected history, but they now seem to have difficulty in keeping up with developments in other parts of the education system. Reform and renewal are urgently called for.

- The colleges themselves need to develop stronger leadership and more effective management, together with a clearer sense of their role and mission. Policies of 'whole college development' might be one strategy for change.

Chapter Nine   **9 Supply, Demand, Efficiency and Costs**

9.0   Summary and Overview

This chapter explores costs and the characteristics of supply and demand for new teachers that condition the policy environment for teacher education. The main research questions that shaped this part of the research were:

➢ What are the national levels of supply and demand for primary teachers?
➢ How are budgets and other resources for training institutions configured?
➢ What are the indicators of internal efficiency in the allocation or resources?
➢ What are the costs of training and how are they profiled?
➢ What is the future demand for initial training and are the costs sustainable?

9.0.1 **Summary of findings**

In summary the data suggest that:

• In Ghana, Lesotho, and Malawi the challenge posed by national targets for enrolment and pupil-teacher ratios is immense. None of these systems can produce enough new teachers to meet projected demand and EFA development targets without expanding output two to four times. The reasons differ – e.g. the need to increase GER to over 100% at primary (Ghana), the small output of the training system (Lesotho), high teacher attrition rates (Malawi). These and other factors interact in complex ways. In contrast Trinidad and Tobago has negative enrolment growth and a diminishing need for new teachers.

• All the countries use budgeting systems that are essentially historic and are not linked closely to enrolment or output. The proportion of the education budget linked to training varies from less than 2% (Trinidad and Tobago) to over 6% (Ghana). Few countries spend more than 6%. If increased output is to be achieved unit costs may have to fall. Few colleges work within medium term expenditure plans and flows of funds can be irregular and unpredictable.

• There is evidence that resources could be used much more efficiently. College enrolment is often limited more by lack of boarding facilities than by teaching space; staff-student ratios are often below 20:1, however working practices often indicate tutors organise teaching in large groups; college size is often small (below 500 enrolled) with diseconomies of scale, learning infrastructure (books, materials and equipment) is often lacking, depleting the quality of the learning experience; teaching practice is expensive but sometimes ritualised, and evidence on trainees' performance raises questions about the extent to which new skills are acquired from college-based work.

---

[39] This chapter is developed from Lewin 2002

9 Supply, Demand, Efficiency and Costs

- Initial training appears to cost between less than 3 times GNP per capita and more than 13 times GNP per capita – a very wide variation. Cost expressed in terms of a multiple of the recurrent cost of a primary school place vary from about 20:1 to 100:1. Large proportions of expenditure are allocated to boarding and to trainees' stipends. These cost levels mean that substantial expansion may not be sustainable within imaginable budgetary allocations.

- Though the detail is complex the simple conclusions are clear. If the national and international targets for universal enrolment and reasonable levels of pupil-teacher ratio are to be met, alternatives to full-time, pre-career training over two or three years may have to be considered. MIITEP gives an insight into one alternative. Though this approach can more closely produce an output of new teachers that matches demand, it reduces time in college, anticipates effective support whilst trainees are working in schools, and implies substantial development costs. Other options may have to be considered which lower unit costs, reduce time in full-time training, extend support into schools at low cost (more print materials to support teachers; better in-school mentoring, more district level assistance to new teachers).

The chapter is organised in three parts. First, some comparisons are made between the countries using financial data to locate subsequent discussion. Second, four country cases – Ghana, Lesotho, Malawi and Trinidad and Tobago, are discussed in terms of supply, costs, internal efficiency, and demand. Finally, some concluding remarks summarise key findings.

9.1 Context

There are a number of good reasons to be concerned about the costs of teacher education. These frame this chapter. Since the World Conference on Education for All in 1990, most low income countries have committed themselves to providing universal primary schooling (Colclough with Lewin 1993). This ambition was endorsed by the Dakar World Education Forum in 2000 and by the widespread adoption of international development targets which include this goal. As a result primary school enrolments have increased rapidly in many of the countries which had low participation rates, creating a rapid increase in demand for teachers. The Education for All process has emphasised that enrolment growth alone is not sufficient to meet development needs, and that concerns for quality and achievement must co-exist alongside enrolment targets. Thus, not only are more teachers needed, but also the new teachers should be effectively trained. This has placed new pressures on the financing of teacher education and its costs. Where the challenges that this has created are not met, the goals of EFA will be compromised by rising pupil-teacher ratios and increased numbers of untrained teachers.

9 Supply, Demand, Efficiency and Costs

An earlier paper outlined more specifically the reasons why the analysis of costs was important (Lewin 1999). First, teacher training can be surprisingly expensive. Pre-career full-time residential training can have costs per student averaging several times the costs of conventional higher education. This may arise as a result of many factors including the length of training, the small size of training institutions, low student teacher ratios, inefficient working practices, and historic budgeting largely unrelated to enrolments. If teacher training is comparatively expensive, and if demand for newly trained teachers is high as a result of enrolment expansion, simple expansion of existing modes of training may be unrealistic. Even if this is not true, high costs per student need justification since they limit the numbers that can be trained.

Second, in many low income countries there are concerns about the quality of new teachers as well as the need to qualify the untrained. Where criticisms are valid, and the content and pedagogy of training need to change to increase the probability of newly trained teachers possessing appropriate competencies, innovations need to be planned which are costed against sustainable budgets. It may be necessary to re-profile the organisation and modes of delivery of training to respond to the need for greater output and the changing characteristics of trainees.

Third, many training systems have their origins in colonial practice, which may or may not have been sensitive to the demands placed on the public budget of the costs of training. In many countries the training college sector developed initially with support from non-government organisations with mixed motives for their sponsorship. The structures that this created may or may not be appropriate to the changed conditions created by mass public education systems. What may once have been rational may no longer meet new needs and resource constraints.

Fourth, studies of the comparative costs and benefits of different methods of training teachers are not readily available in most low income countries. Decisions on modes of training are therefore often made on grounds that are largely independent of these kinds of considerations. It is not that cost and cost effectiveness data should or could be the main basis for policy. It is simply that without considered judgement of what is known of costs and benefits it is unlikely that the best use will be made of public investment. Comparison of costs, and the nature of supply and demand for teachers across countries, can draw attention to some of the main parameters that condition policy, and can suggest alternative ways forward that might not otherwise be considered.

Chapter 3 has outlined the main structural characteristics of the teacher education systems in Ghana, Lesotho, Malawi, and Trinidad and Tobago. This drew attention to the differences between the countries in size, population growth rates, enrolment ratios, and other parameters affecting the demand for new teachers (e.g. pupil-teacher ratios, proportions of

9 Supply, Demand, Efficiency and Costs

untrained teachers). It also noted the current levels of output of the teacher training systems. This descriptive data can be extended to give some indication of how financial resources are allocated and how much initial teacher education costs. Table 7 does this.

Table 7: **Profile of financing for Teacher Education**

	Ghana	Lesotho	Malawi	Trinidad and Tobago
% GDP on Education	3.8%	6%	5%	4.5%
% Public Expenditure on Education	35%	34%	30%	13%
% Education budget on Teacher Education	6%	2.5%	3%-6% (College costs – total costs)	1.8%
Recurrent Public Cost per Teacher Education Student per Year	US$700	US$2500	MIITEP system	US$5500
Recurrent Public Cost of a Trained Teacher	US$2100	US$7500	US$560	US$11100
Recurrent Public Cost per Trained Teacher as a multiple of GNP per capita	5.4 Full-time 3 years	13.1 Full-time 3.3 years	2.8 One fifth time over two years in College; fourth fifths in school	2.6 Full-time 2 years
Recurrent Public Cost per Trained Teacher as % of the Annual Cost of a Primary School Place	45:1	100:1	70:1	18:1

Lesotho and Malawi allocate the greatest amounts of GNP and over 30% of their national budgets to their education systems. Ghana also allocates a high proportion of public expenditure to education. Its college system absorbs 6% of the education budget. Total costs in Malawi are a similar proportion of the education budget. Lesotho allocates less, and Trinidad and Tobago the least (partly because teacher educators are paid secondary school teachers' salaries, unlike in the other countries). Cost per trained teacher as a multiple of GNP per capita are lowest in Trinidad and Tobago, and in Malawi where trainees are mostly working in schools. Ghana has higher relative costs. Those in Lesotho stand out as the highest. Malawi and Lesotho have the highest costs of training relative to the recurrent cost of a primary school child.

9.2   Four Contrasting Case Studies – Supply, Costs and Demand

The case studies presented below analyse the main dimensions of the costs and financing of teacher education designed to meet national objectives for universal primary schooling at

9 Supply, Demand, Efficiency and Costs

acceptable pupil-teacher ratios with a full complement of trained teachers. Each case-study considers questions of supply, costs and demand. Supply is constrained by the capacity of existing physical and professional infrastructure to accommodate and support trainees, and by the numbers of qualified applicants who can be recruited. Most costs arise from the recurrent salary expenditure necessary to support teacher educators and trainees, and from the non-salary recurrent costs of running teacher education institutions. The latter can be greater than the former. Costs determine the numbers of teachers that can be trained for a given proportion of the national education budget. The level of demand determines the numbers of teachers needed and is most strongly influenced by the growth in the school age cohort, ambitions to increase participation rates and reduce pupil-teacher ratios, and the rate of attrition amongst existing teachers. Ghana, Lesotho, and Trinidad and Tobago all have full-time residential training. Malawi organises mixed mode training during which the trainees spend the majority of their time in schools.

9.3   Case-study 1: Ghana

9.3.1 Supply

In Ghana teachers for the basic education cycle are trained through a three-year post-secondary full-time programme which is offered in the 38 teacher training colleges (TTCs). With the exception of the TTC in Accra, all others are residential. All colleges currently prepare teachers for both primary and Junior Secondary (JSS) levels. The 38 TTCs are dispersed among all ten of Ghana's administrative regions and vary in size in terms of trainee enrolment. In 1996, the smallest was Mampong Technical TTC with 241 trainees; the largest Foso with 914. Average enrolment in 1996/97 was 510 per college. The most recent data (1998) indicates there are 1,044 tutors giving an average trainee tutor ratio in 1998 of about 19.5:1, which can be compared with a target figure of 15:1.

The number of new trainees admitted each year is loosely based on a quota allocated by the MOE that does not appear to be linked to an overall analysis of teacher demand. Total TTC output of trained teachers has been between 5,500 and 6,200 since 1995. Female enrolment as a percentage of total enrolment has increased from 33% to 38%. Total enrolment in 1998 reached 20,400 suggesting that the system has a maximum capacity using the current the current mode of training of no more than about 7,000 a year. Minimum entrance qualifications for entry are currently set at Senior Secondary School Certificate level. There is no constraint on applicants arising from a shortage of those with this level of qualification in the labour market. College places are over subscribed and more students could be admitted if places were available.

9 Supply, Demand, Efficiency and Costs

9.3.2 Costs

Ghana allocated about 35% of recurrent expenditure to education in 1998 and nearly 4% of GNP. Basic education (primary and junior secondary schools (JSS) accounts for between 60% and 70% of the recurrent budget. Within this amount about 35% is spent on primary, 20% on JSS and the remainder on pre-schools. Expenditure on senior secondary (SSS) has been rising and now accounts for about 15% of the total despite falling enrolments – the same as tertiary level expenditure. Teacher education has seen its share rise substantially from under 3% to about 6% and this is projected to reach 6.7% in 1999. The evolution of recurrent expenditure by sector is shown in Figure 10.

Figure 10: **The evolution of recurrent expenditure in Ghana**

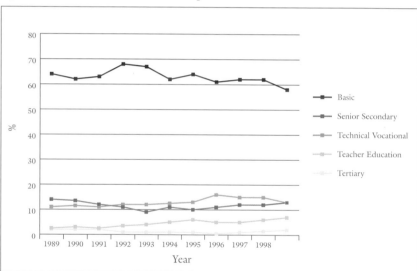

The ratio of annual unit costs at primary to JSS, SSS, teacher education, and university in 1998 were 1:1.6, 1:4, 1:15 and 1:20 respectively. Data from 12 colleges (Akyeampong, Furlong, and Lewin, 2001) indicate that average college costs per trainee per year in 1998 were the equivalent of about US$680 per student. There is a variation from about US$550 to as much as US$ 1,000, which is not related simply to college size. The average cost per trained teacher is about 5.4 times GNP per capita.

The structure of college expenditure is such that that most of the costs lie in expenditure on trainees' stipends. These are comparable with untrained primary teachers' salaries. Data from a fairly typical college in 2000 showed that it had 320 students, 30 teaching staff, and a total of 48 non-teaching staff. 77% of salary expenditure was on trainees' stipends, 13% on teaching staff, and most of the remainder on support and ancillary staff. This confirms the picture from other MUSTER data where typically about 75% of direct costs are in student

9 Supply, Demand, Efficiency and Costs

stipends, 20% in college salaries split between teaching and non-teaching staff about 60/40, and about 5% in non-salary expenses. College running costs are concealed in this budgetary allocation system. Trainees do not receive the entire value of the stipends since a proportion is held back and used by the colleges for operating costs. Our estimates indicate that about 40% is deducted from payments to trainees and allocated to purchases of food, equipment, learning materials etc.

The scope for cost saving is limited by the main parameters identified above. Increasing the college student-staff ratio would reduce costs per student. However, ratios above 20:1 might be thought to be unsuited to conventional curriculum delivery. The only large element of costs that might be reduced relates to students' stipends. Judgements would have to be made whether that proportion which is withheld is efficiently allocated, and whether the proportion of the stipend paid directly to students for living expenses is appropriate. As currently structured, most costs are variable and rise directly with the numbers of students. Increasing average college size from current levels, which are small by international standards, would not result in large savings since it is only perhaps 10% of the costs that could be regarded as fixed within different ranges of enrolment. Currently there appears little incentive in the budgetary system at college level to increase the efficiency with which resources are used.

9.3.3 Internal Efficiency

In Ghana the college teaching year is not as it seems in the sense that the actual number of weeks of teaching delivered in the colleges is well below the theoretical maximum. Although 33 weeks are available a year for teaching, the real number of teaching weeks is much less. Our estimates (Akyeampong, Furlong & Lewin, 2000) suggest that normal teaching takes place for about 24 weeks in the first year, and 13 weeks in the second and third years (excluding a nominal 4 weeks of teaching practice a year). As much as one-third of teaching time is used for other activities, notably very substantial amounts of time allocated to assessment. Fully 9 weeks out of 33 are being used in years 2 and 3 for examination preparation and sitting. This does appear excessive. Increasing active learning time could improve the quality of learning and might lower failure rates. Failure rates of 20%, an average across the colleges, increase unit costs per trained teacher by a similar amount and represent wastage, especially if failure is not retrieved by successful re-sitting.

The way in which teaching is organised has important implications for curriculum delivery and costs. In the training colleges almost all the teaching is organised in a classroom and scheduled according to subject-specific contact hours with tutors. This means that often a tutor's teaching load is viewed strictly in terms of the fixed contact time with students. A common complaint from tutors is that their teaching load is already excessive and that this makes it unrealistic to provide richer quality learning experiences to smaller teaching groups.

9 Supply, Demand, Efficiency and Costs

Ghana Ministry of Education policy stipulates that staff-student ratio should be 1:15 and
tutors should teach between 32 – 36 periods a week (a period = 40 minutes). Teaching loads
expressed in student-periods (number of students x number of periods per week) should be
between 480 and 540 per week. MUSTER has analysed tutors' teaching loads in two
colleges, to ascertain whether the much referred to impact of teaching load on instructional
practice reflects lack of management efficiency or is an organisational problem. College A
has a staff-student ratio of 1:15, whilst College B has a higher staff-student ratio of 1:21.

The average teaching load in student-periods for College A is 458. The estimated contact
time with students is about 11 hours, and the average number of periods taught per week is
17 (ranging from 3 –18). Thus tutors have teaching loads in terms of student-periods which
approach the norms, but their contact hours are much less than the 32 to 36 stipulated. This
is the result of organising teaching with group sizes which average 40. Our data illustrate a
wide range of teaching loads across the tutors which arises from their specialisations, the
elective choices that students make, and choices made about teaching group size.
Inefficiencies arise from uneven work-loads across staff with different specialisations,
whereby some are relatively heavily loaded and others have fewer periods with small groups.
In College B none of the tutors satisfies the MOE minimum teaching load of 32 periods a
week. The average teaching load in student periods a week is 614 which is considerably
higher than College A reflecting the higher staff-student ratio. The overall result is that
tutors teach on average 12 hours a week, the same as in College A, and have larger average
group sizes of about 52 trainees.

Recruitment of staff is done exclusively by the Principal of a College whose only guiding rule
is to keep within the officially recommended staff-student ratio of 1:15. It is clear that the
guideline is also sometimes ignored and that this process can lead to situations where some
departments are understaffed and overburdened whilst others are overstaffed and under-
utilised. Thus, although College A has the full complement of staff (using the 1:15 ratio),
the social studies department has only two tutors teaching a total of 70 periods a week,
whereas the science department has five tutors teaching a total of 48 periods a week. The
Physical Education department has three tutors sharing a total of 27 periods a week. It
would appear from the analysis of teaching load in the two colleges that the problems
emanate from both organisational structure and curriculum demand.

The data we have do indicate that there may be some scope for more efficient utilisation of
staff. Average class contact times of 12 hours per week (2 hours per day) do not seem
excessive, especially when coupled with the large amounts of time allocated to assessment
tasks. Group sizes could be smaller with larger numbers of contact hours, if it was thought
this would improve the quality of learning, and if assessment practices were changed. More
fundamentally the problem of efficient utilisation of staff revolves around the relatively small
size of Colleges, the number of subjects in the curriculum and the willingness and ability of

9 Supply, Demand, Efficiency and Costs

tutors to teach two or more subject areas. A review of policy in these areas might produce opportunities to expand enrolment and maintain student contact and deepen learning experience with modest increases in staff-student contact time. Currently Colleges do not appear to have an obvious incentive to manage staff time more efficiently. Teaching group sizes are not monitored and more rather than less effective deployment brings no clear benefits to the College.

9.3.4 Demand

In Ghana total primary school enrolment in 1998 was 2.29 million, and 1.31 million at junior secondary (JSS). Enrolment rates across the primary cycle averaged about 73% in 1998, having fallen from nearly 80% in the early 1990s. At JSS level, enrolment rates were stable through the 1990s at around 58%. Over the period from 1988 to 1998 the school age population of 6-14 year olds grew by nearly 4% per annum, suggesting the total number of teachers needed was doubling about every 18 years.

The total number of teachers at primary level has fallen over the last ten years, while enrolments have grown by 37%. As a result the average pupil-teacher ratio has increased from 26:1 to 36:1. Interestingly the pupil to qualified teacher ratio has remained fairly constant at about 45:1. At JSS level the number of teachers has increased by 16% and the number of students by 24% Overall pupil-teacher ratios have increased marginally to 20:1 and the pupil per qualified teacher ratio has fallen to 23:1. 12,700 primary teachers and 5,100 JSS teachers are untrained.

Teacher attrition rates are difficult to estimate. Over the period 1988 to 1998, Mereku (2000) estimates that the rate of increase in the number of trained teachers employed was a little below 4% and the rate at which newly trained teachers were being posted was averaging about 9% of the number of trained teachers employed. The difference (9%-4% = 5%) gives an estimate of the underlying rate of trained teacher attrition from all causes.

It is now possible to estimate future demand for teacher training over a ten-year period. Table 8 shows the results using a number of basic assumptions[40]. The number of new teachers that need to be trained each year is indicated in row 10 for 2000, 2005 and 2010. The additional numbers that would be needed to achieve a GER of 100% are indicated in row 12. Lastly, the numbers of untrained teachers requiring training are indicated in row 13. Similar projections have been done for JSS and are reported in detail in Akyeampong, Furlong and Lewin (2000).

---

[40] First the rate of growth of the age cohort at primary is maintained at its historic level of 4%. Second, the pupil teacher ratio remains at 36:1 and teacher attrition is 5% annually. Third, the gross enrolment rate remains constant at 72% in primary.

9 Supply, Demand, Efficiency and Costs

Table 8: **Future demand for teachers at primary level**

	Year	1998	2000	2005	2010
1	Age group 6 years	582223	629732	766166	932158
2	Primary population 6-11 years	3155758	3413268	4152762	5052470
3	Primary Enrolment	2288768	2475531	3011863	3664391
4	Qualified Teachers	50964			
5	Unqualified Teachers	12725			
6	No. teachers needed at PTR of 36:1	63577	68765	83663	101789
7	No. of teachers in post	63689			
8	New Teachers needed as a result of population growth	2543	2751	3347	4072
9	Teacher attrition at 5%	3179	3438	4183	5089
10	Total annual demand for teachers at constant GER 72%	5722	6189	7530	9161
11	Total number of teachers needed for GER100%	87660	94813	115355	140346
12	Additional numbers needed GER 72% to GER100%	24083	26048	31692	38558
13	No. unqualified needing training	12725			

The results of the projections for primary and JSS show that:

1. If the PTRs and GER remain constant, annual demand for new teachers rises from 5,700 to 9,200 at primary and 3,400 to 5,400 at JSS. This is a total annual demand of 9,100 rising to 14,600, over the period from 1998 to 2010.

2. If all untrained teachers were to be trained over a five-year period then annual demand for training, but not new teachers, would increase by about 2,500 at primary level and 1,000 at JSS[41] or 3,500 a year over the first five years.

3. Total annual demand for new primary and JSS teachers rises from about 12,600 a year at the beginning of the projection period to 15,500 in 2005 (the last year of training of the untrained), and to 14,600 by 2010 (after all untrained teachers have been trained). This can be compared to the current total output of about 6,000 per year from the 38 training colleges.

---

[41] This would also temporarily increase the demand for new teachers assuming that replacement cover was organised for those in training.

9 Supply, Demand, Efficiency and Costs

These estimates of demand may be too small.

i). Attrition rates may be rising[42]. If teacher attrition rates were to increase to 10% the number of new teachers needed each year at constant GER and PTR would increase from about 7,100 to 11,700 at primary, and from 4,500 to 7,000 at JSS by 2005.

ii). Drop out rates appear to have been falling from an average of about 8%. If average drop out fell by 1% per year at least 1,000 new teachers a year would be needed.

iii) If Free Compulsory Universal Basic Education (FCUBE) is to achieve its objectives and a conservative target is chosen demand will increase further. The total additional number needed rises from about 24,000 to 39,000 at primary, and from 28,000 to 44,000 at JSS over the period from 1998 to 2010. This implies a total annual demand of as much as 22,000 to 29,000 teachers for both levels depending on the attrition rate chosen.

In summary, the demand for new teachers, and training to reduce the backlog of untrained teachers is more than double the current output from the Colleges of Education. If attrition rates rise to 10% it will rise towards three times current output if PTRs are not to rise. Achieving GER 100% would increase demand to more than four times current output.

9.3.5 Reflection

A policy decision has been made to adopt an 'In-In-Out' model of initial training to replace the current three year full-time 'In' programme. This would reduce the period in college to two full-time years followed by a year of supported teaching practice in schools leading to a final examination and certification. If an 'In-In-Out' system were adopted the consequences might be as follows.

First, output of the colleges would increase by 50% assuming college plant were utilised at the same level of intensity. New trainees could be admitted during the 'out' year Thus each training cohort across the college system would increase from about 6,000 to about 9,000. After three years annual output would rise from 6,000 to 9,000.

Second, assuming no additional teaching staff were recruited to the colleges, college costs per trained student would fall. The reduction would depend on whether staff could cover whatever additional workload was generated by students during the 'out' year.

---

[42] The main reasons for this are that increasing numbers of primary teachers are enrolling on upgrading programmes which often result in them moving on to secondary school teaching or other careers, and that HIV/AIDS may increase teacher attrition.

9 Supply, Demand, Efficiency and Costs

Third, no additional non-teaching staff would be needed unless infrastructure was required to support trainees at a distance.

Fourth, if the frequency of school visiting was increased and more material support needed to be produced (self-instruction manuals etc), costs would rise.

Fifth, about 40% of students' stipends are withheld for college running expenses. Presumably student teachers would receive the whole subsidy if they were working in schools, not the 60% currently paid directly to students.

A simple comparison can be made between conventional three-year training and 'In-In-Out'. Table 9 does this[44]. The result is that the overall cost of a trained teacher falls from US$2,100 to US$1,969 – a reduction of about 6%. The output from 'In-In-Out' would be 9,000 per year, not 6,000 after three years. The total costs of initial training would therefore rise to reflect an increase in overall output[45]. There would be an additional benefit over the three year 'In' system if trainees took sole responsibility for classes during their 'Out' year thus reducing the total number of teachers needed for a given pupil-teacher ratio. This may or may not be permissible.

Table 9: **Comparisons of costs between conventional and 'In-In-Out' (US$)**

	Teaching Staff Salaries	Non-teaching Salaries	Stipends	Non-salary	Overall Unit Cost
First Year College Cost	84	56	525	35	700
Second Year College Cost	84	56	525	35	700
Third Year College Cost	84	56	525	35	700
Total Cost	252	168	1575	105	2100
'In-In-Out'					
First Year College Cost	84	56	525	35	700
Second Year College Cost	84	56	525	35	700
Third Year College Cost	21	6	525	18	569
Total Cost	189	118	1575	88	1969

This case-study leads to a number of conclusions.

First, the teacher education system needs to increase its output substantially if PTRs are not to increase and the proportion of untrained teachers is to be reduced.

[44] The assumptions are that overall unit cost are about US$ 700 per year, in college costs do not vary, and third year support is provided which is costed at 25% of teaching staff salaries, 10% of non teaching staff salaries, and 50% of non-salary costs. Student stipends remain unchanged.
[45] The increase in output is 50% (6000 to 9000); total costs would increase by slightly less since the cost per trained teacher would fall a little. Overall total costs would increase by perhaps 44%.

DFID

9 Supply, Demand, Efficiency and Costs

Second, the magnitude of increases needed is substantial. Between two and three times current output is needed to maintain the existing GERs, and cover demand generated by population growth, attrition and reduced drop out.

Third, achieving GER 100% by 2010 would require an increase in output of three to four times current levels.

Fourth, these levels of demand could not easily be met by expansion of the current system. It is not feasible to assume that the 6% of the education budget allocated to teacher education could be increased to the levels necessary. Nor is it plausible that increased internal efficiency could result in gains in output of these magnitudes, though it remains desirable to pursue the opportunities to improve internal efficiency.

If progress towards EFA goals is to be achieved more radical alternatives may need to be considered that can train greater numbers of teachers at sustainable levels of cost.

9.4   Case-study 2: Lesotho

9.4.1 Supply

The National Teacher Training college was established 1974. The college is the only provider of initial training for primary school teachers in Lesotho. It also trains junior secondary school teachers and secondary school teachers of technical subjects. The college is currently consolidating the three programmes at primary level into a single Diploma of Education, Primary (DEP) course. This is of three years' duration.

In 1999 the NTTC had a total enrolment of about 900 students, of whom nearly half were part-time, giving a full-time equivalent of perhaps 650 including secondary level trainees. There were 106 academic staff working on pre-service and in-service programmes. About 70% of the NTTC staff are female and almost all are graduates. The age distribution of staff indicates that 40% are between 40 and 50, and 29% are over 50 years old. However, fully 50% have less than 5 years service and only 29% have over 10 years. Overall there are 43 teaching staff members in the primary division. The primary staff-student ratio is 14:1.

The fifth Five-Year Plan projected a yearly output of 250 primary teacher graduates for NTTC. However, lack of adequate hostel facilities at the NTTC and other constraints proved to be an impediment in the realisation of this target. The output of newly qualified primary teachers between 1993 and 1997 varied from about 85 to 185. The new DEP programme had a first year enrolment of 100 in 1999. The recruitment for the DEP in 2000 should exceed 150. The intention is to increase the NTTC's capacity from 650 full-time students to 1,100. This would give a total output (including secondary) of just over 350 per

9 Supply, Demand, Efficiency and Costs

year for the three-year courses (primary and secondary). This target has not been met. Many applicants apparently do not have the minimum of four credits and two passes needed at Cambridge Overseas School Certificate level (COSC) and this is one of the reasons for under-recruitment.

About 2,000 students qualify at COSC each year, suggesting that at current levels of recruitment the supply side constraint is a result of small proportions opting for primary school teaching. If enrolment in teacher education were raised to the levels suggested by projections of demand (see below) the picture would change. This would mean up to half of all COSC graduates would need to opt for primary teacher training – an unrealistic expectation.

9.4.2 Costs

The Ministry of Education's share of government recurrent expenditure reached 34% in 1998 and represented about 6% of GNP. The share for primary education has been declining and was 41% in 1998. Allocations have favoured the university level, whilst secondary support has remained fairly constant. Budget allocations to different levels in the past five years are shown in Figure 11. The budget for NTTC in 1997 was between 2% and 3% of the total education budget (not shown). The ratio of annual unit costs at primary to secondary, teacher education and university were about 1:2.9, 1: 20[46] and 1:112 respectively.

Figure 11: **Evolution of recurrent expenditure in Lesotho**

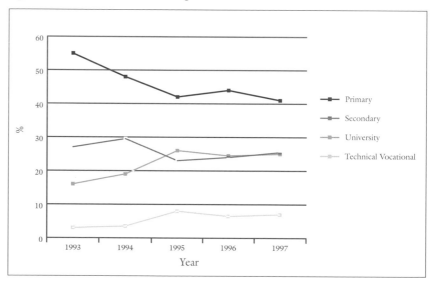

9 Supply, Demand, Efficiency and Costs

The trends in sub-sectoral allocations and unit costs are a cause of concern. They are counter to the intentions of the Five Year Plan to invest more at the first level. They carry implications for the financial support available for the development of teacher education. Budget estimates for 1999/2000 suggest that allocations to primary are planned to rise to 48% of the total, and secondary to 28%, with a consequent fall in tertiary level allocations. NTTC may or may not benefit.

Using 1998 enrolments and costs it is possible to estimate the budgeted cost per student. Across NTTC this amounts to about 10,400 Maloti excluding trainee fees, equivalent to about US$1,500. Some students at the NTTC receive allowances for dependants which gives them a full salary for six months and half salary thereafter. For those who qualify the cost of this is likely to be between M7,500 and M10,000. There are also costs arising from the fact that trainees are in full-time training, and not teaching.

Four further points need noting. First, these are costs per year. The full-time course last for three years and thus the cost per trained teacher graduate assuming no failure is three times greater i.e. about US$4,500, excluding stipends.

Second these unit costs are an average across all programmes at NTTC. The secondary training programmes have smaller enrolments and teaching group sizes. They are therefore more expensive. Primary training is probably about 10% less expensive than the average.

Third, only about one-third of these costs are attributable to lecturers' salaries and the remainder to other costs associated with the operation of NTTC, notably hostel expenses and travel and subsistence.

Fourth, these costs do not include trainees' allowances. We estimate that including these would raise costs to about US$2,500 per year, or US$7,500 per trained teacher. This is as much as 13 times GNP per capita.

It is clear that in principle the costs of a trained teacher could be reduced (or conversely more teachers could be trained for the same cost) if the length of training was reduced, or if the cost of college teaching was diminished. The latter might be achieved by making more use of mixed-mode and distance delivery of some parts of the training programme. It is also clear that some economies of scale should be available in NTTC if it increased its enrolment up to its planned capacity of 1,100 full-time equivalent trainees from its current level of no more than about 750 FTEs.

9 Supply, Demand, Efficiency and Costs

9.4.3 Internal Efficiency

There are 43 teaching staff members in the primary division at NTTC. Each member of the teaching staff teaches on one or two of the primary programmes They usually take responsibility for one or two groups in a programme. Sometimes they cover all the groups depending on the numbers. The overall staff-student ratio at NTTC is 1:14 for the primary division. This should allow the convening of staff in ways that enables a rich curriculum to be delivered to groups of students that are not excessively large. However, the teaching and groups sizes are unevenly distributed over the different programmes and this gives rise to some problems. Staff members who are teaching the diploma groups are handling smaller numbers than those who are teaching the PTC groups and this causes an imbalance in the loads in terms of student-hours. There are also differences between subjects.

An analysis of the number of student-teaching hours delivered was undertaken by MUSTER. In addition to these loads teaching practice preparation and supervision can take five hours a week. Different arrangements are made in different departments to sub-divide year groups. Thus, for example, for PTC year 2 there were 187 students. These needed to receive 3 hours of science per week. The group was taught for one hour as a whole group (187), and then subdivided into three groups of about 62 for two-hour sessions. The total contact time for the students is therefore three hours; the staff member teaches for seven hours. Similar arrangements exist for other groups. The length of periods varies according to department.

The NTTC follows normal government practice and working hours are from 8.00 am to 4.30 pm with a one-hour lunch break. The number of working hours available is therefore 7.5 hours a day or 37.5 hours a week. The data indicates that on average staff have 7.6 contact hours with student groups each week, or about one and a half hours per day. The range is between 2 and 15 hours per week. In addition to this they must prepare and mark work. The overall load in student-hours (the sum of the number of students in each group times the number of hours they are taught) shows that the average load is 780 student-hours per week. This is equivalent to 7.8 hours teaching with a group of 100. The range is very wide and varies between 98 and 2,600 per week.

Teaching group sizes vary widely from 190 to less than 10. There are reasons why some groups are very small. A few students are repeating the first year of the PTC which has no new intake. Some are taking options which attract few students. Large lectures are used for whole year group teaching. When these groups are sub-divided for follow-up sessions group sizes still remain large and are often over 60. This pattern of teaching must constrain opportunities to develop approaches that engage students directly in small group interaction and varied methods of training which cannot be managed with large groups. If more contact hours were taught each week group sizes could be reduced.

9 Supply, Demand, Efficiency and Costs

The first semester of the 1999 academic year was 12 weeks long. At the beginning of each semester students are given two days to register, after which classes begin. The 12 weeks making up the first semester include one week for revision and two weeks of examinations. The actual teaching time is therefore about nine and a half weeks with occasional interruptions due to national holidays.

Students are time-tabled for between 25 and 33 hours a week depending on the course. This allows a limited amount of time for self-study and forms of peer learning. The result of this is that, for example, each group in year two of the PTC has 26 hours of contact time plus 5 hours of teaching practice preparation each week for 9 weeks. Each group has 6.5 hours of free time per week based on the 7.5 hours government/civil service working hours per day. This means that these students are on task 31 hours per week out of the 37.5 government working hours/ time.

An attempt was made to assess the utilisation of space in NTTC. On average teaching space appears to be in use for about 25 hours a week. It should be noted that this analysis is based on periods when the NTTC is in session and students are being taught. Out of session (i.e. about 20 weeks a year) these teaching rooms will not be occupied by normal course students.

In conclusion this analysis of internal efficiency draws attention to the profile of teaching loads (averaging 7.6 hours contact per week at primary); the level of student hour teaching loads (which on average are equivalent to 7.8 hours a week with 100 students); the wide variation in loads between staff members; and the rate of space utilisation (relatively high during semester time). The overall NTTC student teacher ratio is about 14:1 at primary. There are 43 staff allocated to the primary section who will graduate about 190 students in 1999. This translates into an output of a little more than four trained teachers per full-time person year of staff time. A similar analysis for secondary suggests that about 40 staff will graduate a little less than 100 secondary teachers giving a secondary output of about 2.5 trained teachers per staff member per year.

The questions that remain are therefore whether teaching could be organised more efficiently to provide for greater output with similar numbers of staff. Is it possible to timetable courses such that very large group sizes are minimised to allow for more varied training methods which include more inter active work in smaller groups? Can teaching loads be more evenly distributed and should contact hours be revised? To what extent can space be utilised during periods when the NTTC is not in session[47]?

---

[47] This is already the case but no data was available on the extent of utilisation.

9 Supply, Demand, Efficiency and Costs

9.4.4 Demand

Gross enrolment rates at primary are over 100% and about 30% at secondary. There are about 368,000 primary school pupils and 8,100 primary school teachers in post of whom about 1,820 were unqualified. Over 57% of primary teachers are concentrated in the age range 30-50 with only 18% under 30 years old, of which 63% are unqualified. The average age of qualified primary teachers is 44 years and of unqualified teaches 32 years[48]. This draws attention to the high average age of teachers and the age profile of the cadre, which suggests that many are approaching retirement age. Fully 16% are beyond or within five years of retirement age, and a further 9% are within 10 years. 10% of qualified teachers are over 55 years old and will retire soon. 12% of secondary teachers have more than 20 years service. Over 16% are still expatriates, especially in the science area. The supply of newly qualified teachers has been insufficient to reduce the proportion who are untrained.

The number of new primary teachers needed can be estimated with reference to data on the size of the age cohort, the desired pupil-teacher ratio, and the number of unqualified teachers who need to be replaced. Enrolments in primary schools have been declining. From a peak in 1995 of 378,000 they contracted to 368,000 in 1997, the last year for which data is available. This represents a decline of about 1.5% per year. The difficulty is that without knowing the reasons for this decline it is not easy to determine whether or not it will continue. Some analyses seem to suggest that the decline could be arising from permanent or temporary migration of parents and pupils, and reductions in the size of the age cohort as a result of a decline in the birth rate[49].

Table 10 shows the result of projecting teacher demand. This shows that to achieve a pupil-teacher ratio of 40:1 with current enrolments would require 9,225 teachers[50]. This is 1,136 more than the number in post. In addition it would be necessary to replace those who retire, die in service or decide to follow other careers. If the teacher attrition rate is 5%[51] then an additional 461 teachers will be needed; if it is 10% then the number is 923. Thus the total current demand for new teachers would seem to lie between about 1,600 and 2,060, with a subsequent demand of 600 to 1,000 per year. If all unqualified teachers are to be replaced by qualified teachers then it will be necessary to train an additional 1,817 teacher who are already in service in schools over the five year period at, say, 350 per year.

---

[48] Assuming the average age of those over 60 is 63

[49] There is evidence that birth rate and therefore the size of the age cohort is declining. This may be because the propensity to have children has declined and /or because of the effects of high rates of HIV/AIDS in the population. The population projections from the 1996 census have three variants all of which project shrinkage in the cohort. On the other hand migration may be diminishing as a result of changes in the South African economy.

[50] 40:1 has been chosen as the target used in the most recent World Bank simulations (World Bank 1999 Annex 4, Scenario 1).

[51] The World Bank uses 5% attrition. This appears not to factor in the effects of rising levels of HIV/AIDS. It is also lower than previous plan estimates. 10% may be more realistic.

9 Supply, Demand, Efficiency and Costs

Table 10: **Primary teacher projections over 5 years**[52]

		Baseline	Year 2	Year 3	Year 4	Year 5
1	Age group 6-12 years	392800	398500	403100	406600	408700
2	Primary Enrolment	369000	374355	378676	381964	383937
3	Qualified Teachers	6272				
4	Unqualified Teachers	1817				
5	No. needed at pupil-teacher ratio of 1:40	9225	9359	9467	9549	9598
6	No. in post	8089				
7	New Teachers needed as a result of growth and achieving 1:40	1136	134	108	82	49
8	Retirement etc. at 5%	461	468	473	477	480
9	New Teachers needed	1597	602	602	581	560
10	Retirement etc at 10%	923	936	947	955	960
11	New Teachers needed	2059	1070	1055	1037	1009
12	No. unqualified needing training	1817				

9.4.5 Reflection

Our detailed analysis (Lewin, Ntoi et al 2000) suggests that the projections we have made are reasonable. In the medium term the major factors which will influence them upwards (introduction of free education, increased teacher attrition, changes in pensions etc.) seem to outweigh those that could reduce enrolments (significant reductions in repetition, shrinkage of the age group). They may therefore be regarded as minima. It seems unlikely that total demand to sustain the target pupil-teacher ratio will be less than about 800 per year and might exceed 1,200 if enrolments do grow faster than projected[53]. These figures are up ten times larger than current output of new primary teachers and up to five times projected enrolment on the DEP of 250 entrants each year. Unless more teachers are trained pupil-teacher ratios will rise.

It should be noted that the immediate consequence of introducing FPE has caused a dramatic increase in enrolments in grade 1. These increased from 72,000 in 1999 to 111,000 in 2000, implying a need for about 800 more teachers at a pupil-teacher ratio of 50:1. It is reasonable to assume that this is a one-off effect and that new entrants will fall in 2001 to reflect the size of the age cohort.

---

[52] Using baseline data available in 1999.
[53] Even if the higher target of a pupil teacher ratio of 45:1 were adopted, rather than 40:1, this would only make a difference to these estimates of about 200 fewer teachers per year.

9 Supply, Demand, Efficiency and Costs

Policy on teacher recruitment needs to recognise that the limits imposed by the numbers of qualified candidates graduating from secondary schools who are likely to choose teaching as a career. Expanded enrolment may not be possible without an increase in supply of secondary leavers willing and able to enter primary teacher training. It may also need to reconsider admission criteria relating to competence to teach using English as a medium of instruction, since this is a major factor in excluding significant numbers of applicants.

We can note that other analyses (Lewin, Ntoi et al 2000) demonstrate that the demand for new secondary teachers is only likely to grow slowly under current projections and is about 250-425 a year depending on assumptions. Somewhat paradoxically, more secondary teachers are in training than primary, when university enrolments are included in the equation. This suggests at the very least that NTTC might specialise in primary training and thereby fully utilise capacity to train at this level. However, this would still not be sufficient to meet projected demand.

At current costs producing 1,200 new teachers a year in the existing system would require a total enrolment of 3,600 at a cost of about 8% of MOE total expenditure, without including the cost of secondary training, or of qualifying the unqualified. This is unlikely to be achievable without varying the mode of delivery to a lower cost model.

9.5 Case-study 3: Malawi

9.5.1 Supply

The current system of training was introduced to meet the needs for teachers created by the introduction of free primary education in 1994. 18,000 of the 22,000 new teachers recruited were untrained, representing about 42% of the teaching force. The arrangements that were put in place were initially ad hoc. Eventually the Malawi In-service Integrated Teacher Education Programme (MIITEP) was designed with the express aim of training the 18,000 untrained teachers between 1997 and 2000. All other forms of primary teacher training were then suspended. The MIITEP training system and aspects of its current status are described in detail in a number of documents (e.g. Bude et al 1995, DSE 1998, Kunje & Lewin 2000). The profile of planned activity is shown in Table 11 (though this would seem more hypothetical than realisable, (Kunje 2002)).

9 Supply, Demand, Efficiency and Costs

Table 11: **MIITEP programme outline**

Activity	Duration	Notes
Residential block at COE	11 weeks = 390 hours tuition	
Self-study modules	4 terms = 220 hours	Assignments and projects supported by learning materials
Supervised teaching practice	5 terms = 110 hours of supervised practice (concurrent with self-study)	Supervised by school staff
In service training and self-study	12 one day zonal workshops – 60 hours 12 assignments – 36 hours 4 projects – 54 hours (Concurrent with teaching practice)	At Teacher Development Centres and in schools
Residential block and examination	6 weeks	At Colleges of Education

The first term of MIITEP is residential in one of the colleges of education. For the next five terms trainees teach under the supervision of school and zonal level staff and complete assignments and projects. At the end of this period they sit a qualifying exam during a six-week residential period at the colleges. Insights into the initial operation of the programme to orientate untrained teachers are contained in Stuart and Kunje (1996). Further analysis of the MIITEP curriculum in action is available in Stuart and Kunje (2000) and Kunje and Chirembo (2000).

There are six Colleges of Education, which now have about 150 lecturing staff teaching the MIITEP Programme. More than three-quarters of the staff are over 40 years old and well over half have completed 20 years service. Staff-student ratios vary from 11:1 to 21:1. Enrolment capacity in the colleges varies from 300 to 600 with an average of about 450. The total capacity of the colleges at any one time is between 2,500 and 3,000 and is limited by the amount of residential accommodation rather than teaching space. The MIITEP system has the capacity to train about 2,500 per cohort, resulting in an annual output of 7,500 per year after the two-year training cycle. After the sixth cohort was enrolled in 1998, new cohorts were suspended pending resolution of funding difficulties. Output has therefore declined as cohorts complete MIITEP and have not been replaced.

The trainees for MIITEP are required to have a Junior (JCE) or Malawi School Certificate (MSCE) and have taught in a primary school for at least a year. It has always been an ambition to favour MSCE graduates (4 years secondary) and phase out JCE (2 years secondary). In 1997 the total number of pupils graduating from the secondary school system with passes in MSCE was about 8,000. The numbers with credits in English and in mathematics were about half of this. This represents the annual pool of those with this level of qualification. A proportion of those graduating will not enter the labour market for domestic reasons e.g. marriage. A larger number will seek other forms of employment

9 Supply, Demand, Efficiency and Costs

outside the education system. If 25% of MSCE graduates applied to teacher training, about 2,000 would be available each year of which perhaps half might opt for secondary training. This leaves no more than about 1,000 to enter primary teacher training. The number available is larger than this if those leaving school in previous years remain in the labour market and subsequently apply to teach. It does seem that even at existing levels of recruitment most applicants will continue to be JCE holders[54]. This was the case with most of the first six cohorts of MIITEP. Whatever training arrangements are devised, there is a need to recognise this probable constraint.

9.5.2 **Costs**

In 1998 Malawi allocated over 30% of the recurrent budget and 5% of GNP to education. Within these amounts primary education has taken an increasing share as a result of the introduction of Free Primary Education in 1994 and subsequent rapid enrolment growth. (Figure 12). The allocations for Teacher Training only cover the cost of the college training system, not the additional costs of MIITEP whilst students are off site. They also include one secondary teacher training college. Total allocation to the TTCs has fallen as a percentage of the total recurrent budget since 1990. Allocations to the university are consistently more than those made for the secondary school system. Typically twice as much has been allocated to the university than to the secondary schools in most recent years.

Figure 12: **Evolution of recurrent expenditure in Malawi**

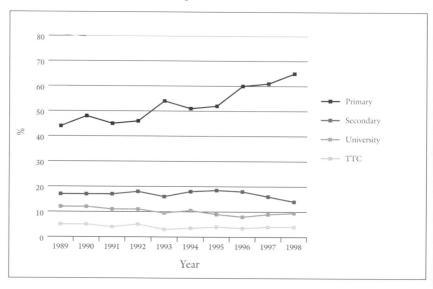

54 The pass rate at MSCE further deteriorated in 1999 to average about 11%, thus worsening the supply side problem.

154

DFID

9 Supply, Demand, Efficiency and Costs

Official estimates of unit costs at different levels give ratios of primary to secondary, teacher education and university in 1997 of 1:6.2, 1:21, and 1:175. The teacher education figure is misleadingly low since it refers only to the college-based costs. Actual costs are considerably more.

The costing of MIITEP is complex (Kunje and Lewin 2000:32). In its first phase a Teacher Development Unit was staffed, a range of Malawian and expatriate advisors were recruited for development work and substantial external assistance was made available. In addition 315 Primary Education Advisors and senior school staff were employed to support trainees[55] through various field activities and in-service events, and college staff were to undertake field visits and assessment tasks[56].

This analysis is concerned with the costs of MIITEP-style programmes and focuses on a forward view of their financial implications and sustainability. It is therefore important to arrive at estimates of the recurrent cost per trained teacher of maintaining such a system, excluding development costs, so that comparisons can be made with alternatives. As a first proxy we have tried to cost elements of the training programme at current rates (January 1999) to establish some guidance as to the cost per trainee that would allow continuation of existing arrangements under existing MIITEP assumptions[57]. The results are shown below (Table 12).

The MIITEP programme appears to cost about MK24,900 per student or US$560 at prevailing exchange rates[58]. These costs are for two years of training and represent about 2.8 times GNP per capita. The cost per cohort of 2,500 is MK 62.3 million (US$ 1.35 million) and for 15,000 trainees MK 374 million (US$8.1 million). This excludes development costs, training of trainers, and international consultant support, all of which have been substantial. The distribution of costs is as shown below in Table 12.

Table 12 gives some indication of the scope for cost reductions. If the basic model of a three-month initial block and a six-week final block separated by school-based practice is retained then cost reductions will have to be found from within the major categories identified. Field support costs could be reduced by sharing costs for zonal meetings and PEA visits, since these are supported from budget headings linked to other development projects. It might

---

[55] The PEAs have more general school support and supervision responsibilities
[56] The World Bank and GTZ provided most of the direct external support for development and implementation. Support from other donors (e.g. DFID) complemented this and normal Government of Malawi expenditure.
[57] Key assumptions include:
    12 zonal meetings occur and that PEAs make 2 visits a term for 5 terms to trainees.
    College lecturers visit trainees in school once each term.
    About 20 weeks of lecturers time is devoted to each cohort over two years (11 week block + 4 week block + visits) and salary apportioned accordingly.
    Trainees receive MK1500 month during training.
    The costs of an initial orientation period are included.
    Materials costs per student are estimated as US$25 for all guides etc.
[58] 1US$ =MK42

9 Supply, Demand, Efficiency and Costs

be possible to reduce these costs by as much as 75%. School visiting by college lectures cannot take place at the frequency originally planned if all cohorts are enrolled simultaneously, since the number of visits needed is well above imaginable capacity. It may also be that such visits add little value to the training process (Kunje & Chirembo, 2000). If this visiting was eliminated in favour of school and PEA-based assessment covered under other budgets, these costs would disappear. Changing the length of the school-based period would not have an effect on costs independent of the number of activities planned. It is more difficult to see how the full-time training costs could be reduced without reducing the time in college. Cost recovery has been suggested related to boarding costs (Government of Malawi, January 2000). If this were set at MK5 per day it would reduce the boarding costs by about MK600. Materials costs are fairly fixed and could not be seriously reduced without degrading the resources available to students. The costs of assessment could be reduced but this would not have much effect on the overall budget. It is probably preferable to re-profile expenditure on assessment to produce more valid instruments of higher quality (Croft, Kunje and Stuart 2000). If these modifications were made the cost per MIITEP trainee over two years would fall from MK24,900 (US$593) to about MK 15,540 (US$370).

Table 12: **Distribution of costs per student over two years**

	MK	US$	Percent
Field Support Costs	9960	237	40.0
Zonal Meetings	1960	47	7.9
PEA Visits	3000	71	12.0
COE Visits	5000	119	20.1
Full-time Training Costs	11300	269	45.4
COE Salaries	1000	24	4.0
Trainees Salaries	6500	155	26.1
Boarding etc	3800	90	15.3
Materials and Assessment	2245	53	9.0
Materials	1050	25	4.2
Assessment	1195	28	4.8
Central Costs	1396	33	5.6
Total	24901	593	100

In summary, what can be said about costs is that MIITEP-style training would cost around MK62.3 million (US$ 1.5 million) for a cohort of 2,500 over two years if it continued to be implemented as originally intended without further development costs. This figure could be reduced to around MK38.5 million (US$ 910,000) per cohort if the field-work costs were reduced and a boarding fee introduced. In both cases this excludes the notional costs of teacher replacement during full-time training. The current annual allocation to teacher education for all the training colleges including secondary is about MK 40 million (US$ 950,000) per year. One cohort costs US S 750,000 per year without cost sharing. Six

9 Supply, Demand, Efficiency and Costs

enrolled simultaneously would cost correspondingly more, and well beyond the current budget. This is unachievable without substantial external assistance. We note that currently infrastructure and staffing are not sufficient to maintain six cohorts simultaneously, and that there are also additional investment costs over and above those needed to support the recurrent budget.

Alternative patterns of organisation for teacher education are being considered as a result of dissatisfaction with some aspects of MIITEP. An illustration can be provided of the most commonly discussed alternatives. The training model could return to a pattern of one-year full-time and one-year school-based, or two years full-time with teaching practice integrated into the programmes. The full-time cost per trainee in colleges can be estimated at about MK 25,200 (US\$ 600) based on existing cost structures. Table 13 estimates costs for a conventional two-year full time programme with 16 weeks of college-supervised teaching practice, and for a one-year full-time course followed by one year of supported school-based teaching practice.

Table 13; **Comparison between different modes of training**

Mode	College cost US\$	Field cost US\$	Teacher Replacement US\$	Full unit cost US\$	Annual Output US\$	Total cost for 7500 US\$'000
MIITEP without cost reduction	350	240	200	790	7500	5926
MIITEP with cost reduction	340	30	200	570	7500	4276
Two year full-time – 16 weeks teaching practice	1200	200	1200	2600	2500	19500
1 yr FT + 1 yr in school - without cost reduction	600	100	600	1300	2500	9750
1 yr FT + 1 yr in school - with cost reduction	570	12	600	1182	2500	8864

Table 13 shows that two-year full-time training is between three and four and a half times as expensive as MIITEP per student. One year full-time followed by school-based training is between two and three times as expensive. The estimates include the cost of teacher replacement. In addition MIITEP is capable of producing three times the output of either of the other options in the same time period without the need for additional facilities. In order to increase output from 2,500 to 7,500 an additional 5,000 places would have to be created in the college system through building new TTCs, or through utilising space in other educational institutions. The alternative modes are therefore substantially more expensive and would require significant capital investment. They would also require the appointment of a considerable number of new college lecturers.

9 Supply, Demand, Efficiency and Costs

9.5.3 Internal Efficiency

The six Colleges of Education currently involved in primary teacher training have staff-student ratios varying between 1:11 and 1:21. MUSTER has analysed teaching loads and the utilisation of space in two of the Colleges. The patterns are significantly different.

In College A (SSR 1:13) lecturers teach on average 12 or 13 periods a week. The least loaded is the Principal with 8 periods per week. The Deputy has only 7 hours per week as a result of combining his classes into double classes, otherwise he would have had 14 hours per week. Mathematics and science lecturers are most heavily loaded with as many as 17 hours per week. This would have been 21 hours if some of the classes were not combined together. Lecturers in foundation studies and arts have the lowest loads. Shortage of staff in the maths-science departments accounts for their heavier teaching loads. In addition to teaching, lecturers in college A are required to supervise teaching practice two hours each week at nearby demonstration schools. Each lecturer has at most 20 students to supervise in the three months period a cohort stays in college.

College B has an SSR of 1:21. Most classes are combined into double size groups with about 80 students. The result is that on average lecturers teach 6 or 7 one-hour lectures per week. The most heavily loaded are time-tabled for 13 hours per week and the least teach 5 hours. In reality some lecturers do teach more and may give additional tuition in the evenings. Each lecturer is also required to supervise teaching practice for two hours per week as in college A. Each lecturer has 24 students to supervise and each student has to be supervised once during a period of three months.

In addition to teaching and supervision, lecturers mark the work of previous MIITEP cohorts whilst they are completing the school-based element of the programme. One consequence is that some lecturers create time to mark by reducing the time they spend on college work, most obviously by not maintaining a college-based system of testing and progress reports. This is also one of the reasons behind doubling-up classes since this halves teaching loads.

Space utilisation in the two colleges is not high. In college A teaching space is utilised less than half the maximum possible time. Combining together two classes for teaching, non-use of some special rooms, and under-use of others account for this. Rooms like the language laboratory, the audio-visual centre and the library are very under-used. There is enough teaching space at the college to more than double the number of teaching periods and/or students. The main constraint on increased enrolment is the amount of boarding space in the hostels which is limited to 300.

9 Supply, Demand, Efficiency and Costs

In College B, which has higher enrolments, space is slightly more efficiently utilised but nevertheless rooms are not time-tabled over 40% of the time available. The doubling of classes reduces overall demand for space but creates pressure on rooms to accommodate up to 80 trainees at a time. As in College A increased enrolment is not constrained by teaching space but by hostel accommodation. Lack of reliable and adequate funding has resulted in deterioration of fabric and services to the point where electricity, water and sanitation are frequently unavailable on a site for 500 students and 25 lecturers.

In summary, internal efficiency in the Malawi training colleges is low. Teaching loads in terms of contact hours are small mainly as a result of large group sizes, not because of excessive student-staff ratios. Physical plant is decaying as a result of a lack of non-salary recurrent expenditure and neglect. The teaching space that is available is more than sufficient to meet current needs. Enrolment is constrained by hostel space.

9.5.4 Demand

In 1997 the eight year primary school system in Malawi enrolled 2.82 million pupils in over 3,700 schools. In 1997 43,400 teachers were listed as employed, about half of whom were classified as unqualified. The Policy and Investment Framework for Malawi targets a pupil-teacher ratio of 60:1 for primary schools which generates a total demand for teachers of about 48,500, without adjustment for the fact that not all teachers teach all the time or that some schools are over-staffed. The demand for primary teachers can be projected[59]. Table 14 shows the result.

Table 14 indicates that an annual output of between 9,000 and 14,000 teachers is needed to sustain universal primary education, if all government objectives were to be met. This is between one and a half and two and half times the output of the MIITEP system. It may be that some of the assumptions are unduly pessimistic and that in any case progress towards targets will be slower than anticipated. This would lower demand. Nevertheless, an output of teachers similar or greater than MIITEP is capable of delivering is likely to be needed for a sustained period. The annual capacity of primary colleges is no more than about 8,000 under the MIITEP system. Under a conventional full-time PRESET system annual capacity would be only 2,700.

9.5.5 Reflection

First, the annual capacity of MIITEP is substantially below what would be needed to meet national plan targets in the Policy and Investment Framework (PIF). Since no new MIITEP

---

[59] These projections take into account the target pupil teacher ratio, the number of primary teachers on the payroll known to be teaching at secondary level, the replacement cost of trainees, and the numbers of untrained teachers needing training. To this can be added the numbers needed to replace those leaving teaching through retirement, resignation or death in-service. The final adjustments are to estimate the effects of school age cohort growth and planned reductions in repetition and drop out. Full assumptions contained in Kunje and Lewin 2000.

9 Supply, Demand, Efficiency and Costs

Table 14: **Teacher demand**

Teacher Demand for 1999		
Current Establishment	52000	As gazetted
Teacher in Post 1997/8	43400	1998 MOE statistics
Number of primary teachers not teaching in primary schools but in MCDE/CDSSs	2500	
MIITEP replacements whilst on course	3000	
Shortfall in 1999	11100	If these were in post ptr would be 54:1
Training Needs - Backlog		
1. Untrained Teachers in system	24000	Within the total of 43400 employed
2. Enrolled in MIITEP	16000	
3. Unqualified teachers needing training not in MIITEP	8000	MIITEP data base 1998 survey
4. Additional teachers needed to reach establishment of 52,000	11100	
5. Training Demand – Backlog in 1999 (3+4)	19100	Number needing training if all 52000 teachers are trained
Annual Recurrent Demand	Per Year	
6. New migration to MCDE/CDSS	500 – 1000	1996-1997 = 500. Could be higher per year if CSS are developed into schools wit much lower ptrs than in MCDE/CDSSs
7. Attrition of primary teacher cadre through retirement and death (attrition 7% or 11%)	3000-5500	1996/1997 attrition rate = 11% = 5,500 loss of teachers
8. Reduction in drop out and repetition	1500-3000	FPE invites reduction in drop out to increase completion rates. Demand depends on rate of reduction and on changes in repetition (see simulation).
9. Cohort growth	500-1000	1-2%
10. Total Annual demand (6+7+8+9)	5500-10500	
11.Backlog of untrained teachers in the system (8000) + teachers needed to reach establishment numbers (14100) = 19100 to be trained over 5 years = per year	3820	Assuming all untrained teachers currently in schools will be trained over 5 years, that MCDE/CDSS teachers will be replaced in primary schools, that MIITEP continues, and that the establishment is filled with new recruits.
12. Training Demand per Annum	9320-13820	
Output of Training System 1999		
13. MIITEP annual net output 1999	6050-6870	15%-25% attrition in MIITEP.

trainees were enrolled for 18 months after cohort 6, the backlog of untrained teachers has remained and teacher attrition has added to demand. In 2000 the plan was to recruit up to 10,000 additional untrained teachers. The immediate consequence of this, and the delay in

---

[60] See Lewin, Keller and Taylor 2000 for more detailed discussion.

9 Supply, Demand, Efficiency and Costs

enrolling cohort 7, will be to increase the proportion of untrained teachers in the primary system. Moreover, the effects of HIV on attrition amongst trainees and teachers have yet to peak (Kadzamira et al 2001). Attrition rates may therefore increase further. This implies that any method of training teachers for the future must be capable of producing similar or greater levels of output than the MIITEP system, unless national targets are to be radically revised.

Second, cohort 7 has been selected but to date (March 2000) residential training has not commenced pending decisions on the future of MIITEP. It consists of a majority of JCE holders who were not called for previous MIITEP cohorts indicating that a supply side constraint remains. Expanded output is likely to depend on recruitment of JCE rather than MSCE holders, with implications for the curriculum, until or unless more graduate successfully from secondary schools and elect to go into primary teaching.

Third, any return to conventional two-year full-time residential training would imply unsustainable increases in costs and tripling or more the number of colleges. MIITEP is clearly more cost-efficient than conventional pre-career training, and is capable of a much higher level of output. Concerns must remain about the quality and effects of this mode of training. MUSTER has identified a number of ways in which these problems might be addressed (Stuart and Kunje, 2000; Kunje and Chirembo, 2000, Kunje and Lewin 2000).

9.6   Case-study 4: Trinidad and Tobago[60]

9.6.1   Supply

Initial training for teachers at the primary level in Trinidad and Tobago is conducted largely at the two government Teachers' Colleges: Valsayn and Corinth. A small amount of training also occurs at the School of Education, UWI and the privately operated Caribbean Union College. Although the course of teacher training offered at the colleges is designed to equip the students for practice at the primary level, some students are allowed to teach at the lower levels of the secondary school system. The training programme takes place over two years full-time.

In 1999, figures indicate Valsayn had 197 students in the first year and 207 in the second. Corinth had 201 and 186, giving a total of 791 in training. Annual output is between 350 and 400 qualified primary teachers. Over two-thirds of trainees were female in 1998. All staff members have professional qualifications in education, many at the post-graduate level. College staff can retire after 33.3 years service or the age of 60 whichever is sooner. The age structure of staff at Corinth shows that about half have reached the age of 50 and are approaching retirement. Valsayn had 32 lecturers in post in 1999 and Corinth 27, giving student-staff ratios of 13:1 and 14:1.

9 Supply, Demand, Efficiency and Costs

An On-the-Job Training (OJT) Programme (George, Fournillier & Brown 2000) extends over a period of about one year and is provided for entrants to the teaching profession prior to college enrolment. This provides some instruction in the Foundations of Education, the Teaching of Reading and the Teaching of Mathematics. This is followed by placement in schools with mentor teachers. Trainees are required to attend Saturday classes and vacation schools. College staff play no role in the selection process for OJTs, or in their subsequent allocation to colleges for training, which is handled centrally in the Ministry of Education. Thus, students entering primary teachers colleges have usually have two to three years of teaching experience in a primary school or, in the case of a small number of students, in a secondary school. Students are selected by the Board of Teacher Training on the basis of seniority in the teaching service and sent to the colleges on scholarship.

The majority of trainees have CXC (Caribbean Examinations Certificate) or O Level passes in five subjects. About 37% have one or more A Level passes. Females are marginally better qualified than males. Between 15,000 and 20,000 candidates take CXC examinations each year in the major subjects of English and mathematics. Pass rates in these subjects are between 30% and 40% suggesting that perhaps 5000 per year achieve the minimum qualifications for entry to primary teacher training of whom perhaps 400 subsequently enter primary teacher training.

9.6.2 Costs

Trinidad and Tobago allocates about 4.5% of GDP and 13% of government expenditure to education. Primary education accounted for 46% of the budget, secondary 38%, post-secondary including Teachers' Colleges 4%, and tertiary 7% (World Bank 1995:112). The ratio of primary unit costs to secondary, teacher education and university costs appears to be about 1:1.6, 1:9, and 1:16 respectively. Student costs per capita as a percentage of GDP were 10%, 16%, 98% and 161% respectively for the different levels. About 95% of the Ministry of Education's expenditure is recurrent, with salaries accounting for about 70%.

Expenditure on teacher training is relatively low compared to the other case-study countries and appears to be about less than 2% of recurrent educational expenditure. This is partly a consequence of the much lower levels of demand for new teachers (see below). It is important to note that the costs of primary teacher education include not only direct college costs but also the salaries of trainee teachers. In 1996 over 70% of the salaries budget covered the salaries of trainees during the period when they are in full-time training. These are paid directly from the Ministry of Education. Other non-salary costs make up a very small proportion of total costs.

The salary scale for lecturers at the training colleges is the same as for graduate teachers at the secondary level which is also a reason for the relative low allocation to teacher education

9 Supply, Demand, Efficiency and Costs

in the national budget. This is an anomaly since the Ministry of Education now demands post-graduate training as a pre-requisite for teaching at the colleges, and no such demand is made of secondary school teachers. Expenditure on goods and services is minimal and averages less than 2% of the total. College libraries are supported from a separate vote from the Ministry of Education that appears to vary unpredictably.

On the basis of these costs it is possible to arrive at an estimate of the recurrent cost per trainee. Since the staff-student ratios are similar, and non-salary costs are small, there is no significant difference in these costs between the colleges. In 1998 enrolments were 791. There were 52 lecturers in post (including principals) and about 20 ancillary staff. Based on average salary costs (including the new salary scales) this would give a cost per trainee per year in 1999 of about $TT35,000 ($US 5,550). Thus a trained teacher would cost about $TT70,000 (US$ 11,100) to produce over two years. This is about 2.6 times GNP per capita.

9.6.3 Internal Efficiency

The two Colleges in Trinidad and Tobago have staff-student ratios of between 1:12 and 1:14. They are in session for 37 weeks per year during which all the teaching takes place. The three terms vary in length between 14 and 11 weeks. The division of teaching time is such that 45% is allocated to teaching, 24% to teaching practice and preparation, and 19% to examinations. Trainees are time tabled for 40 periods per week. However it is not possible to deliver the full time-table as intended. In total about 935 hours of teaching time are time-tabled over two years which can be compared to the 1,565 hours planned. The shortfall arises from a combination of reductions in the number of actual teaching days, the load from assessment, and the disposition of staff.

Students are taught at Valsayn according to a blocked timetable for core subjects which sub-divides each year group of 200 into 3 sub-groups of about 60-70. Electives are taught in small groups. As an approximation there are therefore about 300 periods taught each week across the College during teaching time. This suggests that lecturers on average teach 9 or 10 periods. Corinth organises its timetable in a different way. It mixes whole year group lectures and introductory sessions (up to 200 in a group) with smaller group tutorial sessions with about 35 students per class. As in Valsayn trainees are fully time-tabled throughout the week. Teaching loads seem similar to those in Valsayn. A consequence of the large group sizes and the heavily loaded trainee timetable is that opportunities for working with small groups of trainees are scarce. Most teaching occurs in large lecture-size groups which preclude some styles of teaching.

Teaching practice is conducted in three four-week blocks in Valsayn. College lecturers undertake at least four visits per trainee during each block. Each lecturer is responsible for

9 Supply, Demand, Efficiency and Costs

about 6 trainees and thus makes a minimum of about 24 visits. If school visits take half a day then this represents about 2.5 weeks work per practice. A slightly different arrangement is used in Corinth that involves initial half-day group visits of 5 trainees with a tutor who have jointly planned a lesson. Subsequently trainees undertake block practice in pairs and then individually. It is thought this provides a staged induction into teaching practice that builds confidence and competence. A standard assessment instrument for appraising performance on teaching practice is used in Corinth by all tutors and is made available to trainees.

The implications of the data MUSTER has collected suggest that it should be possible to decrease the size of teaching groups with possible benefits for the quality and richness of the training experience. SSRs of 1:12 to 1:14 should allow teaching group sizes smaller than those indicated for much of the time in College. This would imply greater contact time for staff. The regime of school visits to support trainees in school is time-intensive because of the number of visits to each student. The question this raises is whether the frequency could be reduced, most obviously by sharing support for trainees with practising teachers who are on-site in schools.

9.6.4 Demand

The Trinidad and Tobago education system has succeeded in providing nearly all its children with access to seven years of primary schooling. Currently average pupil-teacher ratios are about 23:1 at primary and 20:1 at secondary. Most importantly for future teacher demand, the cohort of primary school age children is shrinking and attrition rates amongst teachers appear to be low. In the last three years the decline in the size of the school age cohort appears to have been between 3% and 4% per annum. Taken together these factors mean that the demand for new primary teachers is modest and diminishing. Demand for secondary teachers will grow as transition rates increase. Teacher attrition is currently between 3% and 4%. The output of trained primary teachers of about 400 per year represents about 5% of the teaching cadre. Alternative employment opportunities are scarce for primary teachers and it seems likely that attrition rates will remain at these levels.

Our projections, based on official demographic estimates, show that primary enrolment is likely to decline from its present level of around 170,000 in public schools to about 105,000 by 2013. Secondary enrolments will increase if a 100% transition rate into secondary is achieved, and peak at about 120,000 in 2006. The demand for new primary teachers on this projection becomes negative since teacher attrition is less than the rate of contraction in enrolments. Demand for secondary teachers as a result of increased participation peaks at about 400 a year and then falls as the long-term effects of falling school numbers have an impact. The conclusion appears to be that few new primary teachers are needed and that initial training should be on a care and maintenance basis with a small output.

9 Supply, Demand, Efficiency and Costs

However, these projections of teacher demand ignore the need to train those currently untrained in the system. There are over 1,600 untrained teachers in primary schools who will need to become fully qualified. This could be achieved in successive intakes into the existing colleges. If these teachers were retrained over 4 years it would create an additional demand of 400 places per year. At secondary level half of all teachers do not possess a professional qualification. These number about 2,400. If these untrained secondary teachers were to receive professional training over six years this would create an additional demand of 400 trainees per year.

It is also true that if other quality improvements were made in the school system demand for teachers would change. If repetition rates were reduced through a combination of automatic promotion, elimination of the common entrance examination, and more effective schools, teacher demand would fall as pupils moved through the system faster. If the age cohort ceased to shrink at 3% demand would increase, but only after a period of years when the growing cohort was enrolled. If pupil-teacher ratios were to fall to improve quality to 20:1 at primary, and 15:1 at secondary, demand would increase towards current output levels.

9.6.5 Reflection

The demand created by the need to train the 1,600 untrained primary teachers currently in the system, coupled with the need to replace teachers who leave the profession, is probably sufficient to maintain current levels of college output up to about 2004 (Lewin, Keller & Taylor 2000). From then on the recurrent demand for primary teachers may not be sufficient to support more than one college intake. If both colleges are to continue to train primary teachers then there will be a need to re-profile the contribution they make to primary teacher development to include other kinds of support in addition to initial training. Opportunities exist to increase teaching quality and contact time with smaller groups of trainees and to extend the role of college staff into continuing professional development. Because the primary school system is not expanding, and because costs are also low in relation to GNP and to the education budget, there appears to be no problem of financial sustainability. Beneficially there are clear opportunities to improve quality and expand the role of the colleges.

9.7 Concluding Remarks

This chapter has explored the characteristics of supply, costs and demand for teachers in four countries. The overviews provided cannot capture the complexity of each national context which is explored in the discussion papers on which this account is based. They do however allow some general observations to be made.

9 Supply, Demand, Efficiency and Costs

First, in Ghana, Lesotho, and Malawi the challenge posed by national targets for enrolment and pupil-teacher ratios is immense. None of these systems can produce enough new teachers to meet projected demand. Moreover the costs of existing modes of training suggest that simple expansion of existing capacity is financially unsustainable. The Malawi case is the least problematic in the sense that it already has adopted a mixed-mode approach to training which is relatively low cost and high volume. Nevertheless, other factors, notably the high teacher attrition rates and high pupil-teacher ratios, still mean that demand will continue to run well ahead of supply, even if MIITEP becomes fully operational again.

Second, in two of the countries the size of the school age group appears to be shrinking. In Lesotho the potential benefit from this of reduced demand for new teachers is compromised by the small output and high costs of training. Here capacity needs to be increased substantially, not least to respond to the short term increase in demand created by FPE. This could be achieved partly by fuller utilisation of the NTTC for primary training but more would still be needed to maintain enrolment rates and sustain a full cadre of trained teachers. In Trinidad and Tobago demand is small and is not growing. Pupil-teacher ratios are already quite low and enrolment rates high. Here there is a window of opportunity to invest in quality improvement and extending the role of colleges into professional support pre- and post- training.

Third, Ghana has the problem of an under-supply of the number of teachers necessary to maintain current enrolment rates. This is compounded by the fact that it is the country furthest away from achieving universal enrolments at primary and this creates an additional demand of magnitude. The current system, even with a modified 'In-In-Out' system, does not have the capacity to meet demand.

Fourth, the discussion papers on which this chapter depends explore the composition of costs and provide insights into the scope for increases in internal efficiency. From these analyses it is clear that there are opportunities to make better use of staff and physical resources, and that management and accountability systems rarely monitor costs with efficiency in mind. There appear few incentives to optimise the utilisation of staff. Non-salary recurrent costs of colleges are often greater than salaries, except in Trinidad and Tobago where the colleges are not residential. This may also be an area where efficiency could be improved. Student stipends are the major component of recurrent salary costs, and these allowances are often paid at levels comparable with those of teachers' salaries. Only in MIITEP is it the case that trainees are teaching most of the time. In the other systems full-time training implies notional replacement costs of a full-time teacher.

Fifth, though the detail is complex the simple conclusions are clear. If the national and international targets for universal enrolment and reasonable levels of pupil-teacher ratio are to be met, alternatives to full-time, pre-career training over two or three years have to be

9 Supply, Demand, Efficiency and Costs

considered. MIITEP gives an insight into one alternative. It has strengths and weaknesses which other papers explore (e.g. Kunje & Chirembo 2000, Stuart & Kunje 2000). Though this approach can more closely produce an output of new teachers that matches demand, it reduces time in college, anticipates effective support whilst trainees are working in schools, and implies substantial development costs if modified versions of this kind of approach to be considered for different national contexts.

This analysis arrives at an invitation rather than a conclusion. If sufficient new teachers are to be trained to meet demand, a range of options will need consideration in three of the countries. These will have to be considered within a planning climate where the probable length of trained primary teachers' careers is shortening, and where the underlying demographic dimensions of supply and demand are subject to high levels of uncertainty[61]. Whatever the options identified these will have to be appraised in terms of whether they can provide sufficient output at sustainable cost, and whether the quality of what they can deliver is worth the costs of transition.

9.7 Key issues for policy and practice

- Medium term planning of supply matched to levels of demand created by targets set for enrolment rates, pupil-teacher ratios and population growth is the only way to realise goals to universalise primary education.

- In several of the MUSTER countries an adequate supply of new teachers is only achievable if training modalities are reconsidered to lower costs and increase output in sustainable ways. This implies consideration of shorter periods of initial training, greater use of mixed-mode delivery systems, and appropriate curriculum development to match new needs.

- Internal efficiency is often low and there is considerable scope to make more effective use of staff and physical resources.

- The financial systems which support teacher education should move from historic budgeting to programme budgeting linked to numbers of trainees and targets for performance which provide incentives to increase output and efficiency.

- More appropriate balances should be struck between categories of expenditure which direct more investment towards improving the quality of the learning environment in training institutions.

---

[61] Primary teachers' careers may be shortening because fewer trained teachers than in the past remain in primary teaching throughout their careers as the propensity to migrate to teaching at higher levels after up grading increases, and more teachers find opportunities to leave teaching altogether. HIV/AIDs is having substantial effects on both the attrition rates of the cadre of teachers and the numbers of children entering school.

9 Supply, Demand, Efficiency and Costs

- Admission policy has to reflect the realities of the supply of qualified and willing applicants graduating from the secondary school system; new curricula have to recognise these realities.

Chapter Ten   **10 Insights From MUSTER and Ways Forward**

10   Introduction

The MUSTER project grew out of the concerns shared by the research teams outlined in Chapter 1. These drew attention to a lack of evidence-based policy for teacher education in low income countries in a context where commitment to universalise access to primary schools has created high levels of demand for the training of new teachers. At the outset we noted widespread dissatisfaction with levels of achievement and competence amongst newly trained teachers; the slow pace of change in teaching methods in schools despite the aspirations associated with reformed primary curricula, and the lack of research-based insights into the process and practice of teacher education. We also drew attention to the limited extent to which training curricula recognised the changing characteristics of new entrants, the weakness of links between training institutions and schools, and the high costs of much of the training.

The MUSTER research provides insights into all these issues. It is framed by the matrix of research questions which has been used to organise the chapters in this report. This chapter draws together findings within each of the major strands (Becoming a Teacher; Curriculum, Colleges, and Costs and Resources) and arenas (inputs, process, outputs) and uses these to lead into a more general discussion of the key issues, the constraints on policy, and the alternative ways forward.

10.1   Characteristics of Teachers

The first set of questions, which are addressed in Chapter 4, concern the characteristics of those becoming teachers. We have tried to capture both biographical data on new entrants to training and insights into the images they have of teaching and being a teacher. The backgrounds and dispositions of trainees have implications for selection, the design and realisation of teacher education curricula, and for the induction of NQTs into the teaching profession. In summary some general themes that emerge from the data are outlined below.

First, in two of the countries the median age of entrants to teacher education is relatively high, as a result of recruitment practices that enrol untrained teachers. These adult learners have had a gap since leaving school, often have family experience and responsibilities, and have experience of teaching in more or less professionally supportive environments. The training needs of those with this kind of experience are likely to be different to those entering straight from school. MUSTER data suggests that prior experience is rarely recognised explicitly in training curricula or in College transactions.

Second, the majority of entrants in all the countries come from family backgrounds where the cultural and academic capital they bring with them to the training experience is constrained. Many are from households with low levels of parental education and non-

10 Insights From MUSTER and Ways Forward

professional livelihoods. Perhaps predictably, disproportionate numbers do have relatives who are teachers. This may be an advantage - some of the realities and possibilities of teaching should be known to such students; it might also be a disadvantage - the demonstration effects provided by family members who are teachers may present the most compelling role models whatever the college curriculum tries to promote and these may or may not be consistent with new pedagogic aspirations. Trainees who are themselves from impoverished backgrounds may be closer to the children they teach culturally and linguistically, than those from professional backgrounds. Methods of training must recognise the range of trainees' backgrounds and develop curricula which recognise the mix of good and poor quality schooling trainees themselves have experienced, the extent to which trainees have developed effective study skills, and the variety of personal and practical competencies that they bring to training.

Third, the academic level of many entrants is weak. Many have the minimal qualifications necessary for entrance and are unlikely to have secure grounding in core subjects. Low academic achievement in the medium of instruction (in all cases English) is very worrying. None of the teacher education curricula in the countries makes special provision for upgrading language fluency, or for that matter working with pupils in a multi-lingual environment where linguistic code-switching is likely to be common. In most cases simply raising minimum entry qualifications for language or other core subjects would reduce the numbers of qualified entrants and exacerbate supply problems. This suggests that more appropriate strategies may include bridging programmes (to raise the academic achievement prior to entry), and/or enrichment of college curricula to recognise needs for language and subject upgrading from low levels.

Fourth, trainees often do have well-developed images of good primary teachers which focus typically on the personal and affective aspects of the role, rather than methods of effective teaching and learning of content. Many refer to role models exemplified by successful teachers they experienced as pupils. These provide powerful images to aspire towards. Often these models resonate with modes of teaching which are essentially transmission-based, and which stress ordered learning of knowledge and conventional teacher-centred classroom organisation. These images can be contrasted with those found in some teacher education curricula we have analysed which promote more reflective and child-centred (rather than knowledge-centred) methods of teaching, often in response to the aspirations of reformed primary curricula. The images and beliefs of trainees about teaching and teachers constitute a starting point for training. Their qualities and diversity need to be appreciated and incorporated into the curriculum development process.

The final point is to note that the data produces profiles of some of the actual characteristics of trainees, not those idealised or assumed in curriculum and selection documentation. Our qualitative data suggests that often tutors have surprisingly little detailed knowledge of the

10 Insights From MUSTER and Ways Forward

characteristics of the cohorts of students they train, and also of the school environments that newly trained teachers enter. Sometimes the colleges appear to be training students for schools as tutors think they ought to be, rather than for schools as they are. This cannot be an asset in tailoring curricular experience to a realistic appraisal of antecedent conditions and learning needs. Nor can it be a basis for more responsive and reflective modes of training that recognise differences, address questions of motivation and commitment, and prepare trainees purposefully for their first appointment.

10.2 Teacher Education Curricula

Our analyses of teacher education curricula suggest that many suffer from a number of inconsistencies, mismatches and dilemmas.

First, curriculum documentation for teacher education is more often than not patchy and incomplete. In some cases it does not exist in a single integrated form but as a compilation of government circulars, course outlines, teaching timetables, lecturers' notes, and assessment rubrics. One consequence is that the core aims of teacher education programmes can be elusive, extensive, and even contradictory. There is little evidence in the curriculum analysis studies that a consensus exists about the essential knowledge, skills and competencies that new primary teachers should acquire during pre-service training. Often it is not clear what is essential and what is desirable, and what is best acquired during training and what can be learnt later. Some of the espoused aims appear unrealistic within the time available, especially given the qualifications of the entrants. Learning objectives may or may not be consistent in character and quantity with the aspirations embodied in the aims. And characteristically, amounts of content are included which result in an overload of material, and a stronger emphasis on content knowledge rather than professional skills.

Second, to a greater or lesser degree the teacher education curricula we have analysed recognise new approaches to learning. However, the dominant pedagogical stance remains one where trainees are largely regarded as 'empty vessels', with little knowledge or experience of teaching, who need prescriptive advice and guidance from lecturers about how to teach, whether or not the prescriptions appear to suit the learning contexts in the schools where trainees work or the demands of new curricula. One consequence is that opportunities to build on prior learning (especially that as untrained teachers), are often overlooked. The teacher education curricula that have been analysed do not conspicuously engage with the images, metaphors and myths that students bring with them, nor do they recognise that some skills and competencies may already have been acquired as a result of teaching as untrained teachers. The occasions on which trainee teachers were invited to deconstruct and reconstruct their own ideas of teaching in ways that might enable them to understand and internalise new approaches and refine existing good practice, were few and far between.

10 Insights From MUSTER and Ways Forward

Third, trainee teachers need to be confident of their subject knowledge in order to share this with pupils in school in imaginative and flexible ways. The academic expectations of some parts of the teacher education curricula we examined were not well matched to the levels of achievement of new entrants, most of whom only achieved minimum entry level qualifications. As noted above, the difficulties of learning in a second language are under-estimated (and under-researched), and no real allowances are made in many curriculum materials for the difficulties that trainees will experience when they themselves are far from fluent in the medium of instruction.

Fourth, the professional studies components of teacher education curricula are variously weighted in terms of time, and have a wider range of different emphases than do the subject content elements. Rarely are distinctions made which clearly separate that kind of professional knowledge that can be acquired in a college environment, from that which requires an experiential base and cumulative development through practice and reflection. Further, the trainees are often taught subject methods in the form of 'recipes' to be applied regardless of context, rather than being helped to develop 'pedagogic content knowledge' which would allow them to adapt the curriculum to specific classes and pupils. Much of the text material that supports professional studies originates from disciplines (e.g. psychology, sociology, organisation and management theory) whose conceptual structures and exemplars are grounded in the cultures of high income countries. This can mean that some aspects of educational theory are culturally remote; the range of topics may be dislocated in time and space from those current in a particular system; and that some areas critical to current practice (e.g. teaching very large classes, organising multi-grade teaching, coping with pupils of widely differing ability and achievement levels) are neglected or treated superficially. Gender issues are seldom highlighted in the materials we analysed. Approaches are needed the encourage reflection on what it means to be a teacher from a range of different perspectives (e.g. George et al 2002).

Fifth, the pedagogy associated with teacher education curricula may be ill-matched to both the stated aims of training and the characteristics of trainees. We have highlighted the fact that in no case was there serious recognition that trainees are adult learners rather than school students and that prior experience was not foregrounded in the treatment of methods of teaching etc. Most worryingly, although new pedagogic approaches were often advocated and included in aims (e.g. learner-centred lesson development, group work, role play, project assignments, reflective debate) there was little evidence of their application to the training process itself. Decisions on timetable organisation, teaching group size, the format of teaching, and the presentation of text materials often seem to militate against methods which diverged from chalk and talk. Much teaching in Colleges is delivered to passive learners in large groups and seems unlikely to encourage independent learning amongst trainees. It conspicuously does not model effectively many of the novel pedagogic practices advocated for primary school teaching, though it could often achieve this within existing constraints.

10 Insights From MUSTER and Ways Forward

Sixth, analysis of assessment strategies suggests that these are often at variance with curricula aspirations. Most obviously much assessment is narrow in scope, restricted in cognitive level, and paper- rather than practice-based. Where there is continuous assessment its emphasis is frequently on the reproduction of material contained in texts. The assessment of professional studies is widely problematic and it often remains unclear what is being tested apart from the recall of taught material. Professional skills are generally not assessed directly. Though there is some agreement that effective teachers need good interpersonal skills and appropriate attitudes, curricula largely neglect these and other aspects of personal development and growth, and make no attempt to assess them.

Seventh, in no case does there seem to be a system for regular review and improvement of the teacher education curricula. Neither do mechanisms exist to formatively or summatively evaluate their effectiveness. The origins of teacher education curricula are diverse, reflecting historical traditions, sporadic investments in new courses (often motivated by external assistance), and the interests of various groups of stakeholders. The results can appear to lack coherence and balance, and a secure and consistent philosophic and pedagogic base. It sometimes appears that international borrowing can result in curricular ideas being deposited, one above the other, like geological strata, without any of them being critiqued and adapted in the light of local needs and cultures.

10.3 The Practicum: Teaching Practice and School-based Training

The practicum should be at the heart of a professional training since it provides an arena for the development and demonstration of teaching skills and professional knowledge. MUSTER research covered both traditional, college-based pre-service courses where trainees go on Teaching Practice (TP) for relatively short periods of blocked time, as in Lesotho, Ghana and Trinidad and Tobago, and other forms of training more akin to apprenticeship, such as MIITEP in Malawi and the Trinidadian 'On the Job Training' (OJT) pre-service orientation course. The final year 'internship' now being introduced in Ghana provides another variation of practice. Looking across the cases, certain issues recur in different contexts.

Firstly, the studies point up a major conceptual weakness of the so-called 'technical rationality' model (Schon 1983) where theory and practice are taught – and learnt - separately. The programmes we examined generally assume that trainees will go into the schools and 'apply the theory' learnt in college. In reality, this does not happen. Trainees are faced with many confusing situations which they do not know how to deal with, and they often have access to very limited support to help them solve problems. Learning to teach effectively requires that trainees integrate the insights and concepts derived from the public propositional knowledge available in colleges, with the contextual and situated knowledge of specific classrooms and pupils. This can allow the derivation of meaningful generalisations

10 Insights From MUSTER and Ways Forward

for future practice grounded in trainees' needs and experience. This implies that the theoretical and practical elements of the curriculum should be intertwined and presented in a dialogic relationship, rather than as discrete elements. At present this is not so, either in content, or in timing and structure.

A further desirable prerequisite is that the colleges and schools should be in close touch, exchanging information, ideas and even personnel. Nowhere did we find tutors and teachers working as a team to create effective learning experiences for trainees. Relationships between schools and colleges varied from indifferent to mistrustful or even hostile. The colleges dominated, and the schools felt, and were treated as, the junior partner, even when the training was largely school-based.

Secondly, there are real economic and logistical problems when trying to provide appropriate practical experience for large numbers of students in countries with poor infrastructure and where schools are widely scattered over geographical distances. Either students are crowded into schools near Colleges, as has happened in Ghana, or they select their own schools area where they can find accommodation across a wide geographic area, as in Lesotho. If the latter, then it becomes expensive and time-consuming for tutors to visit them. Some systems have 'Demonstration Schools' close to the colleges. However these tend to be few in number and useful only for short, introductory sessions. They do not have the capacity to support trainees over a sustained period where the trainee learns to take responsibility for a class over time.

The third related issue is that of appropriate supervision. Tutors have limited time and transport. Often their visits tended to be badly timed, rushed, irregular, and mostly orientated to assessment. Sustained formative feedback geared to the student's own development does not generally occur. One frequently suggested alternative is to give schools responsibilities for supervision within a framework of school-based training. This is problematic where many co-operating teachers may themselves be un- or under-qualified and lack the skills or confidence to give appropriate advice and support. It may also be the case that primary teachers and principals do not see training as part of their role, and that trainers may resist any attempt to dilute their status through shifting responsibilities to school-level staff. MIITEP in Malawi illustrates sharply these and other problems which arise in trying to shift to more school-based systems of supervision and support. It may be that deploying District Resource Teachers (as in Lesotho) and Primary Education Advisors (as in Malawi) to support trainees is more realistic than expecting schools to be able to provide much professional support. These kind of staff can run local workshops, set and help mark practical assignments, supervise and assess classroom performance, and train school mentors.

Fourth is the problem of assessment. Most of the assessment instruments we saw for the practicum used lists of discrete skills or 'teacher behaviours' which observers graded, usually

10 Insights From MUSTER and Ways Forward

on a 4 or 5 point scale, and then totalled to give a letter grade or percentage mark. In some cases there were moderation systems to guard against bias, but in most cases grades were based on one short visit by a single tutor, raising doubts about validity and reliability. MUSTER research shows that ratings can vary greatly between observers, that reports from school observations are not always collected and collated, and that it is often unclear how TP assessments were incorporated in the final grade. It was noted that very few trainees ever 'fail' TP, and that marks on TP rarely made much difference to final achievement grades despite the cost and effort put into obtaining ratings through visits and observation. An obvious weakness was that none of the assessment regimes we explored captured anything more than discrete behaviours in single lessons. They did not give insight into whether trainees were organising effective learning for pupils, or were learning from their mistakes and developing their practice.

10.4 Post-Training Issues

The evidence so far presents a very complex picture from which it is difficult to draw general conclusions, and still less does it suggest clear-cut policy recommendations. All we can say with confidence is that teacher training does have more of an impact than some of its critics claim, but that its effects are less than many of its proponents desire.

On the positive side, most NQTs value their training. It boosts their confidence, raises their awareness, and provides them with a new discourse – they can 'talk the talk' of teachers. The evidence suggests they have gained some knowledge of curriculum content, and of a range of teaching methods. They have been alerted to aspects of psychology and child development. They have acquired a number of skills - lesson planning, record-keeping, managing children and resources in a classroom, keeping time – which enable them to fit into school routines and work with colleagues. Importantly, they have been provided with or developed their own resource materials in the form of notes, books and teaching aids, which can be used in resource-poor schools. Most principals we interviewed believe that trainees bring a slow but steady stream of new information and practice into schools. Training at its best lays a foundation on which to build.

On the other hand, the training we have explored does not appear to have had dramatic effects on NQTs' behaviour, attitudes or understandings. NQTs seem to teach rather more competently than untrained ones, but not very differently. Their attitudes towards the profession, and towards teaching itself, change only marginally through their college years, and not always in the hoped-for direction. There is little evidence from the programmes studied here that most trainees have gained deep insights into teaching and learning that would enable them to continue to develop and improve their own practice, though there are obviously exceptions and the programmes do vary in their effects.

10 Insights From MUSTER and Ways Forward

We note that first, none of the countries studied had a formal policy for induction of NQTs. Practice varied in the different cases but most commonly it was left to the discretion of head teachers to orient new teachers as and how they thought fit, with varying degrees of support from class teachers. In some cases there was some input from district officials and advisors. The lack of systematic arrangements for guidance and support in the first year on the job was striking It almost certainly contributes to the 'washout' of training, to the extent that NQTs' learning is not reinforced purposefully in their first appointments. It may also lead to problems with morale and lead to career changes if support to overcome problems is not forthcoming. Our studies did not enable us to pinpoint details of the relative importance of school and other environmental factors on the practice of NQTs. We can say that NQTs are likely to benefit from a first placement in schools with basic teaching resources, supportive heads and teacher colleagues, and effective school management. Our evidence, especially that from Ghana, also shows the importance of help with the social and economic aspects of becoming a teacher. For many NQTs establishing appropriate relationships with the local community, finding adequate housing, and getting paid on time are the most important problems which have to be solved before concentrating on becoming more effective teachers.

Second, the research highlights the possible consequences of different practices on the posting of NQTs. Thus for example, in Lesotho NQTs apply for jobs of their choice, whereas in Ghana trainees are posted to where they are needed. Circumstantially those with more choice over where they teach may be more committed to the positions they accept than those posted, especially if such postings are in unattractive locations as can be the case in Ghana. Attitudes of NQTs in Ghana are also shaped by the policy on 'further study' which encourages trainees to think of their first qualification as a springboard to 'better' careers. After three years NQTs can qualify for upgrading, and move into full-time courses leading to degrees which may take them out of primary teaching. It is clear that the transition from a pre-service programme into work is a crucial but neglected stage of training, where new policies are needed.

Third, teacher training is located within a broad socio-economic context. It is one stage of a cycle in which trainees come from schools where they were socialised into certain attitudes, values and practices, enter college where many of these dispositions are only challenged superficially, and move back into schools similar to those they experienced as pupils. It is perhaps not surprising that attitudes are deeply rooted, and may change little over the training period. The question the MUSTER data raises is to reconsider realistically what can be achieved in an initial training programme, over what period of time, with the resources available and the pool of potential new entrants. It also shows the need to be much clearer about which skills and capabilities are essential for the beginning teacher, and which are better developed in mid-career. In none of the MUSTER countries is initial training integrated into a coherent pattern of continuing professional development (CPD) that

10 Insights From MUSTER and Ways Forward

builds expertise and competence throughout a teacher's career. Investment in teacher education is typically heavily loaded towards initial training, despite indications that this may not be the most effective strategy to improve learning and teaching in schools.

10.5 Teacher Educators

The MUSTER study shows the extent to which teacher educators as a group have been ignored, and suggests some of the reasons why most colleges are not playing a more creative and innovative role in their education systems. Some of the key issues that emerged in response to the research questions are summarised below.

Firstly, there are no policies for recruitment and career development for teacher educators in the MUSTER countries. School teachers become teacher trainers in a variety of haphazard ways: in Ghana and Malawi they are 'posted' in ways that imply this is just a further step up the civil service ladder which brings benefits in terms of salary. Elsewhere they apply for the job, sometimes for reasons of status and interest rather than for pay. In Trinidad and Tobago, where tutors are more highly qualified than in the other research sites, teacher trainers are paid the same as school teachers. Conditions for appointment as a teacher trainer, which increasingly require degree or post-graduate degree status, have made it difficult for experienced primary teachers to qualify in the past, with the result that substantial numbers have been secondary-trained. This may be changing slowly.

Secondly, teacher trainers receive no formal Induction or continuing professional development. Some colleges – notably in Malawi – offer some informal orientation and support, but in most places individuals have to rely on curriculum documents – often incomplete – and their own memories of training. In the more bureaucratic systems, in-service support seems to consist mainly of short courses laid on when the Ministry wishes to disseminate innovations. In more open systems some individuals manage to undertake further degrees when time and funding permit, but seldom are these part of an integrated plan for developing colleges as a whole, nor are the new ideas fed back systematically to colleagues.

Thirdly, few of the tutors we have interviewed and few of the colleges seem to have clear models of teacher training to guide their work. Often trainees are treated and taught like secondary students. Many tutors seem to have a 'banking' view of training which simply assumes that trainees need to acquire subject knowledge and standard methods of teaching which can then be applied fairly uniformly in schools. In discussing the kind of teacher they want to produce, tutors seem to share many of the same images and beliefs about the 'good primary teacher' encountered among the entering students, and often emphasise affective rather than cognitive aspects, with rhetoric about personal characteristics and professional commitment. Where tutors espouse theories of student-centred learning, few put these into

10 Insights From MUSTER and Ways Forward

practice in their colleges, or directly help their students do so in schools. It should be noted that many individuals are dedicated and hard-working, and some have developed their own ideas about teacher training and find intrinsic satisfaction in their job. But we also found frustration and low morale amongst substantial numbers of trainers, for reasons connected with lack of policy on teacher education, poor remuneration, uncertain promotion prospects, and poor working conditions.

A final point to make is how difficult it can be for tutors' thinking to transcend the systems in which they are embedded. The intellectual horizons of many college staff seem out of date, narrowly cast, and parochially constrained, for reasons of history and economics. There has been much borrowing of ideas from high income countries, but there is little evidence of critique and adaptive development of key constructs and theories of professional learning. Without the stimulus of further professional development, and an innovative working environment, it is difficult for tutors to pioneer more effective teaching and learning strategies, and to create models of teacher education appropriate to local environments and educational cultures.

10.6 Supply, Demand, Efficiency and Costs

Underlying any policy for teacher education are questions concerning supply and demand, and efficiency and costs. The MUSTER data on these lead to the following summary conclusions.

First, in Ghana, Lesotho, and Malawi the challenge posed by national targets for enrolment and pupil-teacher ratios is immense. None of these systems can produce enough new teachers to meet projected demand. Moreover the costs of existing modes of training suggest that simple expansion of existing capacity is financially unsustainable. Malawi has adopted a mixed-mode approach to training which is relatively low cost and high volume. The other countries retain lengthy conventional full-time pre-career training with limited output.

Second, in two of the countries the size of the school age group appears to be shrinking or static. In Lesotho the potential benefit from this of reduced demand for new teachers is compromised by the small output and high costs of training. It may also be negated by the increased demand which is arising from the introduction of Free Primary Education. In Lesotho capacity needs to be increased substantially, not least to respond to the short term increase in demand created by FPE[62]. In Trinidad and Tobago demand is small and is not growing. Here there is a window of opportunity to invest in quality improvement and extending the role of colleges into professional support pre- and post- training.

---

[62] The World Bank is financing a new distance programme of teacher education which will complement the standard initial teacher education provided by the NTTC. It is currently unclear how the output from this system will grow and how it will articulate with the NTTC.

10 Insights From MUSTER and Ways Forward

Third, Ghana has the problem of an under-supply of the number of teachers necessary to maintain current enrolment rates. This is compounded by the fact that it is the country furthest away from achieving universal primary enrolment, and this creates an additional demand of magnitude. The current system, even with a modified 'In-In-Out' system, does not have the capacity to meet demand.

Fourth, the discussion papers on which this report depends explore the composition of costs and provide insights into the scope for increases in internal efficiency. There are opportunities to make better use of staff and physical resources, especially if management and accountability systems monitor costs with efficiency in mind, which is rarely the case. There appear few incentives to optimise the utilisation of staff. Non-salary recurrent costs of colleges are often greater than salaries, except in Trinidad and Tobago where the colleges are not residential. This may also be an area where efficiency could be improved. Student stipends are the major component of recurrent salary costs, and these allowances are often paid at levels comparable with those of teachers' salaries.

Fifth, though the detail is complex, the simple conclusions are clear. If the national and international targets for universal enrolment and reasonable levels of pupil teacher ratio are to be met, alternatives to full-time, pre-career training over two or three years have to be considered. MIITEP gives an insight into one alternative. It has strengths and weaknesses which other papers explore (e.g. Kunje & Chirembo 2000, Stuart & Kunje 2000). This approach can produce an output of new teachers that more closely matches demand. However, it reduces time in college, anticipates effective support whilst trainees are working in schools, and implies substantial development costs if modified versions of this kind of approach are to be considered for different national contexts.

10.7 MUSTER Key Issues

MUSTER has explored in great detail the process and practice of teacher education across a range of low income countries. It has generated many detailed studies of different aspects of the problems and possibilities that confront teacher educators and policy makers in grappling with the critical issues that will determine future policy, inform innovations designed to increase effectiveness and improve quality, and shape the form teacher education will have in the future. It is now appropriate to go beyond the specific findings captured in this report and in the MUSTER Discussion Papers, and discuss over-arching and cross-cutting concerns that should help frame the options available and the alternatives that may be feasible in reconceptualising teacher education.

This discussion falls into several parts. It is general rather than specific to each country system. The MUSTER country reports provide specific recommendations related to each system.

10 Insights From MUSTER and Ways Forward

10.8 On Policy

The simple observation is that across the MUSTER countries, policy on primary teacher education is fragmented, incomplete, and more often than not simply non-existent. Despite its obvious importance to the achievement of nationally and internationally agreed goals to universalise primary schooling, improve quality, and enhance equity in access and retention, the development of coherent, medium term, financially sustainable teacher education policy tailored to meet the demand for new teachers has been widely neglected. Absence of policy has both practical consequences and symbolic significance (Sayed 2002).

In Ghana, College reform has not been a priority since FCUBE was announced. The recent introduction of the 'In-In-Out' programme to replace the three-year fully residential training has not evolved from a considered strategy to supply the number of teachers needed to meet the objectives of FCUBE. Lesotho continues to train far fewer teachers than it needs to implement Free Primary Education (FPE). The recent establishment of the Task Force on Teacher Education after the Lesotho MUSTER conference is a first step in the direction of a strategic plan. Malawi has grappled with the implication of its FPE programme and has attempted to meet the need for trained teachers through the innovative MIITEP programme of mixed college- and school-based training. The suspension of this programme, with the consequence that no new teachers were enrolled in training in 1999 and 2000, reflects the absence of national teacher education policy. The recent creation of a Teacher Education Division within the Ministry, the inclusion of teacher education more prominently in the Policy and Investment Framework, and the agreement on the funding of three extra cohorts are signs that the importance of a plan for teacher education are now recognised. So also is the formation of a teacher education Task Group. In Trinidad and Tobago the training colleges have seen conditions of service improve and may be moved from the Ministry of Education to Ministry of Human Resource and Development. This creates an opportunity to revitalise the college system and capitalise on its strengths.

It is self-evident that national planning, within or outside the discussions that surround sector-wide agreements with external development agencies, must directly address questions of teacher supply and demand, quality, curriculum and deployment. To be plausible such policy needs to have clarity on its goals (what are the skills and competencies newly trained teachers should possess?), methods (how are these to be acquired?), costs (what resources are needed?) and timescale (how long will it take to achieve the desired outcomes?). This then is the first priority for policy makers. There are a number of others.

The second priority is to recognise that what is possible and sustainable is constrained in different ways in the different countries. Most simply put, any medium term policy has to recognise the realities imposed by demography (which determine the numbers of pupils and hence teachers needed each year), teacher attrition (retirement, alternative career choices,

10 Insights From MUSTER and Ways Forward

the impact of HIV/AIDS), and enrolment rate targets (achieving and sustaining universal enrolment up to a specified grade level). It also has to start from existing training capacity and recognise the constraints of infrastructure on the rate at which output might grow in quality and quantity. Our analyses indicate how different the situations are in the different countries, and also draw attention to some of the constraints and opportunities imposed by history, politics and finance. In three of the four countries the choice is between mass methods that could produce trained teachers in sufficient quantity to meet demand, and those which might improve quality but would limit the number of pupils with access to teachers with any training at all. The MUSTER analyses of supply and demand and of efficiency and costs need refinement, periodic up-dating, and interpretation into frameworks for policy at national level.

A third area of policy concern relates to the mechanisms through which teacher education is resourced, and its performance monitored. Typically budgetary systems use historic budgeting loosely related to actual or projected student numbers. The arrangements vary, but none of those we have explored seem sufficient to provide a stable financial environment conducive to the efficient management of colleges. Where budgetary allocations are unpredictable, release of funds irregular, and auditing and accountability weak it is difficult to see how consistent development can take place. Under these circumstances it is also unlikely that training institutions can develop their own medium term strategic planning and gain the commitment of their staff to a common set of goals. Training systems are not large and complex in comparison with school systems. It should be possible to include teacher education budget lines in Medium Term Expenditure Frameworks and ensure that what is allocated is disbursed regularly. Given the relatively small number of institutions involved there is no obvious reason why they should not stand in a direct relationship with a Ministry department and budget. Where we have observed the effects of decentralising the budget to intermediary levels, this seems to introduce an unnecessary layer of bureaucracy and delay.

MUSTER research has not identified existing funding mechanisms which reward efficiency and penalise waste. Neither, as noted above, is funding generally linked to any formula related to the number of students, or their successful graduation. It is also true that salary costs per student (predominantly lecturers' salaries) vary across training institutions within the same country largely as a result of variations in student-teacher ratios. This suggests that norms on staffing are seldom applied, resulting in under-staffing of some institutions and over-staffing of others. It is also significant for costs that the average size of training institutions is often small, and falls below 500 trainees in many cases. This is often smaller than the size of typical secondary schools and many primary schools. Economies of scale are available if it is possible to increase average size and distribute fixed costs across more trainees. Expenditure on learning resources in training institutions is often minimal and no mechanisms seem to exist to ensure that learning resources are replenished at some minimum level. No ring-fencing or other procedures are used to protect spending on books,

10 Insights From MUSTER and Ways Forward

learning aids etc., with predictable results. There are many mechanisms that could be used to regularise the flow of funds and create at least some incentives to increase efficiency. These could improve the chances that training institutions develop cumulatively within a stable financial environment that could offer better value for money.

Fourth, boarding-related costs are high and often the largest element of training institution costs. These costs may be necessary and can be efficiently managed. The policy questions revolve around the length of time boarding is essential, and whether any element of cost recovery should be introduced. The latter is especially relevant where trainee teachers are paid stipends as untrained teachers, from which they would otherwise have to fund their own living costs.

Fifth, policy on initial teacher education should be linked to that on subsequent INSET and CPD. This is not the case. The main reasons to make these links are that however effective initial training is, it leads into development as a newly qualified teacher, a critical period when new teachers require support and guidance. Training institutions should play a full role in INSET and CPD since these activities should cross-fertilise and feed back into more effective initial training. In principle an initial qualification is precisely that, and not a terminal stage in a career ladder. The balance between the time and money spent on initial training and subsequent INSET and CPD is a critical policy question. If most investment is front-loaded (i.e. at the beginning of a teachers' career), if teacher attrition is high and rising, if teachers' career lifetimes as primary teachers are shortening, and if substantial effort is to be directed to changing school practice through direct support for whole school development, then it may make sense to shorten periods of initial training in favour of more training inputs for NQTs as their careers develop. Amongst other things this has the benefit of directing more investment of training resources towards those on the job and likely to remain so.

Sixth, none of the countries within MUSTER (with the exception of South Africa), has begun to address the question as to whether non-government resources have a role to play in expanded and more effective teacher education. Historically much was provided through not-for-profit non-government institutions. It may or may not be the case that these questions should be reopened. Where resources are a major constraint on teacher education, and internal efficiency of public institutions is low, some forms of public-private partnership need to remain among the options. The detailed articulation of these is necessarily contextually located within each system.

Seventh, clear vision is needed on the appropriate organisational location of teacher education institutions. The most obvious options are directly under a teacher education Division of the Ministry of Education; under provincial or regional governments (where decentralisation is a reality); affiliated to and administered through Universities; and as semi-

10 Insights From MUSTER and Ways Forward

autonomous entities with a large element of self-government. In four cases centralised control under the Ministry is the status quo. In South Africa teacher education has been moved into the tertiary sector and will now be provided by university-affiliated colleges and faculties of education. Integration into the tertiary centre may carry advantages in terms of less intellectual isolation and access to better facilities and learning resources. It may or may not ease funding problems. It might risk the 'academicisation' of professional training. Centralised systems have not been conspicuously successful; indeed MUSTER suggests the opposite. Low prioritisation of funding, moribund curriculum development, and rigid employment structures have been accompanied by policy neglect. But it does not have to be that way. Greater degrees of decentralised administration and accountability might make sense if they succeeded in closing the gap between colleges and the communities of practice they serve, and if the financial base for teacher education could be assured with effective audit trails. However, there are risks that the limitations of infrastructure, competence and vision might have perverse consequences.

Finally, it seems to us, the constructive and effective development of teacher education requires direct access to Ministerial authority, clear lines of administrative control and accountability, and strategic delegation of some measure of autonomy to training institutions, at least in professional arenas. The latter would seem essential if teacher education institutions are to move away from patterns of organisation and operation which closely resemble secondary schools, to become professional development institutions working to facilitate the learning of adults and their induction into new roles as self confident, competent and creative young professionals.

The policy problems we have identified in MUSTER suggest that at their core are several causes. First, primary teacher education policy has often been seen as an afterthought to policy on Education for All. It is almost as if it is a residual concern that has had to be addressed in the wake of policy on universalising schooling, which has had a much higher public profile and much catalysis for development agencies. Second, the locus over control over teacher education has been ambiguous and often a subsidiary function within a department of a line Ministry. Third, and partly as a result, resources have not flowed in ways consistent with demand for newly trained teachers. Fourth, key stakeholders (parents, teachers unions, educational administrators, college lecturers) have been slow to assert the importance of re-conceptualising teacher education in the wake of primary curriculum reform and universal access, as also have been at least some development agencies.

Policy choice is needed as a pre-requisite for the implementation of new strategies. It is of course not sufficient on its own to ensure that the problems we identify will be overcome. Nevertheless without some consensus, and action on the main points above where these are most problematic, it seems unlikely that effective reforms will take place.

---

10 Insights From MUSTER and Ways Forward

10.9 On Selection and Admission

Policy on trainee selection is generally poorly articulated and lacking any evidence base. Predominantly trainees are selected as a result of meeting minimum academic requirements. Other selection methods – interviews, aptitude tests, language tests – are rarely used and are not consistently applied. Yet we can find no studies of the predictive validity of such selection methods. The attempts MUSTER made to test this do not show that school-leaving achievement scores are good predictors of college performance, except perhaps in subject disciplines taught at college level. It is widely argued that academic selection criteria should be raised to increase the quality of trainees. This is unwise unless there is confidence that these are good predictors of subsequent performance. It is unrealistic where there simply are not enough minimally qualified applicants in the pool currently available, which is the case in some countries. Two policy implications flow from this. First, there is a case for considering whether selection should include things other than academic results from secondary school examinations and, if so, what procedures are viable and cost-effective. Second, where academic achievement levels are thought to be too low, the question is whether content upgrading in subjects should be a priority at training institution level, or whether some sort of access programmes at school level might be more effective (school costs are generally much less than college costs). We note that in two of our case-study countries (Malawi and Trinidad and Tobago), trainees are appointed as untrained teachers before initial training. In principle this provides an extended opportunity to assess suitability and base selection on performance as an untrained teacher. However, since trainees are already appointed to the teaching profession, and links between the prior experience programme and the training institutions are weak or non-existent in the two cases, this opportunity is largely lost. It does not have to be.

The second set of issues relates to the characteristics of those selected. The detailed data indicate many factors that shape the starting points from which trainees progress. Some of these may be thought fairly obvious (e.g. low levels of academic qualification), others are not so obvious (e.g. the range and extent of previous experience as teachers, the relatively high ages of some entrants). MUSTER has also provided insights into attitudes and dispositions to teachers and teaching which can be used to inform the process of professional learning. Trainees do not enter training with no preconceptions, but many. How they learn, what they internalise, and how motivated they are to remain teaching in primary schools are all bound up with these cognitive and affective experiences they bring and the attitudes they hold. It is these that, at least from one point of view, frame the 'zones of proximal development' which trainers can use in delivering the curriculum. Yet neither curriculum developers nor tutors seem to take cognisance of what students bring with them, or to seek to understand it more fully. In the worst cases training proceeds on assumptions about the characteristics of those trained which are demonstrably false. The first step in ameliorating these problems is to acquire information and insight about the trainees however they have been selected. It

10 Insights From MUSTER and Ways Forward

is their characteristics that matter in defining their learning needs and shaping the curriculum process.

10.10   On the Curriculum for Initial Training

The MUSTER analyses of teacher education curriculum issues lead to many insights into the quality and relevance of material for existing programmes. The picture these paint is one that suggests that investment in curriculum development is long overdue and that much which is currently available falls short of what is needed and what is possible. Large parts of the teacher education curricula seem to have been adapted from the academic curricula of school or university, rather than designed for adult learners or for the acquisition of professional knowledge and skills. They seldom recognise the role of relevant experiences, nor the different motivation and learning styles of adults. The curriculum needs to be reconceptualised, but in ways that keep in touch with local context and realities. The following are points for consideration.

Firstly, the curriculum must be matched to the needs of the learners, recognising areas of both strength and weakness. Primary trainees are usually a 'mixed ability' group; they will have done different subjects at high school, and a number may well have been 'slow learners'. Many may find maths and science particularly difficult. The subject courses must take this into account, by such means as setting, providing remedial support, self-study materials, or whatever is needed. This could include subject upgrading to school-leaving level through recognised and effective distance learning methods

Second, a fresh look has to be taken at all the traditional components. Curriculum developers have to be realistic about what can be achieved within the given time, taking account of the age, experience and academic level of the entrants. Many programmes seem to assume that everything has to be taught during initial training, and consequently most of the curricula we analysed are grossly overloaded. The resulting stress on both tutors and students tends to lower morale and lead to less efficient teaching and learning.

The curriculum should be slimmed down to concentrate on helping the student acquire relevant core skills and competences, and the basic subject knowledge needed at that stage. This might mean less focus on the subject as a traditional discipline, and more on understanding the main concepts from a learner's viewpoint, as expressed in the terms science education, language arts education, etc. In so doing, students are likely to come to a clearer and more useful, if narrower, understanding of the subject itself, as well as of the primary school syllabus. The languages of instruction should have a special place in the training of primary teachers, especially where lower primary is taught in the vernacular and upper primary in English. Trainees need to be fully fluent and competent in both, and to understand the strengths as well as the difficulties of bilingualism.

10 Insights From MUSTER and Ways Forward

Such a slimmed-down curriculum should, however, include key frameworks drawn from psychology and sociology about how children learn, how individuals differ, and about the role of schools in the society. This is a problem area. Firstly, 'foundations' courses often try to teach far too much of the theory. Secondly, the texts and the research on which they are based are often drawn exclusively from rich country contexts. There is an urgent need here for both research and curriculum development to bring international theories into dialogue with local cultural practices and the students' own experiences of growing up. The aim should be to compare what is universally human with what is culturally specific and contextual, so that students come to understand themselves and their pupils more clearly. Because these topics are relevant and new, students often find them interesting.

Third, the role of the personal in professional education has to be recognised. Trainees, as we have said, do not come empty-handed; they bring much baggage in the form of images, ideas and experiences about teaching. One task for the tutors is to help them unpack and articulate these, so some can be thrown away, others refashioned or replaced. This does not require special techniques or resources, but it does imply an open approach from the tutors, and the use of methods such as autobiographical essays, role-play and discussion, to elicit memories and allow attitudes to be re-examined.

This links to the need for the whole curriculum to pay more attention to the 'affective side'. It is paradoxical that while most trainees teachers and their tutors rate personal attitudes and interpersonal skills as key characteristics of good primary teachers, the training curriculum allows little space or opportunity for fostering personal growth and attitudes conducive to professional responsibility.

Fourth, the processes by which the curriculum are delivered need to be rethought. Theories of professional learning stress how public propositional knowledge, situational understanding, and personal experience have to be brought together. Such theories emphasise the importance of practice, and of reflection on practice, in developing skills. New information, ideas and skills have to be used before they are fully understood and internalised. Therefore, preparing and developing teachers means providing them with appropriate inputs of relevant knowledge, information and concepts stage by stage. Learning to apply and use the ideas and skills needs support, coaching and constructive feedback, thus scaffolding the learning. Therefore learning to teach requires extensive opportunities for guided practice in a conducive environment.

This highlights the role of the school. For practical reasons, most training programmes have Teaching Practice in one or two large blocks, or during an internship year, often at the end of the course. Yet shorter, alternating periods of time on and off campus are more effective, as they allow new information, ideas and skills to be internalised gradually through application and practice; equally, the experiential knowledge gained from attempting to

10 Insights From MUSTER and Ways Forward

teach can be thought about and refined before the next trial. This is difficult logistically, when colleges are residential and/or in rural areas.

Fifth, attention must be paid to modes of assessment. Written terminal exams should be strategically focused on essential summative outcomes. If college assignments were linked more closely to practice in schools, then project and enquiry work could make more use of the classroom as a resource. Ghanaian experience suggests this is difficult, both because of conservative attitudes, and because alternative methods are thought to be too time-consuming to be used with large numbers of students. However difficult, new attempts must be made to find more appropriate methods of assessing professional learning and professional competence. In particular, the assessment of TP is often just a ritual, sometimes a farce. The South African aim of providing holistic assessment of performance in an authentic environment, based on demonstrated competences integrating knowledge, skills and attitudes, may well be appropriate, but difficult to achieve.

Sixth, there is a need for curricula to be more precisely designed for specific contexts. These might be preparing teachers for bilingual teaching, large classes, resource poor teaching environments, or for specific school phases, e.g. infant, junior, or senior primary, or for specific groups of trainees, such as experienced but unqualified teachers, or inexperienced school leavers. One practical approach might be a more modular curriculum, where trainees could follow different pathways and take only those subjects and contents they needed, assuming they could demonstrate mastery of essential skills and competencies in other areas. Care would be needed to ensure integration and coherence, and more time would need to be invested in managing trainees' choices and progress through modules.

Finally, we suggest that in any teacher education curriculum the overall aims and desired outcomes need to be clarified, so that everyone is aware of the kind of teacher they are trying to produce – whether this be framed in terms of an effective instructor engaged to deliver a given curriculum efficiently, or in terms of a more autonomous professional expected to exercise their own judgement reflectively. The curriculum strategy then needs to be consistent with these aims and outcomes, and stakeholders should be supported in understanding and carrying out their roles in achieving it.

There are some general dimensions to curriculum problems raised by the MUSTER research. Amongst the most important are:

The lack of mechanisms for curriculum development, evaluation and renewal.
None of the MUSTER countries have systems for teacher education curriculum development; as a result it is ad hoc and sporadic.

10 Insights From MUSTER and Ways Forward

Teacher Education and Structural Change.

Educational reform focused on schools often proceeds in advance of reforms in teacher education curricula. In principle teacher education should lead rather than lag behind wider reforms, so that new entrants can be prepared to adopt new curricula and teaching methods. It is, however, unrealistic to expect new teachers to be focal points for change as new members of the profession in junior positions. There are risks, exemplified in some of the MUSTER countries, that reforms that simultaneously seek to transform pedagogy, curriculum content, and the organisation of learning and teaching, may over-stretch infrastructure and capacity for change.

Cross-Cultural Borrowing and Innovation.

International borrowing is inevitable and often useful for the development of teacher education. However, models and theories developed in one context should not be imported uncritically to others. Some aspects will resonate more easily across cultures than others. Teacher education curricula are needed that, while sometimes using cross-national insights as points of departure, also build on local teacher knowledge, experience, and examples of good practice, in order to develop culturally relevant and effective teaching strategies. If innovations are to work, they need to be grounded and contextualised, and to make sense to those expected to carry them out (see Croft 2002 for elaboration of these points based on her work in Malawi). Moreover, strategies for innovation should recognise the importance of establishing a favourable climate of opinion to adopt new practices. Innovations that are pushed from the centre, rather than pulled by effective demand from communities of practice, will always be more difficult to sustain.

10.11   **On Colleges**

The college systems that MUSTER has explored have their specific histories which draw attention to the contributions they have made to educational development in the past. The strong impression from MUSTER data is that whatever the historic impact of teacher education institutions had been, those which we researched were no longer playing key roles in the development of their national education systems. There was little evidence that most staff were engaged directly in curriculum development, either at school level or in Colleges. Professional links with school systems were often fragile or non-existent and practising primary teachers were conspicuous by their general absence from activities organised in the colleges. Many colleges can be characterised by physical and intellectual isolation and many appeared held down by the weight of tradition, by lack of vision, and poor management. Any reconceptualisation of teacher education has to consider whether colleges have a role, and if so, what that role should be.

In principle training institutions could be 'powerhouses of change' responsible for a number of different facets of teacher education: initial training, INSET, training of trainers for

10 Insights From MUSTER and Ways Forward

school- and district-based support, curriculum development, research, development of teaching materials, etc. As developmental institutions distributed geographically across school systems they should be ideally situated to be centres of support, inspiration and innovation not only for new teachers but for NQTs and experienced teachers as well. If this were to become a reality then a number of issues need consideration which necessarily differ in detail in different cases. These include:

College governance.

Most colleges exist uneasily in an ill-defined area between Ministries, higher education, and schools. Forms of governance need to be identified that support an academic and professional atmosphere, and which might encourage the development of cultures of research on practice, linking staff and programmes into problems of school development and students' achievement. This may imply some form of University affiliation to provide access to expertise, enhance the status of training institutions, and expand the intellectual horizons of staff.

Staffing.

It is essential to develop a cadre of professional teacher educators, who are capable of working both within and outside the institution in creative and innovative ways. This implies a pay and career structure that recognises the kinds of work they do and the responsibilities they carry. It should be policy to recruit primary trainers from experienced and committed primary teachers and provide the necessary academic upgrading, or if taking secondary trained teachers, to provide appropriate orientation including a significant period observing/teaching in primary schools. Gender issues must be borne in mind to ensure women candidates are not disadvantaged by selection criteria or mode of training. The development of a cadre implies induction programmes for new recruits, and regular opportunities for continuing professional development, including where appropriate post-graduate degrees. Teacher educators should be expected to work with and in schools and carry out research, to keep up to date with international developments and to help adapt these to local conditions.

Links with Schools.

Colleges need to establish closer relationships with schools. We found few examples of good practice. Possible partnership arrangements include: selected 'professional development' schools, near or on the campus; the linking of initial training of students to professional development of the co-operating teachers; the use of trained mentors to undertake part of the supervision and assessment, etc. Tutors could spend in schools time teaching, training, or doing research; equally, experienced teachers could be seconded to colleges for specific tasks.

10 Insights From MUSTER and Ways Forward

College Strategic Planning.

A strategy of 'whole college development' is attractive. Such an approach would require a senior management team with a clear vision of change, and administrative support and resources to carry it out. This presupposes medium term policy on teacher education and confirmation of the role colleges can play. It also assumes the existence or appointment of groups of tutors prepared to commit themselves to their own professional development and that of the training system.

10.12 On Structures

Teacher education systems develop within specific national contexts which condition their form. New ideas for methods and structures have to recognise the realities of differing needs, circumstances and resources. Suggested improvements have to be formulated within the assumptions, processes and expectations of the wider national education system. There is thus no 'one-size-fits-all' solution to the problems of teacher education MUSTER has explored. However there are some structural questions that recur across systems. The basic structural issues for teacher education systems revolve around where training should take place, how long it should take, and what if anything should happen before and after periods of initial training leading to certification.

There are three common options as to institutional location. These are colleges of education, university education departments, or in schools. In reality the choices between these locations are not free. College-based systems for primary training are common in many low income countries and reflect how training systems have developed. Colleges are often the only post-secondary institutions in their geographic area and may be associated with post-secondary opportunities for particular groups who have a political stake in the continuity of the institutions. College systems seem likely to persist unless or until essentially political decisions are made to adopt another arrangement. South Africa has taken the step of making all initial training university-based or affiliated with universities. However, the circumstances under which this has come about are unique (see Lewin, Sayed & Samuel 2003).

College-based systems may have advantages in terms of local location linked to communities or clusters of schools: a focus on a single profession and a responsiveness to educational needs, a role in pre-service and in-service education, and lower costs than tertiary level institutions. Our research suggests that these potential advantages are not necessarily converted into realities. They also have to be balanced against the risks of parochialism associated with the local (especially when colleges are rural, and physically and intellectually isolated), the limits of expertise and insight associated with training institutions divorced from research, and the high costs that may be associated with small size.

10 Insights From MUSTER and Ways Forward

University-based training offers the prospect of inputs from staff with high levels of disciplinary expertise, connection to insights from research relevant to learning and teaching, multi-disciplinary perspectives, and superior teaching resources associated with large-scale institutions. On the other hand critics suggest that university-based training may be a long way removed from the issues of practice in primary schools, high levels of academic knowledge in disciplines are largely irrelevant, and tutors' career advancement is likely to depend more on research recognition than training competence.

School-based training has become increasingly common in rich country systems. There are many good pedagogic and professional development reasons why training located in the work environment is potentially attractive, including its direct links with practical problems, advice from successful teachers, and socialisation into professional norms and standards. However, the basic assumptions of school-based training namely that there are sufficient schools to offer appropriate training environments and enough qualified teachers to act as professional mentors to trainees – are often difficult to meet in low income countries. Most schools may not be appropriately resourced as training sites, lacking both qualified teachers and enough teaching and learning materials. Nor do staff necessarily see their role as including training new teachers and they are unlikely themselves to have any training as trainers. Under these circumstances, school-based training may simply become a form of 'sitting by Thabo', with new teachers simply copying what is done around them whether or not this is good practice. The MIITEP experience does suggest that with enough support, some elements of school based training are possible even in very resource-poor circumstances. But expectations of what can be achieved have to be realistic: serious investment has to be made in print-based handbooks and manuals for trainees and for trainers; field-based peripatetic resource persons and selected members of school staff have to be trained in supervision and support.

School-based training is generally associated with various forms of distance education, as it is in MIITEP. Distance education methods are attractive because they allow teachers to be trained while on the job, which saves the costs of replacement. It should also reduce the direct costs if a proportion of the training is self-instructional and based on print or other low-cost media. However, the problems of distance learning are well known. For primary teachers in rural Africa there are particular problems. The materials have to be at the right language level for ESL learners and cover a wide range of topics, as the trainees may have access to few other printed resources. In so-called predominantly 'oral' cultures students may find book-based learning particularly difficult; aural media such as radio programmes or audio-cassettes may be more effective, if the technology is available and motivation can be maintained. Video is much more expensive, and unlikely to be as cost-effective as alternatives. Though new information technologies based on computers and the internet appear to offer many potential benefits, these are yet to be demonstrated in practice in mass systems of teacher education in Africa. They have high initial costs, very substantial on-costs,

10 Insights From MUSTER and Ways Forward

carry risks of rapid obsolescence of hardware and software, and have great diseconomies for small-scale utilisation. Regular face-to-face contact with peers and a tutor are likely to remain essential components of training, albeit supplemented by other methods as and when these become available at sustainable and attractive levels of cost.

The questions of how long training should take and what should happen before and after the period of initial training are important, but as with the question of where training should be located, there is no single answer. A wide range of possibilities can be imagined, and seven of these are identified in Box 10.1 and Table 15. Descriptively these can be summarised as:

Box 10.1: **Possible Patterns of Initial Training**

Mode 1	Conventional full-time college-based training preceded by no experience, and followed by no structured support
Mode 2	Conventional full-time college-based training preceded by pre course experience and followed by mentored induction into schools
Mode 3	Teaching experience as an untrained teacher followed by conventional full-time college-based training
Mode 4	Mentored pre-training experience on the job, followed by conventional full-time college-based training and mentored induction into schools
Mode 5	Mentored pre-training experience followed by a short period of conventional college-based training followed by school placement with INSET support
Mode 6	Mentored pre-training experience followed by alternating short periods of conventional full-time college-based training followed by mentored induction into schools
Mode 7	Mentored pre-training experience followed by wholly school-based training on the job supported by distance learning and followed by mentored distance support in school

There are many other possible mixes that carry different resource and cost implications. We can note four key observations. First, extended full-time institutional training is only one of many options. Second, what comes before and what comes after core periods of training may

10 Insights From MUSTER and Ways Forward

be just as important as what occurs in the core, though rarely is it systematically considered as part of the training process. Thirdly, there is no necessity for core periods of training to be continuous or front- loaded in terms of costs or training inputs. Fourth, mixed-mode methods, which make use of distance education and learning while working, are clearly options which have potential cost advantages (but which may have other more problematic characteristics (Sayed, Heystek & Smit 2002, Reddy 2002b). The resource implications of different approaches can only be identified when their component parts are specified in particular country contexts.

The analytic questions related to future policy and practice focus on which of these (and other possible modes) are feasible, relevant to short to medium term needs, and are likely to be cost-effective. Is a new and different balance of inputs attractive to meet new needs and disquiet over both costs and effectiveness of existing patterns of delivery? There are opportunities to reconsider how investment in teacher education and training is best organised and delivered, given the constraints on resources, the shortfalls in teacher supply generated by enrolment expansion, the new emphasis in many countries on changing curricula to improve pupils' achievement, and the importance of improving quality and effectiveness.

Table 15: **Some possible training modes**

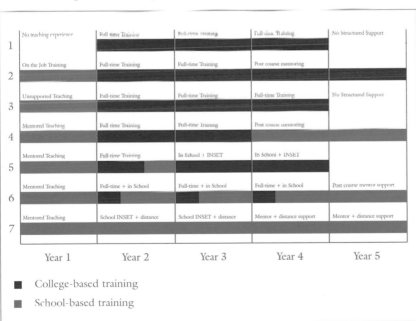

	No teaching experience	Full time Training	Full-time training	Full-time Training	No Structured Support
1					
2	On the Job Training	Full-time Training	Full-time Training	Post course mentoring	
3	Unsupported Teaching	Full-time Training	Full-time Training	Full-time Training	No Structured Support
4	Mentored Teaching	Full time Training	Full-time Training	Post course mentoring	
5	Mentored Teaching	Full-time Training	In School + INSET	In School + INSET	
6	Mentored Teaching	Full-time + in School	Full-time + in School	Full-time + in School	Post course mentor support
7	Mentored Teaching	School INSET + distance	School INSET + distance	Mentor + distance support	Mentor + distance support

| Year 1 | Year 2 | Year 3 | Year 4 | Year 5 |

■ College-based training

■ School-based training

10 Insights From MUSTER and Ways Forward

10.13   On External Assistance

Several issues stand out from the MUSTER research for those who provide external assistance. First, a number of points have already been made relating to the formation of policy on teacher education. Where teacher education, and more broadly the education system as a whole, is partly externally financed, it is incumbent on agency representatives to promote a strategic approach to teacher education and ensure it is appropriately considered in medium term planning. Where such policy does not exist it should be encouraged and the evidence base for its development supported. International development targets related to primary education and the EFA agenda cannot be realised without an adequate supply of qualified and competent teachers. Teacher supply is the main constraint on the achievement of these goals in a good number of the poorest countries.

The second point is that evidently it is not sufficient to make external finance available either through projects or as part of more general budgetary support. Availability is not the same thing as disbursement; disbursement is not the same thing as resources reaching end users in ways that result in valued outcomes. Where teacher education institutions are starved of funds (resulting in erratic and often very low salary payment, near zero allocation to learning materials, and lack of maintenance to the point where facilities are closed for long periods), regeneration of effective training systems is impossible.

The third point is that judgements do have to be made in the round about the profile of external assistance whether within a sector plan or without it. More specifically, assistance directed to school level designed to improve access, retention and quality has to include support for teacher development, since it is teachers who determine, more than anything else, the quality of learning that takes place. How this is articulated with the initial training system, and its institutions, is a core question. Initial training of itself is never likely to result in the transformation of teaching and learning in schools in the short term (new teachers are likely to be less skilled than experienced teachers, their organisational status is such that they have less influence on curriculum and school policy and practice, their numbers are small compared to those established in the profession etc.). Nevertheless, new teachers, and the institutions that train them, are in principle one of the few vectors for introducing new practices to improve pupil learning. Others may exist or be developed (e.g. teachers' centres, peripatetic advisory teachers). So a key question for those who provide external assistance is whether to include initial training institutions in development plans or to by-pass them in favour of direct support into the school system. A strategy of benign neglect of colleges, which does seem by implication to have been followed in some cases, seems an opportunity missed. Unless of course the judgement is made that such institutions really have reached the point where they are largely ineffective and not amenable to significant reform.

Fourth, external support has a comparative advantage in some spheres but not in others.

10 Insights From MUSTER and Ways Forward

Most obviously subsidy of development budgets for capital assets (predominantly buildings) may be the only way in which physical capacity can be expanded. Like other forms of assistance this can of course result in plant which is suited to purpose with appropriate durability and recurrent costs; it may also be poorly designed, expensive and difficult to maintain with local resources. Technical assistance is the other common form of support. This also needs to be tailored to purpose. Few believe that agency support of staff directly delivering services is cost-effective. More attractive is expert assistance with curriculum development, especially in those areas of the curriculum that are most internationalised (e.g. mathematics, science, international languages). This can also give access electronically or otherwise to networks which allow developers to share their experience across institutions and countries. Such international experts need to work very closely with national experts with a view to creating sustainable capacity in the future. This is sometimes easier said than achieved. It needs considerable cross-cultural sensitivity, and commitment to assisting stakeholders develop solutions to problems grounded in national realities.

External support for learning materials production as well as development can also be useful. Views may differ on the value of supporting low volume, low quality domestic production of print material (which often has a high import content), rather than buying in from the lowest cost international provider. The fact is the latter may be considerably cheaper and more cost-effective, but it requires foreign exchange. External assistance is often the only source of staff development for college staff, especially where this involves periods spent outside the country acquiring new skills and evaluating different approaches to training. Training institutions generally account for a small proportion of the education budget and relatively small amounts of external assistance can have a substantial impact on their quality. Their staff ought to be aware of the most recent developments in their fields of study elsewhere and be able to adapt and develop these sensitively and realistically for local use.

Teacher education is a certification process that carries with it a licence to practise, as well as salary benefits. Inevitably this means that curricula in action are heavily influenced by the form and content of the assessment system. MUSTER research identifies this as an area of general weakness. Different arrangements exist in different countries for the setting, taking and marking of assessment tasks, and various rubrics are followed that can include continuous assessment, project work, and assignments alongside the fairly universal fixed-time, closed-book, written examinations, and the assessment of teaching practice by tutors. There is evidence that assessment is narrowly limited and excludes many things identified in curricular materials as valued learning outcomes. Professional knowledge and skill are rarely reliably assessed and much teaching practice evaluation is ritualised to the point where it is unlikely to be valid and reliable. Assessment and certification techniques require expertise and systematic application. External assistance can and should make a direct contribution to the development of reliable and valid examination systems with the objective of ensuring curriculum relevance, technically robust selection, and cost-effective assessment.

10 Insights From MUSTER and Ways Forward

The management of many teacher education systems and their institutions is weak. Few systems provide training or support for senior management, who are likely to have been promoted from teaching positions. None of the colleges we undertook research in had a strategic medium term plan, and as far as we can establish none had been asked to produce one. If they had it is likely they would have needed assistance. Management information systems were also lacking, with basic information often incomplete or simply not collected or retained. The extent to which management expertise, procedures and systems can be transferred across systems depends on differences in organisational culture, infrastructure and resources, and levels of institutional autonomy. However, much is known about more and less efficient and effective management, and external assistance can help such knowledge to be shared in ways which are sensitive to what will and will not make a difference within a particular system.

The list of possibilities for constructive assistance would not be complete without a final observation. Innovation almost invariably requires resources. Poorly financed systems under pressure rarely have these available. Crisis management informs action more often than tested solutions to problems of learning and teaching. External assistance can be crucial to develop work that would otherwise not occur. It can and does also support experiments with innovative curricula and alternative delivery systems which may promise cost-effective methods of meeting expanded demand. This has to be seen as what it should be. It is development support for limited periods beyond which such innovations need to become self-sustaining. If this is not so, then such assistance begins to resemble recurrent budgetary support, which needs a different kind of justification. It should be support for innovations grounded in the systems to which they are applied, not simple transplants of blue-prints developed elsewhere for different purposes.

10.14 On the Prospects for Reform

Teacher education appears to be one of the most conservative parts of many education systems. It seldom is the source of curriculum innovation, theorised pedagogy, or radical reconceptualisations of professional learning. It often lags behind schools in the adoption of new practice and patterns of learning and teaching. This is a signifier that political will and bureaucratic courage may be needed for the implementation of real changes designed to improve efficiency and effectiveness. The case of South Africa, where changes in teacher education were part of more general system-wide transformation, is instructive but unique (see Lewin, Samuel & Sayed 2003). There, the will and the vision has existed to challenge old orthodoxies, wasteful resource allocation, and ineffective training methods.

The MUSTER research leads to much food for thought about future patterns of teacher education in low income countries. One way of encapsulating some of the possibilities is to formulate some possible scenarios. These can then be developed in relation to particular

10 Insights From MUSTER and Ways Forward

policy contexts and tested for professional benefits, pedagogic attractiveness, financial viability, and other criteria that might be relevant to different cases. Three portraits are developed below to encourage debate.

10.15   **Scenario 1: More of the Same – Roosting Egrets**[63]

More of the Same (MOS) is what will happen in the absence of coherent development policy and medium term strategic planning. The strengths and weaknesses will remain, inertia will define curricula and learning experiences, working practices will continue to deliver the curriculum at current levels of efficiency, and increased output will be difficult to achieve where it is needed at sustainable levels of cost.

This scenario is only attractive if there is a reasonable balance between supply and demand for new teachers and the quality of training is regarded as appropriate. The former only applies in Trinidad and Tobago, and the latter in none of the MUSTER countries.

For all the reasons MUSTER has highlighted – e.g. the changing characteristics of new entrants, the gulf between curricular content and process and the realities of schools coping with post-EFA surges in enrolments, the lack of innovation in colleges designed to promote closer professional interactions with schools, the lack of systematic support for induction of NQTs – MOS is not really an option. It is however the default condition and the most likely outcome unless energy, commitment and resources are directed towards the challenges MUSTER has identified.

10.16   **Scenario 2: Managed Evolution - Weaver Birds at Work**[64]

Managed evolution is a real possibility where medium term policy (identifying goals, resources, implementation modalities, and time scale) can be realised and integrated into sectoral plans for education. This is a prior condition since without such policy, updated periodically to reflect changing needs, development cannot be purposefully managed. It implies prioritisation of teacher education as a critical arena for support, manifested through secure forward planning of resource allocation over a long enough period to allow development plans to come to fruition. It also assumes that teacher education has a defined and effective locus of control within Ministry of Education structures (e.g. Departmental status with Director level representation). Though there may be potential in decentralising some aspects of teacher education this may be premature if existing institutions have weak self-management capacity, small size, and common needs.

---

[63] Egrets are birds of habit that return to the same spot each evening to roost day in day out.
[64] Weaver birds in their many varieties both follow set patterns to build nests and display astonishing ingenuity in adapting to different sites with different local conditions to construct efficiently durable nests which all differ in detail but serve the same purpose.

10 Insights From MUSTER and Ways Forward

The incrementalism implied in this scenario invites strategic thinking which identifies those aspects of teacher education that impinge on quality, efficiency and effectiveness and which can be changed without radical reforms and which have gains which outweigh their costs. These may or may not be sufficient to develop systems in ways which respond to the volume of demand for new trained teachers. They may lead to revised timescales for the achievement of EFA goals of appropriate pupil-teacher ratios in schools and the elimination of untrained teachers.

MUSTER identifies a raft of incremental changes that have more or less applicability to different systems. These include:

Improved selection and preparation for initial training

Pre-training teaching experience as an untrained teacher is common. Only in Trinidad and Tobago is this institutionalised as an On-the-Job Training Scheme. The development of OJT-like schemes has several attractions – trainees can be selected partly on the basis of their performance over time, rather than initial academic qualification; trainees contribute to reducing teacher shortages through the work they do; managed OJT schemes could greatly enrich the skills and competencies of those entering training. At the same time, pay and conditions of service need to be improved to the point where they can attract and retain people with appropriate qualities. There appear to be many willing to enter the primary teaching profession, for intrinsic or altruistic reasons, or because it is perceived as an avenue of upward mobility, but also many who are eventually deterred by the low status and material rewards.

Curriculum Development

Teacher education curricula suffer in varying degrees from fragmentation (e.g. lack of integration of subject-based and professional studies, uneven and sometimes contradictory pedagogic assumptions), disjunction with learners' characteristics (non-recognition of prior experience, little emphasis on problems of large class teaching, multi-grade schools, teaching with few learning materials, language issues), and inappropriate assessment schemes (ritualised assessment of teaching practice, recall based written examinations). In most systems curricula are not developed dynamically or incrementally (they remain the same for long periods), neither are they suffused with contributions from teacher educators at college level. Written materials for trainers and for trainees are in short supply and often derived from a variety of sources which lack coherence or consistency in approach. Revitalised teacher education systems could transform this situation through systematic and cumulative approaches to developing and enriching the curriculum and its learning materials base at college level, and through coherent national level programmes to generate more relevant core materials within an agreed framework. This would involve, for example, looking closely at the classroom context for which the students were being prepared, and adapting the college curriculum and teaching methods accordingly.

10 Insights From MUSTER and Ways Forward

Changed Working Practices

Working practices in teacher education differ widely. However, MUSTER data indicates that there is considerable scope to improve quality through more effective management focused on trainees' learning experience. Training institutions need to be much more demand-led, in terms of being responsive to the needs of trainees, rather than to the preferences, priorities and familiar practices of those who work in them. In many cases lecturing to large groups of up to 100 is favoured, though it is not necessary where student-staff ratios are below 20:1. This reflects choices in timetabling to restrict teaching staff contact time with trainees to levels that are low by international standards. Small group work, and structured independent and peer learning is unusual but potentially very valuable. It is often advocated but not practised. Few colleges make much use of experienced teachers drawn in to inform discussions about pedagogy, class management, and curriculum realities. Even fewer college staff spend periods in schools in a professional development role which could help inform their college-based teaching.

Teaching Practice

All the MUSTER training systems include periods of teaching practice in schools. This can have high costs associated with supervision by college tutors. However much of this supervision has the characteristics of assessment and is summative rather than formative. Trainees' experience of teaching practice suggests that it can be very valuable, but that for many learning is not coherently managed, and supportive supervision is not consistently available. There is little clear thinking on what learning outcomes can and cannot be achieved through existing patterns of teaching practice, most of which have not undergone any fundamental reappraisal since they were first introduced. There is considerable scope for improvements, such as integrating teaching practice much more closely and extensively with college work, re-evaluating the merits of college-based micro-teaching and other methods of acquiring professional skill which can be more resource-efficient than largely unsupported teaching practice, and arranging teaching practice placement and support more effectively. Longer internship periods, supervised by mentors or peripatetic trainers, can also be considered.

Infrastructure and Learning Materials

Most colleges in MUSTER countries have poor physical facilities and infrastructure, few learning materials, and under-utilised space (sometimes because of its quality) as a result of periods of neglect. They are nevertheless frequently the only post-secondary institution in an area with a concentration of educational professionals, and thus the only source of advice and support to practising teachers (alongside any teacher centres that may exist). Impoverished facilities compromise the effectiveness with which training can be conducted and have a depressing effect on morale. Relatively small investments could transform at least some of these institutions into much more vibrant, accessible and attractive professional development nodes with outreach capabilities. Non-salary budgets are widely under-funded

---

10 Insights From MUSTER and Ways Forward

to the extent that basic services fail (water, sanitation, electricity), learning materials are unavailable in quantity, and crisis management preoccupies senior staff to the exclusion of any focus on improving the quality of the training experience.

Teacher Educator Staff Development

The college lecturers are a neglected resource. Their main needs are: better personnel management, deployment and induction, and a clearer career structure linked to staff development and promotion opportunities, which would attract, motivate and retain suitable tutors. These things are achievable without excessive costs, but require different approaches to staff development which could improve morale, create incentives and rewards for improved performance, and attract new talent into the profession.

Changes in approaches to learners

Teacher educators may need to develop or rediscover culturally appropriate 'visions' of what an effective teacher is. They should provide opportunities for growth and development of personal attributes that can help trainees become confident and competent in their diverse professional roles. Student teachers need to be treated as adult learners and helped to study in more independent and proactive ways, so they experience themselves new ways of learning and teaching; they need to learn to reflect in ways that enable them to improve the quality and effectiveness of their teaching. To the extent these approaches are culturally unfamiliar, they raise much broader questions about the relationships between children and adults, role models and aspirants, and professionals and those for whom they provide services. Such issues need to be opened up and debated so that culturally appropriate ways are found to develop curricula and pedagogy consistent with the demands of Education for All.

10.17   **Scenario 3: Radical Reform – Soaring Eagles**[65]

Radical reform requires vision, courage and persistence to reshape teacher education in fundamental ways. It will usually require substantial investment up-front before benefits are apparent, and the conversion to new approaches of those embedded in the comfort zones of the old. It is the most exciting but the most risky option as entrenched interests rarely embrace new practices without strong incentives; such changes are usually linked to wider political reforms.

Some possibilities here are:

Reprofiling the structure and length of training

Conventional teacher education systems are heavily front-loaded in terms of the investment of resources i.e. most if not all the resources are committed to pre-career full-time residential training. This has several disadvantages e.g. it leaves few resources for investment in

---

[65] Eagles cover large distances with remarkable skill and adapt to different environments with apparent ease, flexibly applying themselves to the problems of survival in different and changing environments.

10 Insights From MUSTER and Ways Forward

managed induction and subsequent continuing professional development, a proportion of those who enter training may qualify but seek and find other jobs, and some kinds of professional skill and competence may be best acquired after experience on the job rather than before. Where demand is high long periods of pre-career training will be expensive and slow to produce large numbers of new teachers.

Alternatives which provide shorter periods of introductory training, followed by periods of work as assistant teachers interspersed with subsequent training inputs building on the base acquired from school experience, could be both more efficient (those who are trained are on the job, therefore costs are lower), and more effective (theory and practice are placed in dialogue, college-based work has to respond to real problems and skill needs). It is therefore possible to conceive of training which is 'drip fed' over time rather than provided in a single long period pre-career. There are many possibilities of detailed configuration which could include short intensive (e.g. 3 months) residential training, vacation workshops, complementary distance learning support, local cluster groups to support trainee teachers on the job etc. If this were linked to incremental progression up the career structure – e.g. trainee teacher, assistant teacher, junior teacher, fully qualified teacher – it could provide incentives to stay with the programme and accumulate skills and competence.

A variant of this approach could seek to move the locus of training activity to schools, as is the case in many high income countries. Conceptually it is easy for this to appear attractive. However, MUSTER empirical evidence draws attention to some important stumbling blocks. These include: the scarcity of school locations representing good practice relative to the numbers of trainees, the shortage of those likely to possess mentoring skills at school level and their willingness to invest substantial time in the activity, and the difficulties of moderating the school-based experience and ensuring appropriate and valid assessment and certification. Circumstances will differ and it may be that some of these problems can be overcome. More realistically in the short to medium term it is possible to imagine movement towards more school-based training through alternating periods of On-the-Job training and college-based work. Where colleges are located in areas where it is feasible to 'adopt' a cluster of schools large enough to provide meaningful school-based training, the opportunity exists to re-organise the curriculum accordingly. Peripatetic trainers based in Teachers' Centres rather than colleges have proved effective if given good training, support and management.

Mixed-mode training programmes, which combine college-based work with different types of distance learning, already exist. MIITEP in Malawi is an example. The research on MIITEP indicates the many difficulties that exist in realising the technically coherent model in practice where infrastructure is weak. Many planned support activities simply do not happen and such systems have to be engineered with characteristics that are realistically sustainable. However, where infrastructure is more adequate, they have many attractions.

10 Insights From MUSTER and Ways Forward

MUSTER countries do not currently use ICTs in teacher education. The reasons for this in the African countries are self-evident. The costs are high, (especially the on-costs of systems that remain functional), connectivity is low, and relevant content is yet to be created. This situation may change over the next decade. Until it does it will remain the case that print material offers far more durable opportunities for support for training at a distance, though of course it lacks the interactivity that ICTs could potentially provide[66]. If infrastructure improves to the point where connectivity at sustainable cost can be assured, then ICTs clearly have a complementary role to play in training. This is likely to be most often the case on site in college locations.

In restructuring teacher development, attention needs to be paid to what happens before, during and after training. A coherent policy would ensure that the activities and experiences were complementary within and between the three phases. The visual presentation in Fig. 13 below suggests some of the alternatives which can be 'picked and mixed' to suit local conditions and resources.

Figure 13: **The Three Phases of teacher development**

PRE-TRAINING

1. Unsupported teaching
2. Targeted subject upgrading
3. Short orientation course prior to entering school
4. On-the-Job apprenticeship training; combination of courses, distance learning and mentor support

INITIAL TRAINING

1. 1, 2 or 3 year residential College-based course with short TP
2. Combination of College and college-supervised Internship year: e.g. In-In-Out, or In-Out-In
3. Mixed-mode course with intensive residential study periods and school experience
4. School-based course with distance learning, vacation courses, and local support
5. Combinations of 3 and 4

---

[66] Interactivity is only of value where it suits the purpose (i.e. it provides a pathway to desired learning outcomes), and is available at affordable price levels. Interactivity that requires responses from people can quickly become very expensive in staff time, or simply inoperable when the volume of messages requiring considered response overloads the capacity to respond.

10 Insights From MUSTER and Ways Forward

POST-TRAINING

1. Short school- or district-based induction course
2. Probationary or locally-supervised Internship year
3. Regular recurrent INSET, district- or region-based.
4. INSET leading to further qualifications, or completion of those begun during IT

Traditionally, most time, effort and money has gone into the middle, Initial Training, phase. Given that in low income countries many teachers have to be recruited without training, that full-time residential college-based courses, as we have seen, do not seem to provide value for money, and that all teachers benefit from on-going professional development, it might be useful to direct more attention to the first and the last phases.

A different conceptual model of learning to teach

The transformations sketched above require more than structural changes. The map of learning and knowledge would have to be redrawn. Many of the curricula we analysed seemed premised on the idea that if students are given enough knowledge and skills at college these can be applied unproblematically, like 'recipes', to any classrooms. A more useful model is one that sees teaching as interactive problem-solving, requiring a thoughtful and reflective approach to one's own practice. Thus learning to teach means acquiring not only knowledge and skills, but also a situated understanding of pupils and how they learn, along with repertoires of skills and strategies for dealing with unique and ever-changing circumstances. The aim of the training should be the development of professional reasoning ability, rather than the acquisition of pre-defined behaviours (Akyeampong 2001). Such a model requires an epistemological shift towards a view of knowledge that recognises the value of teachers' personal, experiential and craft knowledge as well as the public propositional knowledge offered in college. For such a different model to take root will require time, debate, and professional development among lecturers, curriculum developers, MOE personnel, and the wider educational community. This is consonant with the new more learner-centred and constructivist-based approaches to teaching and learning in many reform programmes for school curricula, and would be a more suitable preparation for them.

Transforming College Practices

Two radical suggestions emerge from MUSTER data. First, none of the colleges in the research have strong and free-flowing professional links with schools. They play little role in curriculum development and implementation at school or any other level, and seldom provide central resources for teachers' INSET and CPD. With a different mandate, managerial commitment, and appropriate resources they could become developmental institutions with substantial outreach to schools. Their staff could acquire responsibilities to

10 Insights From MUSTER and Ways Forward

improve learning and teaching at school level directly as well as through the training of teachers.

Secondly, and even more radically, college lecturers could be appointed on different types of contracts than those which prevail. Most college staff are drawn from the ranks of practising teachers in mid-career. For many this becomes their occupation through until retirement. Employment practices usually favour those with higher levels of academic qualifications and this can have the effect of excluding those with extensive primary experience in favour of those who have taught at secondary level and who are more likely to have degree level qualifications. The staffing of a developmental college might not look like this. It could be staffed by experienced and effective teachers, given appropriate professional development, and seconded from primary schools for, say, five year periods. Permanent college staff could be required to work in schools periodically to give them relevant and recent experience and ensure that their training activities were closely grounded in the realities of schools and learning problems. With imagination groups of staff could be periodically tasked with development activities related to curriculum implementation, improving training effectiveness and supporting the induction of NQTs. In the long term, most countries will probably aim to have an all-graduate teaching profession. As part of the preparation for this, colleges could be more closely affiliated to local universities. This will help provide more chances for staff development, and open access to wider frames of reference.

Changing the Relationships between Content and Professional Skills and Competences.
All the college systems MUSTER has researched have difficulties in striking an appropriate balance between up-grading content skills in subjects (and in the medium of instruction), and developing pedagogic and professional skills. Most attempt both simultaneously with more or less successful integration. Where the entry level characteristics of trainees suggest that subject-based knowledge and skill, or language fluency, are inadequate, the radical choice may be to develop pre-course bridging programmes focused specifically on these. This could be in the training institution. But it could also be undertaken in nominated secondary schools given this task. The latter is likely to be more cost-effective. If initial training programmes really could assume students' mastery of basic content and language skills, then they would be free to focus sharply on professional and pedagogic competencies.

A Flood of Materials

Learning material for trainee teachers and NQTs located within national contexts in MUSTER countries is scarce. Yet print material is relatively cheap, durable and can be immensely helpful to those starting teaching in school environments where good practice may not be common and informed advice is difficult to come by. Colleges, which could and should be a major source of such material, often do not produce text material in volume and are unable to ensure trainees leave with a portfolio of supporting manuals, enrichment materials etc. This problem is more readily resolvable than textbook supply to all children

10 Insights From MUSTER and Ways Forward

since the numbers are much smaller. The radical proposition may not sound radical – flood the trainee teachers with quality support materials. It is radical in the sense that it has yet to be prioritised or realised in the systems we have researched (although a start was made with the Student Handbooks in Malawi).

10.18 Concluding Remark

The last scenario has explored some of the more radical options available that would challenge current practice and can provide an agenda for reform. These include:

- Strategic use should be made of untrained teachers supported by orientation programmes and school-based apprenticeship-like relationships (on-the-job training). If this process was managed effectively it could become a step on a pathway to initial qualification. The experience of working as a teaching assistant would discourage some, reinforce the aspirations of others, and allow the unsuitable to be selected out.

- Initial training could be organised in a more modularised way to allow training to be acquired as and when needed. Investment in skill and competency would be cumulative and could take place through a variety of routes (full-time, part-time, day release, residential, distance etc) and in a variety of locations (in school, at teacher centres, in colleges and universities). It would have to be linked to a progressive career structure that regulated promotion to different grades to experience, qualification level and competence. The important difference is that it would not be a single-shot qualification process but a continuous pathway leading to higher levels of competence.

- A staircase of training linked to posts of responsibility and rewards offers the opportunity to embed the training process more firmly in the school and the learning needs of its pupils. So also might the modularisation of the training curriculum, at least in part. It would make it possible for more training to take place in closer proximity to professional practice both in space and time. It might allow possibilities for schools (and colleges) to acquire some of the attributes of learning institutions. It could obviate the need for special induction and support of NQTs if a seamless web of Continuing Professional Development began to develop which could include the induction of NQTs.

- Teacher educators at all levels, whether school or college-based, need to have induction and continuing professional development. This should ensure that they are aware of recent developments, can judge whether these should be incorporated into training, have perspectives that run beyond their direct experience, and have a rich range of material to draw on to support and stimulate trainee teachers.

10 Insights From MUSTER and Ways Forward

- Colleges could then move away from being monotechnic institutions focused purely on residential long course qualifications, towards becoming dynamically integrated nodes of innovation, professional development activity, and advisory support. They could be challenged locally and nationally to make a real difference to learning in schools and the development of the human potential of the populations they serve.

Whether these kinds of proposals are feasible or desirable is necessarily a question for different systems to address. It may be that incremental changes based on the kind of evidence that MUSTER has accumulated, are both more attractive and more likely to gain political support. The teacher education systems MUSTER has undertaken research on are 'not broken but they do need fixing'. If teacher educators are to retain public support for their activities, if EFA and the MDG targets are to be realised, and if new approaches to learning and teaching which have developmental significance are to be adopted, then all the options should be aired and considered judgements made about which will make a real difference to the next generations of learners and teachers.

Appendix 1: List of MUSTER Researchers by County

Ghana Team

Lead Researcher:	Kwame Akyeampong
Associate Researchers:	Joseph Ampiah, Jonathan Fletcher, Nicholas Kutor, Ben Sokpe

Lesotho Team

Lead Researcher:	Pulane Lefoka
Associate Researchers:	Mantoetse Jobo, Rene Khiba, Puleng Mapuru, Mamotebang K.Molise, Baatswana Moeti, Mabaphuthi J. Moorosi, H. Johnson Nenty, Vuyelwa M. Ntoi, Bolelang Qhobela, Edith M. Sebatane

Malawi Team

Lead Researcher:	Demis Kunje
Associate Researchers:	Joseph Chimombo, Shadreck Chirembo

South Africa Team

Lead Researchers & Coordinators:	Michael Samuel and Yusuf Sayed
Research Contributors:	Nazir Carrim, Luis Crouch, Ken Harley, Jan Heysteck, Jonathan Jansen, Elizabeth Mattson, Ben Parker, Daisy Pillay, Dirk Postma, Labby Ramrathan, Vijay Reddy, Maureen Robinson, Brigitte Smit, Reshma Sookrajh, Crain Soudien, Mark Steele, Tania Vergnani,

Trinidad and Tobago Team

Lead Researcher:	June George
Associate Researchers:	Marie-Louise Brown, Janice Fournillier, Arthur Joseph, Michael Kallon, Carol Keller, Samuel Lochan, Jeniffer Mohammed, Jeanette Morris, Susan Otway-Charles, Lynda Quamina-Aiyejina, Balchan Rampaul, Jocelyn Rampersad, Patricia Worrell

Sussex University Team

Keith Lewin, Yusuf Sayed (1999 onwards), David Stephens (1997-1999), Janet Stuart

Research Fellow:	Julie Coultas (1998 1999)
Doctoral Researchers:	Alison Croft, Dominic Furlong, John Hedges (Research Fellow Jan.- Sept. 2001)

Appendix 2: Other Publications

Edited Book:

Lewin K M , Samuel M and Sayed Y (eds) (2003) *Changing Patterns of Teacher Education in South Africa – Policy Practice and Prospects*, Heinemann Press, South Africa.

This book explores policy and practice in Teacher Education in South Africa and their implications for the future. It arises from the work of the Multi Site Teacher Education Research Programme (MUSTER) co-ordinated by the University of Sussex in five countries, of which South Africa is one.

Teacher education in South Africa is in transition. The first wave of educational reform rightly focused on the need to develop a post-apartheid school curriculum and the new structures that were needed to support different approaches to learning. Teacher education was made a Provincial competence and left largely untouched until new norms and standards and a regulatory framework began to be developed. Recent developments in the governance, funding and rationalisation of post school professional development and training have now begun to address the pressing needs to convert ideas into structures and learning opportunities. The incorporation of Colleges of Education into the higher education system and the reform of the national curriculum for schools invite a reappraisal of methods and content.

No contemporary, empirically grounded and policy-orientated studies of teacher education in South Africa exist. The National Teacher Education Audit was the last major review and that has now been overtaken by events. The signs are that demand for teachers is set to rise sharply as a result of increased attrition and demographic changes. If this demand is to be met at affordable costs and through programmes of appropriate quality new thinking is needed.

This book will fill an important gap for students of teacher education and for those with an interest in transformation and the implementation of ideas into action. It explores recent developments, anticipates future needs and reflects on underlying aspirations and conundrums. The contributors include many key individuals with a direct stake in teacher education policy in South Africa. A Symposium at the University of Pretoria in April 2001 brought together authors of the various studies commissioned by the MUSTER South Africa team.

Appendix 2: Other Publications

Doctoral theses

Croft A (2002) 'Teachers, student teachers and pupils; a study of teaching and learning in lower primary classes in Southern Malawi', Unpublished D.Phil.Thesis. University of Sussex.

Hedges, J. (2002) 'Becoming a Teacher in Ghana: a qualitative study of NQTs in Central Region, Ghana',Unpublished D.Phil thesis, University of Sussex.

Furlong D (forthcoming) 'Teacher education in Ghana: efficiency and equity in resource allocation'. Unpublished D.Phil thesis, University of Sussex.

Special Edition of International Journal of Educational Development
Vol. 22 Nos.3-4 May/July 2002
Guest Editors: Janet S. Stuart and Keith M. Lewin

Contents

Appendix 3: National Conferences

MUSTER Dissemination Conferences

All the Country Research Teams involved in MUSTRER have organised national conferences based on their work designed to disseminate findings and provoke policy dialogue between stakeholders. Proceedings are available from the Principal Researchers in each country.

Ghana: 'Teacher Education and Development in Ghana: Reformulating Policy for Effective Practice', Hotel Dodowa, July 10-12th, 2002 hosted by the Institute of Education, Cape Coast University.

Lesotho: 'National Conference to disseminate the MUSTER findings and to facilitate the formulation of policy on teacher education in Lesotho' at the Maseru Sun Hotel, April 2nd-3rd, 2001, hosted by the Institute of Education at the National University of Lesotho.

Malawi: 'The National Conference on Teacher Education', at the Management Institute of Malawi, 18th-20th November, 2001 hosted by the Centre for Educational Research and Training, Chancellor College, Malawi.

South Africa: National Symposium: 'Teacher Education Policy in South Africa: Rhetoric and Reality' at the University Pretoria, April 5th-7th hosted by University of Durban Westville, and University of Pretoria.

Trinidad and Tobago: National Symposium on 'Critical Issues in Primary Teacher Education in Trinidad and Tobago' at The School of Education, UWI, St. Augustine, Jan. 11th-12th, 2002.

England: MUSTER Research in Progress Seminars at the Oxford International Education Conferences in September 1999 and 2001.

References

Akyeampong A.K. (1997) 'Continuous Assessment in Post-Secondary Teacher Training in Ghana: a case-study evaluation'. Unpublished Ph.D thesis, University of Nottingham.

Akyeampong K. & Stephens D. (2000) "On the Threshold': The Identity of Student Teachers in Ghana' *MUSTER Discussion Paper No 4*, Centre for International Education, University of Sussex.

Akyeampong K. & Furlong D. (2000) 'Ghana: A Baseline Study of the Teacher Education System'. *MUSTER Discussion Paper No 7*, Centre for International Education, University of Sussex.

Akyeampong K., Ampiah J., Fletcher J., Kutor N. & Sokpe B. (2000) 'Learning To Teach In Ghana: An Evaluation Of Curriculum Delivery'. *MUSTER Discussion Paper No 17*, Centre for International Education, University of Sussex.

Akyeampong K., Furlong D. & Lewin K. M. (2000), 'The Costs and Financing of Teacher Education in Ghana', *MUSTER Discussion Paper No 18*, Centre for International Education, University of Sussex.

Akyeampong K. (2001) 'Teacher Training in Ghana – Does it Count?' *MUSTER Research Report No 1*, Centre for International Education, University of Sussex.

Akyeampong K. & Lewin K.M. (2002) 'From student teachers to newly qualified teachers in Ghana: insights into becoming a teacher' in *Researching Teacher Education: The Multi-Site Teacher Education Project*. Special Issue of the *International Journal of Educational Development* 22 (3/4).

Akyeampong K. & Stephens D. (2002) 'Exploring the backgrounds and shaping factors of beginning student teachers in Ghana: a case for contextualising teacher education' in *Researching Teacher Education: The Multi-Site Teacher Education Project*. Special Issue of the *International Journal of Educational Development* 22 (3/4)

Avalos B. (1991) *Approaches to Teacher Education - Initial Teacher Training*, London: Commonwealth Secretariat

Avalos B. & Haddad W. (1981) *A Review of Teacher Effectiveness research in Africa, India, Latin America, Middle East, Malaysia, Philippines, and Thailand: Synthesis of Results*. IDRC, Ottawa, Canada.

Ball S. J. & Goodson I. F. (eds.) (1985) *Teachers' Lives and Careers*. London: The Falmer Press.

Beeby C. (1980).. 'The thesis of stages fourteen years later'. *International Review of Education* XXVI pp. 451-474.

Bude U., Coombe C., Muwowo B., & Nashire N. (1995) *Teacher Development for Free Primary Education in Malawi*, Bonn: Deutsche Stiftung für Entwicklung

Bullough R. V., Knowles, J. G. & Crow N.A. (1997) *Emerging as a Teacher*. London & New York: Routledge

Burke C. (1996) 'The changing agenda in Teacher Education in Papua New Guinea' *International Journal of Educational Development* 16 (1) pp.41-51.

Calderhead J. & Shorrock S.B. (1997) *Understanding Teacher Education*, London: Falmer Press

Chakanyuka S. (2002) 'Mentoring and the Professional Development of pre-service primary teacher training students of Masvingo Teachers' College' Unpublished D.Phil thesis, University of Sussex

Colclough C. with Lewin K.M. (1993) *Educating All the Children: Strategies for Primary Schooling in the South* Clarendon Press, Oxford

Coultas J. & Lewin K.M. (2002) 'Who Becomes a Teacher? The Characteristics of Student Teachers in Four Countries' in *Researching Teacher Education: The Multi-Site Teacher Education Project*. Special Issue of the *International Journal of Educational Development* 22 (3/4)

References

Croft A. M. (2000) 'Gender Gaps in Schools and Colleges: Can Teacher Education Policy Improve Gender Equity in Malawi?' *MUSTER Discussion Paper No 14*, Centre for International Education, University of Sussex.

Croft A. M. (2002a) 'Teachers, student teachers and pupils; a study of teaching and learning in lower primary classes in Southern Malawi', Unpublished D.Phil.Thesis. University of Sussex.

Croft, A.M. (2002b) 'Singing under a tree: does oral culture help lower primary teachers be learner-centred in Malawi?'in *Researching Teacher Education: The Multi-Site Teacher Education Project*. Special Issue of the *International Journal of Educational Development* 22 (3/4)

Croft A., Kunje D. & Stuart J.S. (2000) 'An Analysis of MIITEP Assessment in Malawi'. MUSTER unpublished working Paper. CIE: University of Sussex.

Crouch L. with Lewin K. M. (2001) 'Turbulence or Orderly Change? Teacher supply and demand in South Africa - current status, future needs, and the impact of HIV/Aids' *MUSTER Discussion Paper No 26*, Centre for International Education, University of Sussex.

Daniels H. (1996) *An Introduction to Vygotsky*, London: Routledge

Dove L. (1985) *Teachers and Teacher Education in Developing Countries: Issues in Planning, Management and Training*, London: Croom Helm

DSE (1998) *The Project Progress Review, Malawi Integrated Inservice Teacher Education Programme (MIITEP)*. Bonn: Deutsche Stiftung fur Entwicklung

Elliott J. (1999) Editorial introduction: 'Teacher Education Reforms in an age of globalisation', *Teaching and Teacher Education* 15

Eraut M.R. (1994) *Developing Professional Knowledge and Competence*, London: Falmer

Eraut M.R, 1976, 'Some Perspectives on Curriculum Development in Teacher Education', *Education for Teaching*. 99

Furlong D, (forthcoming), Teacher education in Ghana: efficiency and equity in resource allocation. Unpublished D.Phil thesis, University of Sussex.

George J., Fournillier J. & Brown M. (2000) 'On-the-Job Training: Pre-service Teacher Training in Trinidad and Tobago', *MUSTER Discussion Paper No 19* Centre for International Education, University of Sussex.

George J., Worrell P., Rampersad J., Rampaul B. & Mohammed J. (2000) 'Becoming a Primary School Teacher in Trinidad and Tobago, Part 1 The Curriculum in the Teachers' Colleges' *MUSTER Discussion Paper No 20*, Centre for International Education, University of Sussex.

George J., Worrell P., Rampersad J. & Rampaul B. (2000) 'Becoming a Primary School Teacher in Trinidad and Tobago, Part 2: Teaching Practice Experience of Trainees' *MUSTER Discussion Paper No 21*, Centre for International Education, University of Sussex.

George J., Mohammed J., Quamina-Aiyejina L., Fournillier J. & Otway-Charles S. (2001) 'Primary Teacher Trainees in Trinidad and Tobago: Characteristics, Images, Experiences and Expectations'. *MUSTER Discussion Paper No 22*, Centre for International Education, University of Sussex.

George J. & Quamina-Aiyejina L. (2002) 'An Analysis of Primary Teacher Education in Trinidad and Tobago: The MUSTER Project' *MUSTER Research Report No 4*, Centre for International Education, University of Sussex.

George J., Worrell P., & Rampersad J. (2002) 'Messages about good teaching: primary teacher trainees' experiences of the practicum in Trinidad and Tobago' in *Researching Teacher Education: The Multi-Site Teacher Education Project*. Special Issue of the *International Journal of Educational Development* 22 (3/4)

References

Goodson I. (1992) *Studying Teachers' Lives*, London: Routledge.

GTZ (1995) *Malawi German Basic Education Project – The Malawi Integrated Teacher Education Programme, Appraisal Report* June 1995. Bonn: Gesellschaft fur Technische Zusammenarbeit.

Hedges J. (2000) 'The Importance of Posting in Becoming a Teacher in Ghana' *MUSTER Discussion Paper No 13*, Centre for International Education, University of Sussex.

Hedges J. (2002a) 'Becoming a Teacher in Ghana: a qualitative study of NQTs in Central Region, Ghana', Unpublished D.Phil thesis, University of Sussex

Hedges J. (2002b) 'The importance of posting and interaction with the education bureaucracy in becoming a teacher in Ghana' in *Researching Teacher Education: The Multi-Site Teacher Education Project*. Special Issue of the *International Journal of Educational Development* 22 (3/4)

Hopkin A.G. (1996). 'Evaluation of the Teaching Practice Programme, NTTC', unpublished consultancy report, Maseru: NTTC

Kadzamira E., Banda D., Kamlongera A. & Swainson N. (2001) *The Impact of HIV/AIDS on Primary and Secondary Schooling in Malawi*. Rockefeller Foundation and Centre for International Education, University of Sussex.

Kelchtermans G. (1993) 'Teachers and their career story: a biographical perspective on professional development'. In C. Day (ed) *Research on Teacher Thinking: understanding professional development*, London: Falmer Press

Kunje D. (2002) 'The Malawi Integrated In-service Teacher Education Programme: an experiment with mixed-mode training' in *Researching Teacher Education: The Multi Site Teacher Education Project*. Special Issue of the *International Journal of Educational Development* 22 (3/4)

Kunje D. & Stuart J.S. (1996) *Final Report on the Evaluation of the Emergency Teacher Programme in Malawi*, London: Overseas Development Administration, British Development Division for Southern and Central Africa.

Kunje D. & Chimombo J. (1999) 'Malawi: A Baseline Study of the Teacher Education System' *MUSTER Discussion Paper No 5*, Centre for International Education, University of Sussex.

Kunje D. & Chirembo S. (2000) 'The Malawi Integrated In-Service Teacher Education Programme and its School-based Components' *MUSTER Discussion Paper No 12*, Centre for International Education, University of Sussex.

Kunje D. & Lewin K. M. (2000) 'The Costs and Financing of Teacher Education in Malawi' *MUSTER Discussion Paper No 2*, Centre for International Education, University of Sussex.

Kunje D. with Lewin K. M. & Stuart J. S. (2002) 'Primary Teacher Education in Malawi: Insights into Practice and Policy' *MUSTER Research Report No 3*, Centre for International Education, University of Sussex.

Lefoka J.P, Jobo M., Khiba R., Liphoto N., Mapuru P., Molise M., Moeti B., Moorosi M., Nenty H. J., Ntoi V., Qhobela B., Sebatane, E. & Sephelane T. (2000) 'Lesotho: A Baseline Study of the Teacher Education System'. *MUSTER Discussion Paper No 8*, Centre for International Education, University of Sussex.

Lefoka J.P. with Jobo M., Moeti B. & Stuart J. S. (2000) 'The Experience of Training: a Study of Students at The National Teacher Training College in Lesotho'. *MUSTER Discussion Paper No 24*, Centre for International Education, University of Sussex.

Lefoka J.P. & Stuart J. S. (2001) 'Analysis of the Curriculum as Documented at the National Teacher Training College in Lesotho'. *MUSTER Discussion Paper No 23*, Centre for International Education, University of Sussex.

References

Lefoka J.P. with Jobo M. & Moeti B. (2001) 'Teaching Practice at the National Teacher Training College in Lesotho'. *MUSTER Discussion Paper No 25*, Centre for International Education, University of Sussex.

Lefoka J.P. with Molise M. K. Moorosi-Molapo J. M. & Sebatane E. (2001) 'Who Becomes a Primary School Teacher in Lesotho: Characteristics and Experiences of the DEP Student Teachers upon Entry in NTTC'. *MUSTER Discussion Paper No 28*, Centre for International Education, University of Sussex.

Lefoka J.P. & Ntoi V. (2002) 'Primary Teacher Education in Action: a peep into the TTC Classrooms at the National Teacher Training College, Lesotho'. *MUSTER Discussion Paper No 29*, Centre for International Education, University of Sussex.

Lefoka J.P. with Sebatane E. M. (2002) 'Initial Primary Teacher Education in Lesotho' *MUSTER Research Report No 2*, Centre for International Education, University of Sussex.

Lewin K. M. (1999) 'Counting the Cost of Teacher Education: Cost and Quality Issues' *MUSTER Discussion Paper No 1*, Centre for International Education, University of Sussex.

Lewin K.M. (2002) 'The costs of supply and demand for teacher education: dilemmas for development' in *Researching Teacher Education: The Multi-Site Teacher Education Project*. Special Issue of the *International Journal of Educational Development* 22 (3/4)

Lewin K. M., Ntoi V., Nenty H. J. & Mapuru P. (2000) 'Costs and Financing of Teacher Education in Lesotho', *MUSTER Discussion Paper No 10*, Centre for International Education, University of Sussex.

Lewin K. M., Keller C. & Taylor E. (2000, revised 2002) 'Teacher Education in Trinidad and Tobago: Costs, Financing and Future Policy'. *MUSTER Discussion Paper No 9*, Centre for International Education, University of Sussex.

Lewin K.M. & Stuart J:S. (2002) 'Editorial Postscript' in *Researching Teacher Education: The Multi-Site Teacher Education Project*. Special Issue of the *International Journal of Educational Development* 22 (3/4)

Lewin K. M., Samuel M. & Sayed Y. (eds) (2003) *Changing Patterns of Teacher Education in South Africa – Policy Practice and Prospects*, Heinemann Press, South Africa.

Lockheed M. & Verspoor A. (1991) *Improving Primary Education in Developing Countries*, World Bank/OUP

Lortie D.C. (1975) *School Teacher*, University of Chicago Press

McLaughlin D. (1996) 'Who is to retrain the teacher trainers? A Papua New Guinea case study'. *Teaching and Teacher Education* 12 (3) pp.285-301.

Mereku D. K. (2000) *Demand and Supply of Basic School Teachers in Ghana*. Department of Mathematics Education, University College of Education of Winneba.

Morris J. & Joseph A. (2000) 'Newly Qualified Teachers: Impact On/Interaction with the System in Trinidad and Tobago' *MUSTER Discussion Paper No 15*, Centre for International Education, University of Sussex.

Ntoi V. & Lefoka J. P. (2002) 'NTTC under the microscope: problems of change in primary teacher education in Lesotho' in *Researching Teacher Education: The Multi-Site Teacher Education Project*. Special Issue of the *International Journal of Educational Development* 22 (3/4)

NSE (2000) *Norms and Standards for Educators*, Department of Education, Pretoria

Osler A. (1997) *The Education and Careers of Black Teachers: Changing Identities, Changing Lives*. Milton Keynes: Open University.

References

Parker B. (2002) 'Roles and Responsibilities, Institutional Landscapes and Curriculum Mindscapes: a partial view of teacher education policy in South Africa, 1990-2000' *MUSTER Discussion Paper No 30*, Centre for International Education, University of Sussex.

Perraton H. (2000) *Open and Distance Learning in the Developing World*, Routledge

Quamina-Aiyejina L., Mohammed J., Rampaul B., George J., Kallon M., Keller C. & Lochan M. (1999) 'Trinidad and Tobago: A Baseline Study of the Teacher Education System' *MUSTER Discussion Paper No 6*, Centre for International Education, University of Sussex.

Reddy V. (2002a) 'Face-to-Face Training in a Conventional Preservice Programme: a case study at Edgewood College of Education in South Africa'. *MUSTER Discussion Paper No 34*, Centre for International Education, University of Sussex.

Reddy V. (2002b) 'South African College for Open Learning: a model of an Inservice Distance Education Programme for Initial Teacher Education'. *MUSTER Discussion Paper No 35*, Centre for International Education, University of Sussex.

Robinson M., Vergnani T. & Sayed Y. (2002) 'Teacher Education for Transformation: the case of the University of the Western Cape, South Africa'. *MUSTER Discussion Paper No 32*, Centre for International Education, University of Sussex.

Rogers A. (1996) *Teaching Adults*, Milton Keynes: Open University Press

Russell T. & Korthagen F. (Eds) (1995) *Teachers who Teach Teachers*. London: Falmer Press

Rust V.D. & Dalin P. (1990) *Teachers and Teaching in the Developing World*, N.Y.: Garland

Samuel M. (2002) 'Working in the rain: pressures and priorities for teacher education curriculum design in South Africa: a case-study of the University of Durban-Westville' in *Researching Teacher Education: The Multi-Site Teacher Education Project*. Special Issue of the *International Journal of Educational Development* 22 (3/4)

Samuel M. & Stephens D. (2000) 'Critical dialogues with self: developing teacher identities and roles – a case-study of South African student teachers' *International Journal of Educational Research* 33 pp.475-491

Samuel M. & Pillay D. (2002) 'Face-to-face initial Teacher Education Degree programme at University of Durban-Westville, South Africa'. *MUSTER Discussion Paper No 31*, Centre for International Education, University of Sussex.

Sayed Y. (2002) 'Changing forms of teacher education in South Africa: policy symbols and policy practice' in *Researching Teacher Education: The Multi-Site Teacher Education Project*. Special Issue of the *International Journal of Educational Development* 22 (3/4)

Sayed Y., Heystek J. & Smit B. (2002) 'Further Diploma in Education (Educational Management) by Distance Education at the University of Pretoria, South Africa'. *MUSTER Discussion Paper No 33*, Centre for International Education, University of Sussex.

Schon D. (1983) *The Reflective Practitioner*, London: Jossey Bass

Sebatane E. M. & Lefoka J.P. (2001) 'New Teachers on the Job: the Impact of Teacher Education in Lesotho', *MUSTER Discussion Paper No 27*, Centre for International Education, University of Sussex.

Shilambo P. & Dahlstrom L. F. (1999) 'Critical-practitioner inquiry and staff development for teacher educators'. In K.Zeichner & L.Dahlstrom. (Eds) *Democratic Teacher Education Reform in Africa: the case of Namibia*, Boulder: Westview Press.

Shulman L.S. (1987) 'Knowledge and Teaching: Foundations of the New Reform', *Harvard Educational Review* 57 (1)

References

Stuart J. S. (1999) 'Primary Teacher Education Curricula as Documented: A Comparative Analysis'. *MUSTER Discussion Paper No 3*, Centre for International Education, University of Sussex.

Stuart J.S. (2002) 'College tutors: a fulcrum for change?' in *Researching Teacher Education: The Multi-Site Teacher Education Project*. Special Issue of the *International Journal of Educational Development* 22 (3/4)

Stuart J.S. & Lewin K.M. (2002) 'Editorial Foreword' in *Researching Teacher Education: The Multi-Site Teacher Education Project*. Special Issue of the *International Journal of Educational Development* 22 (3/4).

Stuart J.S. & Tatto M.T. (2000) 'Designs for Initial Teacher Preparation Programmes: an international view'. *International Journal of Educational Research*, 33 (5)

Stuart J. S. & Kunje D. (2000) 'The Malawi Integrated In-Service Teacher Education Project: an analysis of the curriculum and its delivery in the colleges' *MUSTER Discussion Paper No 11*, Centre for International Education, University of Sussex.

Stuart J. S. with Kunje D. & Lefoka J.P (2000) 'Careers and Perspectives of Tutors in Teacher Training Colleges: Case Studies of Lesotho and Malawi'. *MUSTER Discussion Paper No 16*, Centre for International Education, University of Sussex.

Tabulawa R. (1997) 'Pedagogical Classroom Practice and the Social Context: the case of Botswana'. *International Journal of Educational Development* 17 (2) pp.189-204

Tafa E. (2001) 'Teacher Socialisation in Botswana Secondary Schools: a critical qualitative analysis of the teaching methods of seven new teachers', Unpublished Ph.D. thesis, University of Birmingham

Tatto M.T., Nielson D., Cummings W., Kularatna N., & Dharmadasa K. (1991) *Cost effectiveness and Teacher Education in Sri Lanka*. BRIDGES Report. Harvard School of Education/ USAID Washington. Report Number 10.

Tatto M.T. & Dharmadasa K.H. (1995) 'Social and political contexts of policy formation in teacher education in Sri Lanka' in M. Ginsburg. & B. Lindsay (eds) *The Political Dimension in Teacher Education: comparative perspectives on policy formation, socialisation and society*, London: Falmer

Wideen M.F. & Grimmett P.P. 1995, (eds) *Changing Times in Teacher Education: restructuring or reconceptualising?* London: Falmer Press

Wideen M., Mayer-Smith J., & Moon B. (1998). 'A Critical Analysis of the Research on Learning to Teach: Making the case for an Ecological Perspective on Inquiry'. *Review of Educational Research*, 68 (2) pp 130-178.

World Bank (1978) *Teacher Training and Student Achievement in Less Developed Countries*. World Bank Staff Working Paper No 310, World Bank, Washington.

World Bank (1995) *Basic Education Project Report* Staff Appraisal Report Trinidad and Tobago; 14865-TR Washington DC.

World Bank (1996) *Basic Education Sector Improvement Program*, Staff Appraisal Report, Republic of Ghana, Population and Human Resources Division, West Central Africa Department, Africa Region. World Bank: Washington D.C.

The MUSTER Discussion Paper Series

No 1   *Counting the Cost of Teacher Education: Cost and Quality Issues*
        (January 1999) Keith M Lewin

No 2   *The Costs and Financing of Teacher Education **Malawi***
        (March 2000) Demis Kunje & Keith M Lewin

No 3   *Primary Teacher Education Curricula as Documented: A Comparative Analysis*
        (July 1999) Janet S Stuart

No 4   *"On the Threshold": The Identity of Student Teachers in **Ghana***
        (April 2000) Kwame Akyeampong & David Stephens

No 5   ***Malawi**: A Baseline Study of the Teacher Education System*
        (December 1999) Demis Kunje & Joseph Chimombo

No 6   ***Trinidad & Tobago**: A Baseline Study of the Teacher Education System*
        (July 1999) Lynda Quamina-Aiyejina, Jeniffer Mohammed, Balchan Rampaul, June
        George, Michael Kallon, Carol Keller & Samuel Lochan.

No 7   ***Ghana**: A Baseline Study of the Teacher Education System*
        (September 2000) Kwame Akyeampong & Dominic Furlong

No 8   ***Lesotho**: A Baseline Study of the Teacher Education System*
        (September 2000) J Pulane Lefoka et al

No 9   *Teacher Education in **Trinidad & Tobago**: Costs, Financing and Future Policy*
        (August 2000) Keith M Lewin, Carol Keller & Ewart Taylor

No 10   *Costs and Financing of Teacher Education in **Lesotho***
        (June 2000) Keith M Lewin, Vuyelwa Ntoi, H J Nenty & Puleng Mapuru

No 11   *The **Malawi** Integrated In-Service Teacher Education Project: an analysis of the
        curriculum and its delivery in the colleges*
        (February 2000) Janet S Stuart & Demis Kunje

No 12   *The **Malawi** Integrated In-Service Teacher Education Programme and its School
        based Components*
        (June 2000) Demis Kunje & Shadreck Chirembo

No 13   *The Importance of Posting in Becoming a Teacher in **Ghana***
        (June 2000) John P Hedges

No 14   *Gender Gaps in Schools and Colleges: Can Teacher Education Policy Improve
        Gender Equity in **Malawi**?*
        (August 2000) Alison Croft

No 15   *Newly Qualified Teachers: Impact On/Interaction with the System
        (**Trinidad & Tobago**)*
        (March 2000) Jeanette Morris & Arthur Joseph

No 16   *Careers and Perspectives of Tutors in Teacher Training Colleges: Case Studies of
        Lesotho and Malawi*
        (November 2000) Janet Stuart with Demis Kunje & Pulane Lefoka

No 17   *Learning To Teach In **Ghana**: An Evaluation Of Curriculum Delivery*
        (August 2000) Kwame Akyeampong, J. Ampiah, J Fletcher, N. Kutor & B. Sokpe

No 18   *The Costs and Financing of Teacher Education in **Ghana***
        (December 2000) Kwame Akyeampong, Dominic Furlong & Keith Lewin

No 19   *On-the-Job Training: Pre-service Teacher Training in **Trinidad & Tobago***
        (August 2000) June George, Janice Fournillier & Marie-Louise Brown

No 20   *Becoming a Primary School Teacher in **Trinidad & Tobago**, Part 1 The Curriculum
        in the Teachers' Colleges*
        (October 2000) June George, Patricia Worrell, Joycelyn Rampersad, Balchan
        Rampaul & Jeniffer Mohammed

The MUSTER Discussion Paper Series

No 21 *Becoming a Primary School Teacher in Trinidad & Tobago, Part 2: Teaching Practice Experience of Trainees*
(October 2000) June George, Patricia Worrell, Joycelyn Rampersad & Balchan Rampaul

No 22 *Primary Teacher Trainees in Trinidad & Tobago: Characteristics, Images, Experiences and Expectations*
(January 2001) June George, Jeniffer Mohammed, Lynda Quamina-Aiyejina, Janice Fournillier & Susan Otway-Charles.

No 23 *Analysis of the Curriculum as Documented at the National Teacher Training College in Lesotho*
(May 2001) J. Pulane Lefoka & Janet S. Stuart

No 24 *The Experience of Training: a Study of Students at The National Teacher Training College in Lesotho*
(August 2000) J. Pulane Lefoka with Mantoetse Jobo, Baatswana Moeti & Janet S. Stuart

No 25 *Teaching Practice at the National Teacher Training College in Lesotho*
(May 2001) J. Pulane Lefoka with Mantoetse Jobo & Baatswana Moeti

No 26 *Turbulence or Orderly Change? Teacher Supply and Demand in South Africa – Current Status, Future Needs and the Impact of HIV/Aids*
(June 2000) Luis Crouch Edited and Abridged by Keith M. Lewin

No 27 *New Teachers on the Job: The Impact of Teacher Education in Lesotho*
(September 2001) Edith M Sebatane and J Pulane Lefoka

No 28 *Who Becomes a Primary School Teacher in Lesotho: Characteristics and Experiences of the DEP Student Teachers upon Entry into NTTC*
(January 2002) J. Pulane Lefoka with M.K. Molise, J.M. Moorosi-Molapo, Edith Sebatane

No 29 *Primary Teacher Education in Action: a peep into the TTC classrooms at the National Teacher Training College, Lesotho*
(June 2002) J.Pulane Lefoka and Vuyelwa.M. Ntoi

No 30 *Roles and Responsibilities, Institutional Landscapes and Curriculum Mindscapes: a partial view of teacher education policy in South Africa, 1990-2000*
(March 2002) Ben Parker

No 31 *Face-to-face Initial Teacher Education Degree Programme at University of Durban Westville, South Africa*
(May 2002) Michael Samuel and Daisy Pillay

No 32 *Teacher Education for Transformation: the case of the University of the Western Cape, South Africa*
(May 2002) Maureen Robinson, Tania Vergnani and Yusuf Sayed

No 33 *Further Diploma in Education (Educational Management) by Distance Education at the University of Pretoria, South Africa*
(June 2002) Yusuf Sayed, Jan Heystek and Brigitte Smit

No 34 *Face-to-Face Training in a Conventional Preservice Programme: a case study at Edgewood College of Education in South Africa*
(August 2002) Vijay Reddy

No 35 *South African College for Open Learning: a model of an Inservice Distance Education Programme for Initial Teacher Education*
(August 2002) Vijay Reddy

The MUSTER Research Reports

No 1   *Teacher Training in **Ghana** – Does it Count?*
(December 2001) Kwame Akyeampong

No 2   *Initial Primary Teacher Education in **Lesotho***
(January 2002) J.Pulane Lefoka with E.Molapi Sebatane

No 3   *Primary Teacher Education in **Malawi**: Insights into Practice and Policy*
(March 2002) Demis Kunje with Keith Lewin and Janet Stuart

No 4   *An Analysis of Primary Teacher Education in **Trinidad and Tobago**: The MUSTER Project* (May 2002) June George and Lynda Quamina-Aiyejina

No 5   *Researching Teacher Education: New Perspectives on Practice, Performance and Policy.* **Report on the MUSTER Project**
(June 2002) Keith M.Lewin and Janet S.Stuart

The discussion papers are downloadable from the following web address:

http://www.sussex.ac.uk/usie/muster/list.html